HOW TO WIN THE BACHELOR

HOW TO WIN THE BACHELOR

The Secret to Finding Love and Fame on America's Favorite Reality Show

CHAD KULTGEN and LIZZY PACE

GALLERY BOOKS

New York London Toronto Sydney New Delhi

G

Gallery Books
An Imprint of Simon & Schuster, Inc.
1230 Avenue of the Americas
New York, NY 10020

Illustration Credits: Rose by Juan Pablo Bravo from the Noun Project: 1, 23, 51, 91, 119, 151, 167, 191, 209, 219, 235, 243; Ring by Marco Livolsi from the Noun Project: 21, 310; Heart by Three Six Five from the Noun Project: 30; Cross by ade from the Noun Project: 30; emoticon by Caesar Rizky Kurniawan for the Noun Project: 31; Rose by Tatiana from The Noun Project: 31; Rose by SBTS from the Noun Project: 31; pray by AliWijaya from the Noun Project: 31; Microphone by Maxim Kulikov from the Noun Project: 31; twin by Adrien Coquet from the Noun Project: 91; droplet by AlePio from the Noun Project: 310.

First Gallery Books hardcover edition January 2022

GALLERY BOOKS and colophon are registered trademarks of Simon & Schuster, Inc.

For information about special discounts for bulk purchases, please contact Simon & Schuster Special Sales at 1-866-506-1949 or business@simonandschuster.com.

The Simon & Schuster Speakers Bureau can bring authors to your live event. For more information or to book an event, contact the Simon & Schuster Speakers Bureau at 1-866-248-3049 or visit our website at www.simonspeakers.com.

Illustrations by Matt Johnstone
Data Assistant – Katie Finnigan

Manufactured in the United States of America

1 3 5 7 9 10 8 6 4 2

Library of Congress Cataloging-in-Publication Data has been applied for.

ISBN 978-1-9821-7294-7
ISBN 978-1-9821-7296-1 (ebook)

The only way out is through.

CONTENTS

INTRODUCTION

If you're reading this, chances are good that you're a *Bachelor* fan. And if you're a *Bachelor* fan you know that can mean a lot of different things.

Maybe you're a casual fan. You catch a few episodes near the end of a season every once in a while. You know the names of some of the most recent Bachelors and Bachelorettes, but you don't think about it much more than that.

Maybe you're a devoted *Bachelor* fan. You look forward to every season. You do your very best to watch every episode as it airs and sometimes you even go to Monday night viewing parties with an equally devoted group of friends who have put together a fantasy league.

Maybe you're even a hard-core *Bachelor* fan. The world would have to end for you to miss an episode. You throw the viewing parties and run the fantasy league. You follow everyone from the show on all social media platforms and *Us Weekly* is your *New York Times*.

And maybe, god help you, you are a *Bachelor* superfan. For you the show isn't a frivolous guilty pleasure to be enjoyed over wine and popcorn. It is a way of life. You find it difficult to watch the show with other people because you need to rewind and pause incessantly in order to scrutinize every frame of the document. You started a separate Instagram account just to follow some of your favorite *Bachelor* contestants a few years back and over time it has become your primary account. You know everything about all of their lives, including the names and IG follower counts of their babies. You listen to twenty hours of *Bachelor*-related podcasts per week, whether the show is in season or not. And when a friend casually tells you they're "obsessed" with *The Bachelor*, your first impulse is to grab them by the shoulders, shake them as hard as you can, and scream into their face, "No. You're. Not!"

When we (Chad and Lizzy) first met we were squarely in the casual fans category, just two coworkers who bonded over our mutual interest in the show and started watching together with a few other friends during Season 19 of *The Bachelor*. We'd have a few drinks, have a few laughs at Chris Soules's expense, and back then we still had the audacity to talk over the show, engaging in conversations that weren't even related to *The Bachelor* at all. Oh, how things would change.

At the end of Kaitlyn Bristowe's season of *The Bachelorette*, we started to augment our Monday night viewing ritual. Chad began taking pictures of the TV screen with his phone and making memes of the funny moments from the show. Lizzy started writing short recaps for a blog that also highlighted the humorous elements of *The Bachelor*. It was all innocuous at first, just some new ways to engage with what we thought was a harmless guilty pleasure and enhance our experience as viewers. Completely innocent fun.

But by Season 20, Ben Higgins, Chad was compulsively photographing the TV screen literally thousands of times per episode to make thirty to forty memes every week and Lizzy's recaps were averaging more words than a featured article in the *New Yorker*, complete with dozens of GIFs she made from footage of the show. But that was only the beginning. When the memes and the recaps weren't enough to satisfy our deepening obsession, we did the unthinkable: We started a *Bachelor* podcast.

When a friend or family member asks you what you've been up to lately, the last thing they want to hear is, "I started a podcast." And then they *really* do not want to hear, "It's about *The Bachelor*." So we endured reactions that ranged from halfhearted, empty promises to listen to our show to sincere concerns for our mental health. But we weren't deterred. The more we talked about *The Bachelor*, the more time we devoted to the study of it, the more we uncovered . . . the more we knew we were on to something.

Season after season of intense, almost frame-by-frame scrutiny and hour after hour of impassioned podcast discourse about the minutiae of *The Bachelor* began to reveal repeating patterns that led us to a conclusion that has changed how we watch the show forever. Alongside baseball, football, basketball, and hockey, we have come to understand that *The Bachelor* is a professional sport. And after twenty-five seasons, we knew there was a robust enough body of statistical data to be gathered that we could determine the best players of all time and the best plays to be made in any given situation. Even beyond that, we realized that literal strategies could be derived from the analysis of past plays to help any potential player win the entire game. This eye-opening revelation would ultimately take us where no *Bachelor* fan has gone before. In order to get that data and make sense of it, someone was going to have to go through eighteen years' worth of episodes and meticulously record every Steal, every kiss, every Tattle, and every tear. And as much as we didn't want to admit it, we knew that someone had to be us. There simply was no one else who would willingly subject themselves to a *Clockwork Orange*–style force-feeding of the entire show.

So we pushed ourselves to a level of engagement with *The Bachelor* that we believe has never been achieved before in the history of humanity: the Hyperbinge. Over seventy-four days, we watched every episode of *The Bachelor* ever made, from Season 1, Episode 1, to Season 25, Episode 12, in order, on 2x speed. We mainlined the entire oeuvre, every day all day. We tried not to take any breaks, but sometimes the breaks took us. The wave of relief and the sense of accomplishment that washed over us when we finally finished was indescribable. A memory we will each cherish for life, proof that we are capable of literally anything. But even as profound as the experience was, we emerged from the Hyperbinge with something far more valuable than simply fulfillment or newfound confidence. We generated a body of data, composed of literally thousands of pages of notes and complex spreadsheets in which we recorded every play that has ever been made in the history of the game. It is, to our knowledge, the most complete and detailed record of the game in existence.

What lies on the pages before you is everything we've learned about the unspoken rules of the game, its history, and how best to play it in the current era. No matter where you find yourself on the scale of *Bachelor* fandom, this book will take you deeper. And if you're a prospective player in an upcoming season, this book will give you all the tools necessary to make a deep run and possibly walk away with a Neil Lane engagement ring, or maybe even be crowned the next Bachelorette.

So with that said . . .

Trust the process, turn the page, and let the journey begin.

THE HISTORY OF

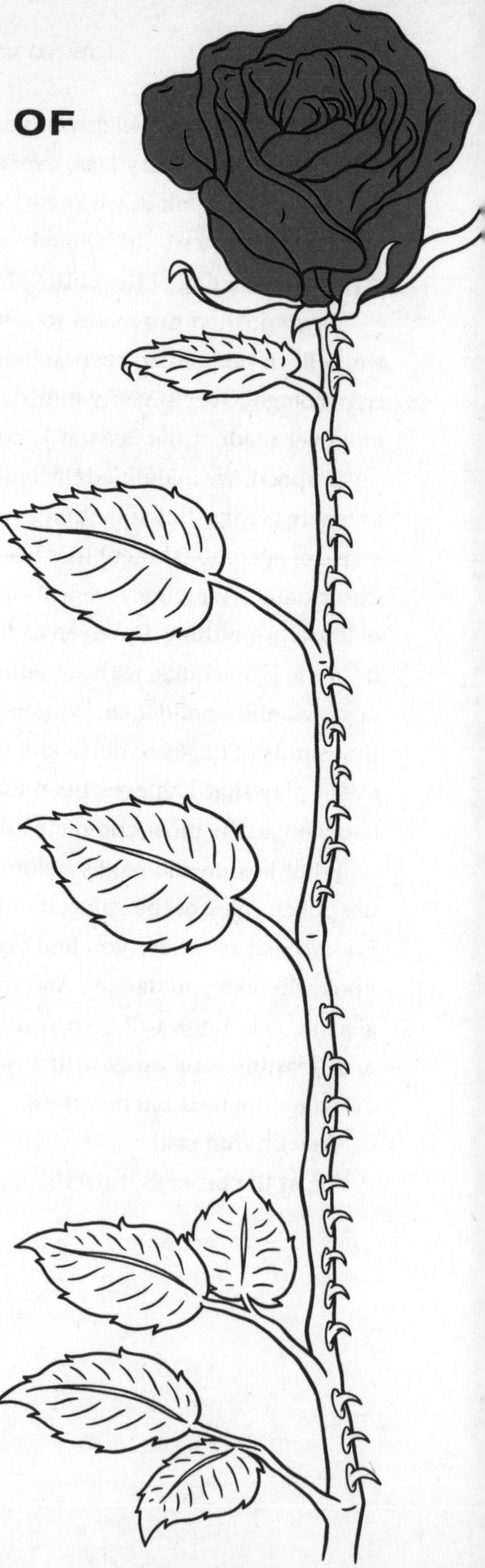

The Professional Era
(2020—Present)

The Paradise Era
(2014—2020)

The Modern Era
(or Mesnian Era)
(2009—2014)

The Experimental Era
(2003—2008)

The Classic Era
(2002—2003)

OUR BELOVED GAME

Season 25 Matt James — the first Black Bachelor
Season 24 Peter Weber — rise of the Fourth Audience player (Madison Prewett/ Hannah Ann Sluss)

Season 23 Colton Underwood — the virgin Bachelor
Season 22 Arie Luyendyk Jr. — reversed his final decision in a Mesnian switch
Season 21 Nick Viall — most diverse cast at that point
Season 20 Ben Higgins — first Bachelor to say "I love you" to both finalists before the Final RC
Season 19 Chris Soules — first season after Paradise, players aware of IG

Season 18 Juan Pablo Galavis — first Villain Bachelor
Season 17 Sean Lowe — first marriage Ring Winner, Catherine Giudici
Season 16 Ben Flajnik — first Villain Ring Winner, Courtney Robertson
Season 15 Brad Womack (2) — increased player pool to 30
Season 14 Jake Pavelka — first appearance of Neil Lane
Season 13 Jason Mesnick — starts common practice of all susbsequent Bachelors coming from prior *Bachelorette* seasons

Season 12 Matt Grant — first product tie-in with the movie *Made of Honor*
Season 11 Brad Womack (1) — first season shot at the mansion
Season 10 Andy Baldwin — first lead to say "I love you" to both finalists
Season 9 Lorenzo Borghese — Rome
Season 8 Travis Stork — Paris
Season 7 Charlie O'Connell — New York
Season 6 Byron Velvick — 2 Bachelors
Season 5 Jesse Palmer — origin of FIMP Rose
Season 4 Bob Guiney — first Bachelor who was a player from *Bachelorette*

Season 3 Andrew Firestone — first Fourth Audience Player, "Tina Fabulous"
Season 2 Aaron Buerge — paid for the ring with his own money
Season 1 Alex Michel — Genesis

On the island, I told her that I didn't like playing games. How could I look into her eyes and say anything without sounding disingenuous? Then again, we were, in fact, playing a game . . . *The Bachelor*.

Excerpt from The First Time: Finding Myself and Looking for Love on Reality TV, *by Colton Underwood, the twenty-third Bachelor*

AUTHORS' NOTE

This book is not endorsed or written in affiliation with *The Bachelor*, ABC, or any production entities involved with the show. All commentary is the opinion of the authors and all data presented has been collected by the authors by watching every episode of *The Bachelor*.

Chapter 1

FUNDAMENTALS

When one man is involved with more than one woman there's bound to be trouble.

Chris Harrison, *The Bachelor*, Season 1, Episode 1

The most common response we get when we tell somebody *The Bachelor* is a sport is something along the lines of, "You've been talking about *The Bachelor* for three hours; can we please talk about anything else?" The second most common response is something along the lines of, "It's not a sport because people actually fall in love on *The Bachelor*." Indeed they do and we are by no means suggesting that the game elements and the sincere pursuit of finding a soul mate are mutually exclusive. In fact, we're suggesting the exact opposite—that in order to fall in love and end up living happily ever after with the Bachelor of your dreams, you must not only play in a ten-round game of attrition that combines competitive group social dynamics, emotional obstacle courses orchestrated by Producers, and navigating the fickle court of public opinion, but you must also win it by any means necessary.

The Bachelor is not just a regular sport. It is not merely a game of winners and losers decided by simple measures like hitting a ball or running around in circles. Oh no. *The Bachelor* is by far the most complex of all sports because the rules and regulations are not as apparent as the foul lines on a baseball diamond or the end zones of a football field. They are instead hidden from view, buried under ceremony and spectacle, a secret shrouded behind the curtain of *The Bachelor*'s stated premise—that this is a process designed to help people find love, nothing more. The rules have never been outright expressed, formally displayed, or even discussed anywhere by any official production entity, network executive, or representative of the franchise. And even the growing number of journalists covering a wide variety of the game's various aspects hasn't ever gone so far as to analyze *The Bachelor* as the game it is . . . until now.

In this chapter we humbly present what we have identified as the rules, objectives, and structural components that combine to form the sport of *The Bachelor*. We must make it clear that this is different from either *The Bachelorette* or *Bachelor in Paradise* (*BIP*). Although we will reference those games in this book as they influence or relate to *The Bachelor*, they each have their own rules and statistics requiring their own future Hyperbinges.

You will notice as you progress through this book that we have coined a variety of terms and phrases to describe a wide range of game elements in much the same way other professional sports have languages unto themselves. We will define each new term upon first use, but we've also included a lexicon at the end of the book where you can reference all terms in alphabetical order. With that said, here are the fundamentals.

Roses

Over countless millennia of the evolution of human courtship, these botanical icons of love and devotion became the most common gift of romance in our society, and they are the lifeblood of *The Bachelor*. They make up the in-game currency, the points, the awards given to successful players in each round that grant them immunity from dismissal. But not all Roses are created equal. The many different types come with a wide array of strategies to secure each. From the uniquely exotic First Impression Rose (or FIMP Rose), of which there is only one in the entirety of any season, to the anxiety-inducing Group Date Rose (GDR), securing any Rose that's made available each week is the primary goal. The Rose is safety. The Rose is victory.

The "Rose Quotient" (RQ): Measuring a Player's Skill at Winning Roses

Sure, it might seem a little . . . obsessive to create a statistical metric that allows you to illustrate a player's raw ability to acquire non–Rose Ceremony Roses. But every sport goes through a moment when outside observers start taking a closer look at how the game works and how it can be measured. Sportswriters invented RBIs and the ERA for baseball in the early 1900s. A panel of statisticians created the quarterback rating for football in the 1970s. And now in 2022, we give you the RQ for our beloved game—the lower the number, the more successful the player. You can calculate a player's RQ by assigning point values to all Roses in the game, which are as follows:

All Roses outside a Rose Ceremony have a value of 0. This includes FIMP Roses, One-On-One Date Roses (1O1Rs), Group Date Roses (GDRs), Two-On-One Date Roses (2O1Rs), Knock-Knock Roses (KKRs), the Final Rose (FR), and any Special Roses (SRs).

We assign all Roses acquired during a Rose Ceremony a value equal to their order given. So the first Rose of any Rose Ceremony, which we designate "First Flower," has a value of 1. The second Rose has a value of 2, and so forth, all the way to the last Rose, which has the highest value of the night.

Add up the value of all Roses and average it over the number of total Roses received to derive your RQ. Importantly, you must have acquired at least five Roses for your RQ to be valid. And the lower your RQ score, the better you are at acquiring high-value Roses. A perfect RQ score would be 0, which has never been achieved by any player in history.

The top five RQ scores since Season 7, which was the first season to offer players the opportunity to acquire each of the main 0-point Rose types (FIMP, 1O1R, and GDR) are:

PLAYER	RQ	SEASON	PLACE
Kaitlyn Bristowe	0.714	19 (Chris Soules)	3rd
Nikki Ferrell	0.8	18 (Juan Pablo Galavis)	Ring Winner
Sarah Brice	0.857	7 (Charlie O'Connell)	Ring Winner
Caelynn Miller-Keyes	1	23 (Colton Underwood)	4th
Tenley Molzahn	1.14	14 (Jake Pavelka)	2nd

ROSES (Numbers indicate the numerical value of Rose Ceremony Roses)	**BACHELORETTE**
1, GDR, 101R, GDR, 2, GDR, 2	Yes
2, 2, GDR, GDR, 101R, 1, 1, 1, 1, FR	No
1, 101R, GDR, 101R, 1, 1 FR	No
1, 3, GDR, 101R, 1, 2, 101R	No
FIMP, 3, 3, GDR, 1, SR, 1	No

All of these players are legends in the game who achieved Top 4 status. Kaitlyn Bristowe sits at the top of the list with the best RQ score in history. She is arguably the greatest player to ever set foot out of a limo, and future players would do well to review every play she's made over the course of her career. She is the blueprint for a perfect modern player on and off the field.

Structure

As with any sport, *The Bachelor* is played over the course of a season. From January to March every year a new crop of rookies competes in four distinct periods of escalating vigor. Night One, the regular season, the play-offs, and the finals are all collectively played over the course of ten rounds. Twenty-five to thirty-two players (with some rare exceptions) begin the game, trying their best to survive each round in a series of attrition-based psychosocial events, or dates. Each of these rounds serves the same function as games in single-elimination tournament sports like basketball or tennis. Similarly, *The Bachelor* produces one "winner" at the season's end, although players can find more ways to victory in our beloved game than just by standing in the champion's circle with the Final Rose in hand.

Night One

A game unto itself, the first night of play features the ceremony of Limo Exits, the challenge of forced social engagement with both the Bachelor and the other thirty-plus players, all while you must endure the sink-or-swim circumstance of standing in front of a TV camera for what is very likely the first time. This grueling opening round lasts through the night and well into the next day, testing your physical stamina as much as your game sense and strategy. You face one of the most difficult challenges to overcome in the entire season in Night One, which eliminates almost a third of the player pool, so you must do everything in your power to get a Rose by daybreak.

The Regular Season

The next six rounds of the game comprise the regular season, which includes Group Dates, One-On-One Dates, head-to-head competition on Two-On-One

Dates, domestic travel, and in most modern seasons international travel. The regular season is where Villains vill and most players will shed more than a few tears while divulging their most painful secrets. Each of these rounds culminates with a Rose Ceremony, at which multiple players are eliminated simultaneously. Surviving the regular season all but guarantees a player's invitation to the subsequent *BIP* season and therefore another opportunity to gain new IG followers. Making it through the regular season is as much a game of attrition as it is aggression. Know when to be visible and when to relent to avoid unwanted attention while still being able to capitalize on your time with the Bachelor.

Regular-Season Dates

The Group Date

If two's company and three's a crowd, how would one begin to describe eighteen? Yes, eighteen players competed on the largest Group Date in history during Season 25. The Group Date usually requires up to a dozen or more players to simultaneously compete for the Bachelor's attention and for screen time, while engaging in some kind of mandatory activity. Group Dates are almost always divided into two parts. The daytime activity comprises Part One. Producers present players with situations that will require artistic performances, athletic endeavors, forced violence, and even nudity, so you need to be ready for anything and everything in order to find the balance between reserved nonchalance and aggressive over-participation. Part Two is almost always a formal cocktail After Party at which the Bachelor speaks with everyone separately. Although the Bachelor traditionally grants only one player the GDR, a good GD performance can all but assure a Rose at the next Rose Ceremony.

The One-On-One (1O1)

The cause of instant jealousy and ire from the other players, the 1O1 allows a single player to spend time alone with the Bachelor, which is absolutely necessary in order to progress through the regular season. Like Group Dates, 1O1 Dates are also divided into a day and night portion. In the early part of a season, a 1O1 Date is a virtual guarantee for a Rose, but as the season progresses it can be used by the Bachelor as an execution. Most important, a 1O1 is your greatest chance to build solo screen time, which is a crucial element in building IG followers.

The Two-On-One (2O1)

The most dreaded event in all of the sporting world, a 2O1 is a date most players do everything in their power to avoid. This no-holds-barred, head-to-head forced competition almost always requires one or sometimes both players to be sent home before the date's end. Producers design 2O1s based on manufactured rivalries between two players. Learn to recognize the signs of Producers trapping you in a rivalry to either avoid being sentenced to the perilous 2O1 or to embrace it as a final attempt to gain followers and secure an invitation to Paradise by orchestrating an explosive and memorable exit.

Play-offs

The eighth and ninth rounds of the game are the play-offs. The rules of the game change radically in these two all-important weeks, forcing you to rely on the approval and integration of your friends and families into your relationship with the Bachelor during the Hometown round. If you advance to the second week of play-offs, the Fantasy Suite round, you will almost certainly jet-set away to an international location where you will be required to devise and enact a chemistry strategy to be compared against the other players' within a matter of days. You will also face the Bachelor alone, off-camera, for the only time all season. A successful run through the play-off weeks grants a player a berth into the finals.

Play-off Dates

The Hometown

In the first round of play-offs you will be forced to take the Bachelor to a location that was meaningful to you in the town where you grew up before bringing him home to meet your family. Conscript mothers, fathers, siblings, aunts, uncles, and best friends into supporting your strategy. This stage of the game usually eliminates only one player of the remaining four, so general odds of progression are high, but one miscue from an overly protective brother, one admission of distrust for the process from a mother, or one refusal to give a blessing of a proposal from a skeptical father can immediately destroy your chances to move into the next round.

The Fantasy Suite

Even more crucial than the game's Finale, the Fantasy Suite week begins for each player with a romantic 101 in whichever exotic locale the Producers have selected. At this date's culmination the Bachelor presents you with the option of spending a night with him without cameras recording your behavior, the implication being that this false privacy can foster an environment conducive to sexual activity. You must rely heavily on your chemistry game in this second round of play-offs to possibly make a run for the Ring or, if you choose, the *Bachelorette* Crown.

WTA

The Women Tell All (WTA) is akin to an All-Star game in other sports. It has no effect on the outcome of the season and isn't part of standard play but gives high-level players who didn't make it to the play-offs a chance to show off their skills one more time in the hopes of generating a few more IG numbers or showing the Producers that they're Paradise ready.

The Finals

In the final round, the two players remaining must meet and impress the Bachelor's family, then wait until he decides which of them he will claim as the Ring Winner and which he will eliminate as the runner-up. Although it might seem like a loss here would be devastating for a player who has come so close only to be dismissed, if played properly, a late-season dismissal can be the perfect strategy for becoming the next Bachelorette.

Final Date

In the game's final round, the two remaining players have to meet the Bachelor's family for a head-to-head comparison. In this high-stakes meeting of strangers, you must mind your p's and q's, because one slipup can fan the flames of parental doubt and leave the door wide open for the other finalist to slip in and steal the Ring. After the grueling hours of forcing a smile for his family, you will receive a final night date with the Bachelor on which you can make your last, all-important plays. Then in the following forty-eight hours, you must don a formal dress and take turns with the other finalist, standing before the Bachelor's judgmental gaze to either receive the Ring in a rushed and awkward proposal or endure a public dumping, clinging to the hope that you've done enough over the course of the season to warrant the adornment of the *Bachelorette* Crown.

The Three Objectives

Since the first season of *The Bachelor* in 2002, players have experienced fame as a potential by-product of appearing in the game. As celebrity itself has transformed into a monetizable commodity over the past decade in the arena of social media, fame has become the primary objective for most players in more modern seasons. And even for those players who view whatever social media audience they might gain as nothing more than an added benefit of pursuing a genuine relationship with the Bachelor, they all fully embrace the job of influencer and therefore all players now clearly and openly indulge this goal. One of the things that makes *The Bachelor* more intricate and complex than any other sport in the world is that it provides three separate objectives in service of attaining that goal.

The Ring

For any player who genuinely seeks to start a lasting relationship by playing our beloved game, the Ring is the only prize that matters. In most cases the Ring is a literal diamond engagement ring the Bachelor gives to the last player remaining after the conclusion of all ten rounds of play, although in some rare cases it may be symbolic if the Bachelor can't find the courage to get down on one knee and give us all what we came for. But whether there's a proposal or a halfhearted agreement to keep dating, we consider the recipient of the Final Rose to be the Ring Winner of a season. At this point in the game's history, Neil Lane supplies all rings and some are valued in excess of $100,000. As long you remain in a publicly romantic relationship with the Bachelor for a contractually determined period of time after the final episode, you get to keep the Ring. If the relationship dissolves before that contractually defined period of time, at least publicly, then you have to give the ring back.

We often muse to ourselves about a room that must exist somewhere with a little glass case where all the rings of the broken Bachelor engagements are kept. Only one Bachelor has married his Ring Winner—Season 17's Sean Lowe, who married Catherine Giudici. While the Ring might seem like the most valuable form of the three possible victories, it is actually the worst in terms of IG benefit. Certainly all Ring Winners experience an influx of followers and spon-con opportunities, but since *BIP* ushered in a new era in the game, the average IG follower count for Ring Winners comes in under 1 million at 982K. This is the lowest average of the three groupings of victors. Another detrimental effect of winning the Ring is a statistical ban from ever setting foot in Paradise or coming back for a second tour as a player in a subsequent season. Only three players in history have won the Ring and then the Crown—a feat we have dubbed the Full Royale: Jenn Schefft won the *Bachelor* Season 3 Ring, then wore the third Crown; Emily Maynard won the fifteenth-season Ring and then wore the eighth Crown; and Becca Kufrin won the Season 22 Ring, then wore the fourteenth Crown. And Kufrin only gained the Crown after an incomprehensibly special circumstance materialized when then-Bachelor Arie Luyendyk Jr. revoked her Ring in favor of Season 22's runner-up, Lauren Burnham.

Top 4

For those players who are not as interested in finding love as they might be in selling dry shampoo in their IG stories, making the Top 4 is the primary goal. Of course, a deep run into the play-offs grants you more screen time and therefore more followers, but it does so much more. A Top 4 finish all but guarantees a secondary appearance in some other Bachelor Franchise game. Since the start of the Paradise Era, 94 percent of all Top 4 finishers have appeared on a season of *BIP* or have played in another season of *The Bachelor*. And it's in that second season of play that Top 4 finishers see their social media following grow the most, with an average IG count of 1.05 million. With the exception of Hannah Brown and Katie Thurston, the last eight Bachelorettes have all been Top 4 finishers, and Season 18 (Juan Pablo Galavis) produced two Bachelorettes from the Top 4—Andi Dorfman and Clare Crawley. In addition, more and more players form long-term relationships in Paradise and go on to exploit parasocial power-couple status as influencers and podcast hosts, which allows them to stay relevant within Bachelor Nation for several years after their time in-game.

The Crown

The highest honor a player can receive—yes, even more so than being the Bachelor's final choice—is to become the next lead and wear the Crown of the Bachelorette. This is also the most difficult form of victory to attain because it depends not only on a near-perfect season of play but on circumstances outside your control as well. What direction the Producers are moving the game, the tastes of ABC's executives, and even the social climate of the day all contribute to the decision on who will get to feel the awesome power of the Crown resting atop her head. But for those outstanding few who enter the royal sorority, the reward is unparalleled. Not only does the Bachelorette embark on a journey to find real love if that should interest her, but she also enjoys an average of 1.4 million IG followers since the start of the Paradise Era. Rachel Lindsay is the only Bachelorette in this era who has yet to break the 1 million follower mark, but she has arguably benefited the most from her time under the Crown, as she now serves as on-camera talent for *Extra* and MTV. She also hosts a successful podcast called *Higher Learning* and she was the co-host of the most listened to Bachelor Franchise podcast in America—*Bachelor Happy Hour*. And on top of her impressive résumé, she also found love in her season and married her Ring Winner, Bryan Abasolo. Winning the Crown grants a player a tidal wave of magazine covers, spon-con opportunities, possible appearances on *Dancing with the Stars*, and a permanent place in the pantheon of the game's most important players of all time.

The Four Audiences

To the layperson's untrained gaze, *The Bachelor* might seem like a straightforward game of weekly winners and losers, competing in a game of attrition that pits each player against all others, but this is just a surface observation. The trivial goals of lesser sports are checkers to *The Bachelor*'s four-dimensional chess, and the truth is there are no real opponents at all in *The Bachelor* but instead a collection of four audiences. You must engage in a constant and simultaneous dance of psychological manipulation with these four separate but related groups of interested parties to achieve the final goal of being accepted and hopefully even adored by each of the four audiences.

The First Audience—the Bachelor

This is the most important audience for any player who wants the Ring, and it is conversely the least important audience for a player with any other goal. Despite the presentation of the Bachelor as all-powerful within the game, the truth is that he only wields one element of absolute control, the selection of the Ring Winner. Producers determine virtually everything else in the game, including the order of most eliminations. That said, you have to make it seem like you want the Ring and therefore must engage in as strong a First Audience game as possible, not only for the sake of appearance but also in the rare case that the Bachelor truly is confused about who he wants to select as his Ring Winner. A good First Audience game includes playing to the Bachelor's preferences in conversation and behavior. Consider fully and enthusiastically indulging the Bachelor's whims on every date. Questioning the Bachelor's decisions is an extremely high-risk strategy that usually ends in horrific failure. Just like each of the players, the Bachelor is aware that his actions will be viewed by the public, and your job is to make him feel like he's always doing the right thing and that he will have your support no matter the situation or perceived personal cost.

Keep the goal and purpose of the Bachelor in mind at all times (as it is with each of the four audiences). The Bachelor has one job—the elimination of every player from the game except one. Many past Bachelors like Nick Viall have revealed that they knew on Night One who their Ring Winner would be, so for the rest of the season they were just waiting for the other players to give them reasonable justification to walk them out to the black SUV to drive off into the cold dark of night. An argument, a temper tantrum, not leveling up the emotional stakes at the right time, and any other behavioral misstep all constitute errors that allow the Bachelor to eliminate you on righteous grounds.

The Second Audience—the Other Players

Many players throughout the history of our beloved game have made the simple mistake of treating their fellow players as opponents. While yes, in raw terms all players engage in competition with one another, it is not as simple as a head-to-head, kill-or-be-killed, last-woman-standing-wins tournament. In *The Bachelor* the other players simultaneously fulfill the roles of competitive rivals and helpful teammates, equally capable of rendering a crushing defeat or elevating another player to glorious victory. And perhaps most important, the Second Audience has the awesome and terrible power of cursing any player who cannot conform to the basic group identity with the damning title of Villain. Although past Villains have progressed to later rounds in the game and in the case of Courtney Robertson (Season 16—Ben Flajnik) even won a Ring, in more recent seasons all leads have taken caution of the player who can't get along with the others. Avoid the Not Here To Make Friends strategy at all costs, as it paints you into a corner with virtually no escape.

The Second Audience always recognizes the front-runners and the Villains and therefore determines the pecking order by elevating players who are agreeable and sabotaging those who are not. The Second Audience provides Tattletales to sow seeds of doubt in the Bachelor's mind about players who go against the grain and also provides support to the players who go with the flow. Befriend as many players as possible to guarantee good standing with the Second Audience. Even beyond the game, this helps solidify a strong base of other players to engage for postseason social media opportunities.

The Third Audience—the Producers

Although they are the most invisible part of the game from a spectator standpoint, the Producers have the most power of all of the audiences because they control every aspect of the game and a player's life, constructing and orchestrating all scenarios that you endure during the course of a season. They generate story lines among the players and the Bachelor that exploit the fundamental nature of perceived rivalries, past traumas, sexual attractions, or burgeoning friendships. Each stage of the game presents Producers with new opportunities to force players into a variety of perilous situations designed to propel their stories forward. As much as the players compete in our beloved game, so too do the Producers compete to prove who among them can choreograph the most outrageous conclusions to the stories they conceive.

In order to achieve their goals, Producers uniformly present themselves as friendly confidants who are exclusively concerned with helping you through the process, but nothing is further from the truth. A Producer's only loyalty is to the show and their desire to produce big ratings. So as friendly as they may seem, they will betray you. They orchestrate situations specifically designed to undermine your goals and even the Bachelor's preferences in service of creating what they refer to as "good television," which invariably includes induced moments of trauma and suffering. And if the Producers don't get what they want, they won't hesitate to use a practice known as Frankenbiting, in which they recut audio to create sentences and phrases players never actually said.

Despite all of this, do not avoid the Producers. Quite the opposite, because they determine which players get screen time and how they will be edited. The Producers wield so much power in deciding which players will make deep runs in each season that you must placate them and even counter-manipulate them in order to stay in the game as long as possible and receive a favorable edit. While the process is difficult to master, you must learn to walk the line between believable unwittingness and clear-headed opposition to their Machiavellian schemes.

The Fourth Audience—Bachelor Nation

Players never come in contact with the Fourth Audience during the season. Made up exclusively of the millions of people who tune in to the game every week, the Fourth Audience contains two distinct elements. Some think the game is not a game at all. This section of the audience believes all players to be 100 percent sincere in their attempts to find love and never realizes that Producers or editors play any role whatsoever in designing the images and situations they see on their TV screens. The show effectively deceives this portion of the Fourth Audience with its stated premise. But for the other portion, they clearly see what we understand to be the historically racist casting practices, the overtly orchestrated situations in which players find themselves, and in some cases the players' calculated actions. This part of the Fourth Audience knows they are watching a game and watches because it is one, celebrating their favorite players and the astounding plays they make.

You must play to both halves of the Fourth Audience simultaneously, maintaining believable sincerity for those viewers who demand it while always finding a moment to flash a symbolic wink to those viewers who revel in knowing a player knows she's playing a game.

Ultimately, the Fourth Audience influences your postgame career most significantly. They determine if you receive a large enough social media following to maintain a career as an influencer or if you will simply be forgotten after your playing days are finished.

Tools

As in all sports, you must proficiently learn to use certain game-specific pieces of equipment. Baseball has its bats. Football has its helmets. Tennis has its rackets. Soccer has its ball. So, too, does *The Bachelor* have five distinct tools with which every player enters the game and can use at will.

1) THE PERSONAL TRAGEDY CARD (PTC)

From the unexpected end of a past relationship to the death of a loved one, all players have endured some emotional trauma that they will need to share with the Bachelor at some point during the course of play. Your trauma is your PTC and you can play it for extreme benefit in a variety of situations. There are twelve main categories of PTCs:

1. Death
2. Divorce (parental or personal)
3. Heartbreak
4. Infidelity
5. Addiction
6. Medical
7. Abuse/Assault
8. Estrangement
9. Bullying/Racism
10. Injury
11. Incarceration
12. Mental Health Struggle

The PTC is among the most powerful and versatile of all your tools. You can use it offensively at dinner on a 1O1 in order to assure a Rose, defensively in the unfortunate event of another player attacking you in order to garner a sympathy Rose, or even as a means by which you can overcome the gravity of another player's PTC on a Group Date in order to secure a GDR. Time it well to maximize your PTC's benefits and save it for later stages of the game if possible. Never leave a PTC unplayed.

Very often, playing a PTC invokes the use of another tool that is integral to every successful player's strategy. . . .

2) WALLS

Traditionally, walls stand the test of time, stay strong, and never come down. But the walls in our beloved game serve the exact opposite purpose. Erect them specifically and only to take them down at the exact most opportune moment. Walls are emotional obstacles, often the result of the lasting effects of a PTC, which threaten to keep the Bachelor at a romantic distance from you if not overcome. Different players can play them for longer periods of time than others and in different situations, but if you properly play a wall game, it can last for one or two rounds, allowing you to convey progress being made toward a closer relationship with the Bachelor once you decide to take them down. In almost every case, the Bachelor rewards a player who takes her walls down at the correct moment with a Rose, and very often this wall-lowering moment offers a natural transition into the use of another tool. . . .

3) THE LOVE LEVELS

The goal of the game is to fall in love. So to progress through the game you not only have to believably fall in love; you also have to continually verbally announce increasing attachment to the Bachelor at various points throughout the season or risk elimination. There are four very distinct Love Levels, although if you're aggressive you can skip one or more. The four Love Levels are:

Love Level 1—I Like You

LL1 includes anything from the literal phrase "I like you" to "I'm surprised I'm feeling so strongly about you already," or "you give me butterflies," or "I'm smitten," or anything that confirms an emotional affinity forming on your behalf. Play this beginning level as early as Night One.

Love Level 2—I'm Starting to Fall for You

LL2 also includes the variant "I'm starting to fall in love with you" or "I can see myself falling in love with you." The most crucial elements of Love Level 2 are the words "starting" and "fall." LL2 escalates from LL1 and conveys that the process of falling in love has begun. Most players underuse and therefore waste this Love Level, as many skip it in favor of moving straight to Love Level 3.

Love Level 3—I'm Falling in Love with You

LL3 also includes the variant "I'm falling for you." We define Love Level 3 by the use of the present tense of the verb "fall." You're actively engaged in the process of falling in love and progressing to the final goal of the ultimate Love Level.

Love Level 4—I'm in Love with You

LL4 includes a wide variety of variants from "I'm head over heels in love with you" to "I frickin' love you so much," or any statement of final arrival at the state of being in love with the Bachelor. Most wait until play-offs to play this final Love Level or in some cases throw it out there as a last-ditch, Hail Mary attempt to avoid a premature dismissal.

4) TEARS

Whether they be caused by joy or sorrow, use the invaluable tool of tears, because unlike the others we've already mentioned, you can use them endlessly. Furthermore, playing tears all but guarantees you precious screen time, as Producers feature crying players in promotions for the show 100 percent of the time and virtually every round of the game contains at least one heavily featured incidence of crying.

Tears produce a wide variety of responses. On a Group Date they can generate valuable 1O1 time with the Bachelor as he seeks to console a distraught player. On a 1O1 they can punctuate the play of an especially powerful PTC or the lowering of a well-constructed wall. For a strong Second Audience game you can use them to diffuse a possible rivalry or express concern over another player's false intentions. But above all, utilize tears to convey sincerity, which plays to all four audiences simultaneously.

Tears make up such an important part of your repertoire that in recent years some All-Stars who revolutionized tear play have been honored by the game. The nation knows Ashley Iaconetti primarily for two things—her virginity and her ability to play tears often and effectively in Season 19 (Chris Soules). Her tear play became a story line in multiple episodes and even helped propel her to Paradise, where she eventually accrued over 1 million IG followers, an influencer career, and her husband, Jared Haibon. Producers brought her back on Season 24's WTA to give a "Best Crier" award to that season's fourth-place finisher, Kelsey Weier, who cried in almost every episode.

As important a role as tears play in a wide variety of situations, you have another tool at your disposal that is perhaps even more paramount. . . .

5) KISSES

During the very first season, LaNease Adams performed the first kiss in the history of the sport with Alex Michel on a GD gondola ride in Las Vegas. Countless players have smooched since and some seasons have generated higher total kiss counts than others, but in every case players have used the kiss as the primary method for establishing their chemistry game. In general, kiss early and often, as waiting too long for the first kiss can result in other players establishing chemistry games that you cannot overcome. Always position yourself physically close to the Bachelor at Cocktail Parties and GD After Parties to make this leap smaller. Prepare Kiss Lead-In lines and actions to help yourself cross this barrier as soon as possible. Before Kelly Jo Kuharski in Season 4 (Bob Guiney), no one had ever broken that barrier on Night One, but since she made history many skilled players consistently touch lips with the Bachelor shortly after their Limo Exits in the Modern Era.

In a best-case scenario, use these tools at a measured pace to ensure steady progress through all ten rounds of the game, doling out one tool at every opportunity you get to be alone with the Bachelor. But it should be noted, tears and kisses augment the strength of the other tools and so in reality you only have six plays to stretch evenly over ten rounds—the four Love Levels, your PTC, and your walls. Time and conserve these precious tools.

The Host

A constant in the game since its very first season, the host of the show appears at various moments for a variety of reasons. Until very recently the host has always been Chris Harrison, whom most players viewed as a harbinger of doom. But in actuality, no matter who the host is, their primary function is simply to signal the beginning and end of each new round of the game, to deliver Date Cards, and to explain the rules of various dates. Most of the host's other duties are largely superficial and ceremonial. They can sometimes serve as an on-camera confidant for the Bachelor and high-level players in times of crisis or reflection. Perhaps most important, the host represents the incarnation of the Producers' will on-screen. Placate the host or entertain them with a funny sound bite or gesture, because history shows that players who cross the host usually find themselves the victims of a speedy exit while those to whom the host takes a liking find their way to high sand placement in Paradise.

Rules

As complex as the rest of the fundamentals might be, the rules that govern our beloved game maintain elegance in their simplicity because every player, the lead, and even the Producers must all abide by only one rule.

For The Right Reasons (4TRR)

The entire game's foundation consists of a conceit that maintains the illusion that *The Bachelor* is not a game but instead a viable and sincere effort to help bring two people together to find love everlasting. Players and the Bachelor alike repeat this mantra woven into the fabric of the game, again and again, that all persons involved must be there "For The Right Reasons." This phrase echoes through time all the way back to the very first season, when it was uttered by Cathy Grimes, who never could have known that it would become the de facto statement of all players to prove their sincerity. The "right reasons" demand that each player conveys she is only participating in the game to find love, that the IG followers, the trips, the prizes, the celebrity, and all material gain associated with an appearance in the game remain circumstantial. Do everything possible to avoid having your motivations questioned by the other players or by the Bachelor, because any player accused of being in the game For The Wrong Reasons (4TWR) rarely outlives the accusation.

The "right reasons" make up such an unassailable property of the game that they can never be questioned and allow players to use them to defend against character attacks or just as easily use them to attack other players who haven't firmly asserted their motivations for participation. The "right reasons" bind even the Bachelor and he will have no choice but to oblige any player's request in service of appearing to also be there 4TRR.

To say that 4TRR is the only, all-important rule of our beloved game doesn't properly describe it. For The Right Reasons governs the game. It is the ball with which the game is played. It is the field on which all players play and it is the identity of the game itself.

That's it. Those are the basics, the mechanics, the way the game works. And now, with a firm grasp of the fundamentals, we're going to move into what's really the first phase of playing the game for any serious prospective player—preparation.

Chapter 2

THE PRESEASON

On to more important things . . . like spending $40,000 on clothing for the show . . . which is f*%king insane!!! . . . The girls do have to bring all of their own clothing and, of course, they want to be wearing the best clothes EVER to be seen on TV in!!! I had re-mortgaged my house and I spent something like $8,000 on clothing.

Jillian Harris, third place in
Season 13 (Jason Mesnick) and the fifth Bachelorette

The Hyperbinge revealed the structure of the game to us, the mechanics, the rules, the prizes, and the strategies. But as we descended into the next level of fandom of our beloved game, we found ourselves wondering: When do you actually start playing?

We always thought Night One was your big debut. You step out of the limo, you try to make a good first impression (possibly in a full-body sloth costume), and you start mingling with the competition. But our growing understanding of everything related to *The Bachelor* started to take us into areas of research beyond just watching every episode of the show and we realized something incredibly important. You start playing this game months before you ever step out of the limo.

Just like Jillian Harris said, figuring out what to wear on the show and, even more important, figuring out how to pay for it is just one small part of what you must do during the preseason to set up your best possible season.

At the dawn of the Professional Era (which began with Season 24—Peter Weber), the days of players joining the game and "winging it" are dead. Everyone who plays the game in the Professional Era knows the structure and the rules and has at least some basic idea of an initial strategy. So to maintain an advantage in today's game, you must complete thoughtful and thorough preseason preparation that includes branding yourself to get through the multiphase casting process, preparing makeup and wardrobe (even and especially if you're on a budget), physical training to not only get camera ready for the obligatory bikini date but also to gain strength and agility helpful for participating in mandatory physical violence that Producers will undoubtedly design into one or more Group Dates, and so much more.

If you are serious about getting the most out of this experience, create the pre-written performance and brand material we've outlined to bring into the game like poems, essays, comedic anecdotes, and catchphrases. And perhaps most important, we discuss strategies for tying up all loose ends in your life, in person and online. As soon as you enter the game your social media will fall under a level of scrutiny so intense that politicians would shake in their boots. The Fourth Audience never sleeps and one of its primary functions during the course of a season is to unearth *everything* about every player, especially those who make deep runs. Something as seemingly insignificant as a like on a questionable IG post can derail your season before it even really begins.

Pre-casting Round 1—Research and Discovery/Branding

Every person is a brand, and before the actual application process, the first step for any player looking to enter this game is self-reflection to discover what their brand will be. Examine your personal qualities and various skills to help determine the branding and story line that will work best. Make a list of the particular attributes you bring into the game and think about how each of these can be expanded upon, exaggerated, and exploited to make a TV-ready character that will appeal to the casting Producers. Below we include categories along with some questions and guidelines designed to help you build a strong preseason player identity.

Background

Where are you from? Can you augment your hometown into a character trait through an exaggerated accent, a costume, quirky eating habits, et cetera? Do you have a regional or colloquial nickname that succinctly encompasses your brand? If not, can you create one?

Family, Friends, Coworkers

What unique people in your life might the viewers get to meet if you make it to Hometowns? Are you particularly close with anyone? Can you weave this person or people into a character trait or a reusable topic of conversation on dates?

Skills

What hobbies and activities do you engage in that would make "great television" and help further romantic connections? Do you have any high degrees of proficiency at a sport or other activity that could serve as the foundation of a 101 Date like Madison Prewett (Season 24—Peter Weber), who had basketball expertise?

Emotional Strengths

Are you funny? Are you good at giving advice? Are you the life of the party? Do you know a lot of fun facts? Do you perform a heartwarming community service activity? You should know your strengths in group social dynamics and build an identity that will allow you to use them as often as possible.

Emotional Weaknesses

What kind of trauma have you endured and how can it be used to inform your story line or create pre-planned moments to raise or lower walls? What are your phobias? If none, what fictional phobias could you manufacture to give Producers easy and obvious ways to exploit them on dates?

Quirks

Do you engage in any abnormal compulsions or activities that might entice the Producers to include them in the tag of an episode or even to create a minor story line in an episode? We've seen chronic hiccups in the past, but options like humorous sleep-talking or a bizarre workout routine would work perfectly for you to garner screen time.

Archetypes

In the same way other sports rely on teams made up of different positions, each playing different but essential roles, so too does *The Bachelor* rely on players with separate identities, skill sets, and associated tropes. We saw the same basic archetypes play out again and again while conducting the Hyperbinge. Producers always choose the identities, but they are very usually based on inherent traits possessed by the players. Although a player's archetype can change over the course of a season, it's important to know the twelve basic types and enter the game with one in mind as a blueprint. Listed here are the twelve archetypes and some examples of players who played them well:

1. The Villain—Courtney Robertson, Tierra LiCausi
2. The Fool—Annaliese Puccini, Alexis Waters
3. The Foreigner—Kristina Schulman, Magi Tareke
4. The Professional—Rachel Lindsay, Sharleen Joynt
5. The Good Girl—Madison Prewett, Becca Tilley
6. The Free Spirit—Kaitlyn Bristowe, Lucy Aragon
7. The Single Mother—Emily Maynard, Chelsea Roy
8. The Bumpkin—Raven Gates, Tia Booth
9. The Weirdo—Kendall Long, Ashley Salter
10. The Pageant Queen—Hannah Brown, Caelynn Miller-Keyes
11. The Princess—Corinne Olympios, Victoria Larson
12. The Dynamic Duo—Becca Tilley/JoJo Fletcher, Ashley Spivey/Ashley Hebert

Talented players dip into different archetypes as needed and even apply novel flair to their play through the use of a variety of thematic augmentations like seductive, Christian, artistic, face player, competitive, athletic, emotional, family oriented, et cetera. We will cover the twelve archetypes and their associated themes in the regular-season chapter.

Hero Players

Currently anyone and everyone can watch and study twenty-five seasons of play in their entirety. Some are harder to come by than others, trust us, but a variety of streaming services offer all seasons from the Paradise Era forward, making them mandatory viewing for any prospective player because they offer invaluable information about the different tropes and player archetypes the Producers most commonly use to develop stories and seem to prefer. And beyond that, they offer case studies in how the greatest players of all time were able to handle the various situations they encountered in any given season. More and more modern star players select one or more former Hero Players to emulate every season. And the best players don't just mimic the styles of the greats; they also evolve them, adding to the legacy of that specific style and making it their own, like Katie Thurston (Season 25—Matt James), who added to Kaitlyn Bristowe's original blue humor Limo Exit to include prop work with a vibrator. Although you can learn things from every player's time in the game, generally mirror only those players who were Top 4 finishers.

Pre-casting Round 2—Social Media Preparation

After you complete your research, choose a Hero Player, and develop your brand, your natural inclination might be to apply, but there is still more preseason work to be done! Perhaps the most important element of your preseason strategy is the complete overhaul of your social media. Casting Producers use Instagram for scouting potential talent as well as for deep dives once prospective players submit applications. Producers primarily use Instagram to gather information about prospective players, but you should recalibrate your TikTok, Facebook, Twitter, YouTube, and all other platforms to present only what you want a Producer and ultimately the entirety of the Fourth Audience to eventually see, because they will see it all.

Instagram is the modern résumé, head shot, and audition all rolled into one. Convey a fun, dynamic, charismatic, bold, and clear picture of the archetype you have chosen to represent with your posts. The same holds true for IG stories, reels, and highlights as well. Embrace the phrase "kill your darlings." No matter how much you might love a post for any reason, even sentimental, if it doesn't fit with the strong and specific character and brand that you are trying to portray, *archive it*! This includes most pictures with beloved friends, family, food, landscapes, inspirational quotes, exes—almost anything that is not you alone! We permit an occasional second person if they help convey one of the main themes of your brand. If you choose a Good Girl archetype, for example, include an image of you helping others for a nonprofit or celebrating holidays with your family. If you determine that you don't have any posts that match these criteria (and *many* IG feeds do not), delete your profile and start over from scratch, unless you already have a large social media following (10K plus). Starting from scratch gives you several benefits, including the ability to precisely curate a profile and the added bonus of not needing to delete all your likes and tags. The only real benefit of keeping an original Instagram is that the inclusion of older posts raises fewer red flags about the possibility of you entering the game simply for fame.

The Parasocial Gaze

When we look into our screens we want to feel like we're friends with the person staring back. This is the foundation of all parasocial relationships, and developing a strong parasocial gaze during the off-season enhances the effectiveness of your social media dramatically. A strong parasocial gaze requires you to look directly into the camera with nothing obscuring your eyes—no sunglasses, no hats. You can smile, look pensive, work out, or engage in any kind of activity or emotional state as long as you're looking directly at the viewer, giving them the feeling of an intimate moment between you, a personal connection. Study and mimic the parasocial gazes of your Hero Players to help develop your own.

And don't stop there. Hero Players from past seasons offer much more to study. Comb their social media or parasocial plays for even more knowledge. Mimic everything from their picture format, tone, types of stories/highlights, and how often they post as closely as possible. This holds especially true for the highest-level parasocial players who have the most IG followers, starting at the top with Hannah Brown, who currently has more than any other player in history at 2.5 million.

The Basic Scrub

Just like a trip to the spa includes an exfoliating scrub to reveal the new glowing skin beneath, so too should your initial basic IG scrub remove the nonessential posts to let the new, glowing version of you shine through. While you must perform a heavier scrub once you're cast, this initial culling serves primarily to streamline the casting process for any producers who might be looking. Archive or delete any and all posts that do not fit your prescribed brand and archetype. Remove any posts that do not meet at least the impression of a professional-level photograph and caption. If the image works but the caption doesn't, rewrite the caption. Delete any hashtags that suggest you are looking for followers (#followforfollow, et cetera). Remove tags from any and all posts that do not fit your chosen archetype, and especially posts that have any kind of potentially problematic content. And this scrub extends far beyond just the posts themselves. The *Bachelor* subreddit community will heavily scrutinize likes, reposts, and, of course, photos in which you are tagged. The Fourth Audience infamously outed Victoria Fuller (Season 24—Peter Weber) as having modeled for a clothing line with shirts that said "White Lives Matter" after tagged posts surfaced in which she was wearing the shirt.

If you decide to leave up a tagged post, perform a thorough scan of the person's profile that you are linking to yourself to make certain no questionable likes surface on that person's page. While this is more apt for the post-casting Deep Scrub detailed later in this chapter, assume that Bachelor Nation will heavily scrutinize your entire family, friends, exes, and even pets' IG pages—it is up to you to convince them to clean up or privatize their profiles as well.

Professional Photo Shoot

You will probably need to conscript the services of a professional photographer to create a series of suitable images unless you have been prepping for this for a long time or already make a living on Instagram. If you're on a budget, do your best to imitate professional-level quality with a friend or a tripod. There is a time of day that begins an hour before the sun sets when the light dances in a hazy amber aura around all those who find themselves in its magical embrace. Take literally all of your photos during this "Golden Hour." Prepare for the shoot by selecting bold backgrounds in interesting locations and by bringing multiple wardrobe changes. Strike as many common influencer poses as possible, which you can find by casually scrolling through any Hero Player's Instagram. Attempt to re-create these Heroes' images exactly, down to the cropping.

Feature every single type of outfit you might wear on the show (athletic, formal, swimsuit, casual, et cetera) in this shoot and environments that will be shown on the show if possible (hot tubs, boats, helicopters, mansions).

These images help casting Producers see exactly what you would look like on any number of dates they might arrange. If you have a special skill that can be conveyed visually, include it. Change your lighting and hair to maintain the illusion that your photos were taken on different days. Pose alone in most of your IG posts, though a couple images with a family member or friend can remain as long as they will star as central figures in a backstory element to be used in the game. The ideal profile includes a mixture of professional glamour shots and more "casual" down-to-earth shots that are still perfect but slightly less staged. And if you settle on the Fool archetype, you can throw in one or two perfectly lit, designed, and cropped "silly" photos.

The Perfect Bio

Your bio should be short, witty, and further define your brand. Change your IG handle to your full name or "The Real [Full Name]" to make it instantly clear for any member of Bachelor Nation seeking out a new player's profile that it is indeed the correct "Lauren Smith" so that their browsing converts to clicking "follow" as quickly as possible. Bachelor Nation journalists publish lists of IG handles once they discover the player pool, so change your handle as early as possible to avoid having a broken IG link. Perhaps the greatest parasocial player of all time, Season 17 Bachelorette Katie Thurston, changed her handle from @ventwithkatie to @therealkatiethurston a few weeks before her season started airing. Many successful players choose to include Bible verses in their bios, which we strongly recommend if you have selected a Christian thematic element to complement your archetype. Only tag a brand or company in your bio that you want discussed and dissected publicly and don't include links to a Venmo account or any requests for donations unless they are for specific charities that are widely publicly acceptable. And when it comes to emojis, less is certainly more, with a hard ceiling of three. Here are a few examples of professional player bios as they appeared at various times:

Hannah Brown (Bachelorette Season 15, Most successful IG player of all time - 2.5M Followers)

♡ I'm still Alabama Hannah // ✞ And Jesus still loves me //

⇩ New YouTube Video

Hannah Ann Sluss (Season 24 Ring Winner, 1.2M Followers)
southern charm with a side of sass ☺ follow my journey through the streets of LA! food, flowers, + fashion are my passion 🌹 email contact below

Madison Prewett (Season 24 Runner Up, 1.7M Followers)
love greatly // be a voice for the voiceless // always stand up for what you believe in // Proverbs 31:8 | Romans 5:8

Tayshia Adams (Season 23 3rd place, Bachelorette Season 16 Crown, 1.8M Followers)
——— TAYSHIA ADAMS ——— // The Bachelorette 🌷 //
🙏 : Psalm 46:5† // 🎙 Co-host on @clickbaitbn // #goodtrouble

Brand Blossom

Going forward, treat your account as your *Bachelor* audition page, targeting your future audiences. If you'd like, keep a separate, private account for personal use. The Fourth Audience will follow your friends and family (even private accounts) to try to find your problematic likes and posts. Hypervigilance will be rewarded. Create and stick to a consistent photo schedule that includes a post at least once a week and ideally multiple posts a week, along with daily IG story additions, the best of which you should save to clear, organized IG highlights. Assume that any interaction you have with people, be it in person or via DM, will be made public by someone looking to parasocially capitalize themselves on knowing a player going on the show. Many people have created viral TikToks by claiming to know certain players, for better or worse. Some strangers have even publicly posted their interactions with players on dating apps, saying that certain people "ghosted" them. Welcome to the wild world of Bachelor Nation.

Casting Round 1

Once you've selected an archetype and crafted an Instagram that supports it, the next step is to make first contact, to let the Producers know you are ready to enter the game, because there is only one way any prospective player finds herself stepping out of the limo on Night One—she has to be cast. There are four ways to get cast: the application, the recommendation, the open call, and the cold call.

The Application

Producers provide two main types of applications to players. One is a form found on the official *Bachelor* producers' website: Bachelornation.com. The other is submitting a video, which requires sending a copy to the casting office. To be eligible for either type, you must be at least twenty-one years old, though it is recommended that you should wait until age twenty-four if you want to be in contention for the Crown without first doing a stint on *BIP*. You must be from the United States or Canada, have a valid passport, and have no felony convictions. The fine details of eligibility are included in the following link: https://bachelornation.com/pages/eligibility/.

The online form requires basic information about employment, former marital status, children, if you have applied before, et cetera. Deliver all answers in accordance with your archetype and themes already selected. For example, if your family currently resides somewhere more interesting and important to your brand than wherever you might have grown up, choose that location as your hometown.

Producers request Facebook and IG links, but they are not mandatory. They will let you upload a recent and accurate photo and luckily you just took a bunch of high-quality pics, hopefully with a professional photographer, so you're all set!

There is a single essay question on this specific online form: "Why do you want to be on *The Bachelor*?" There is no one perfect response. It will vary greatly according to the individual player, their particular brand/story, and who the Producers have cast as the Bachelor if this information is known. Make the Producers' jobs easy by crafting your own seasonal arc and allowing them to do less work when they pitch you to their superiors, who will find it easier to visualize you on-screen in a number of the various scenarios they are already engineering.

Key Points of Interest

- If you want to include humor in your essay, crowdsource your jokes to make sure they are universally appealing and easily understood. And above all, they should never undermine the sincerity of your essay or the genuine tone.
- Paint a vivid picture of your background, including where and how you were raised and why that makes you ready for mar-

riage. You can include endearing details about a colorful family figure who might pop up on your potential Hometown Date.

- Include your beliefs about love and relationships and how you came to hold those beliefs.
- Include an expression of what you hope to get from this experience (true love) and possibly how it relates to past players, e.g., wanting what Catherine Lowe has (a husband and a family). This is an outstanding way to convey you are 4TRR.
- A statement of your strong belief in the power of the process, backed up by personal anecdotes about the success of accelerated romantic relationships among people in your own life, is a fantastic strategy. Perhaps your parents or friends met in an unorthodox manner, so you "know that it's possible to find love in unexpected ways."
- If your parents have been together for a long time, express a desire to have what your parents have.
- Conversely, if your parents are not together, craft a statement acknowledging how intentional you have become about picking the right person. You know firsthand how important it is to make the right decision because you have seen how the incorrect decision can negatively affect children.
- Definitely include a full description of your PTC or multiple PTCs that you will play at some point in the game.
- And easily the most important thing to do in this essay is convey a *story* that the Producers can use to craft a longer arc for you with the Bachelor that will be interesting and emotionally fulfilling and ultimately culminate in true love or eviscerating heartbreak. Easy!

Key Points to Generally Avoid (Exceptions for Experimental Applications/Villain Goals)

- Instagram
- Desire to be famous
- Connections to people who work in entertainment
- That you know this is a game (or use any game-related words like "winning"). Similarly, you will want to not mention this book or the podcast *Game of Roses*.

- Political extremes
- Crimes committed
- Non-Christian religion. Players have practiced other religions but have not generally gone as far in the game. You could focus on a non-Christian religion as an experimental strategy.

If you opt for the video form of application, shoot the video in a landscape view and utilize all of the same points of interest described above in a direct address to the camera. This is where your parasocial gaze comes into play. Make sure the lighting is good and the audio is clear enough for the Producers to hear every word easily, and look directly into the lens. You can also add subtitles. We recommend video applications over the standard online form application due to the smaller number of videos received and the ability they grant a player the opportunity to show the Producers what the player would potentially look like on television.

Keep your video no longer than ten minutes and preferably under seven. Use a light and fun tone and smile as much as possible. Include shots of your pet, your unique brand-supporting hobbies, your work, or your fun family members. You can easily find some casting videos of ex-players online like Ashley Iaconetti. Study and mimic them if possible. However, the most helpful videos to watch in service of crafting an effective casting tape are the intros. At the beginning of almost every season as the players are being introduced in the Night One episode, Producers include short intro videos for six to ten players. Imitate these videos as closely as possible when creating your audition tape in order to show Producers how you might fit seamlessly into an upcoming season.

The Recommendation

In some cases players had no idea they were being nominated into the game by friends or family members until they received a call from Producers who were interested in getting to know them. This powerful method of application implies 4TRR from the get-go. If you are unaware you are even being considered for the game, then there is no possible way you could have ulterior motives for playing. Submissions for approval in this manner have produced several top players and even the greatest male player of all time, Nick Viall. It is worth noting that this method of nomination does not have to be genuine.

Conscript the aid of friends or family to nominate you to the casting process. You can even fill out the application yourself in the voice of an interested third party as long as that third party is willing to go along with the ruse if the Producers call to get information about you. This is an easy way to enter the process with an elevated sense of sincerity.

The Open Call

The only method of application that allows players the opportunity to meet Producers immediately is the open call. Producers hold these meet-and-greet-style events throughout the year in malls, hotels, and similar venues that can comfortably manage a high volume of people. If you plan on attending an open call you should come prepared. In addition to wearing the proper outfit, bring food and water to last for several hours, as the process is long. The first thing you must do upon arrival is fill out the same application found online. Then they will photograph you and eventually you will come to sit in front of a casting Producer who will ask a lot of the same questions you just answered in the application. The difference is that this time they record your answers on video. Treat this interview like it's taking place during the course of the regular season. Imagine this footage is going to be used in the show itself as one of the confessional-style segments between in-game events, which are known as ITMs or In The Moments. The Producers don't just want to know how you will answer the questions at an open call; they also want to see what you will look like on-camera while you answer them. As always, convey a high degree of 4TRR.

The Cold Call

Increasingly, casting Producers are discovering players by searching through Instagram randomly, looking for anyone who has the right set of photos and videos. This is why the first phase of preseason preparation is your social media transformation. It might happen that just as you are sitting down to fill out the application, you receive a DM from a casting Producer and you can bypass the insincere process of attempting to convince the Producers of your value through an essay. This is by far the most desirable manner in which to begin the casting process because it elevates you to a position of advantage. The Producers in this case must convince you to come into the game. The exact opposite holds true with both the application and the recommendation, which place the burden of convincing the Producers of your value on you. So if you receive a cold call you should enjoy the moment and feel absolutely free to play a little hard to get, thus raising your level of value in the Producers' eyes, which will hopefully help you once the game begins.

Casting Round 2—Producer Interviews

This is the moment in which you get to have a conversation and ultimately meet a member of the Third Audience for the first time, assuming you didn't begin your casting process at an open call. Although Producers follow a basic casting protocol, no two players' interview processes are exactly alike and in some cases even the number and location of interviews varies. Normally, though, they will conduct your first interview via phone call or video chat.

The producers use your initial interview and any subsequent interviews as opportunities to dig deeper into your personality profile. This is where they begin to excavate pieces of information they can use to start building possible narratives in the upcoming season. Assume that these interviews are being recorded and, even though you're not technically in the season yet, you are already playing the game.

Before attending an in-person casting interview, do a practice interview in the same outfit you are going to wear to make sure you are comfortable. Answer a list of basic interview questions to a camera, ideally to a friend who asks follow-up questions. Watch these tapes repeatedly and practice your answers over and over until they sound genuine and confident, eliminating any distracting mannerisms or excessive use of "ums" and "likes" (unless that is part of your brand). Use colorful metaphors to describe your life, especially your love life. Ideally, walk the fine line of being TV ready and being obliviously genuine. Watch ITM footage of your Hero Players from past seasons. Reach out to veteran players via DM in order to get some advice leading into this process. Many modern players befriend and receive coaching from former players. Season 23 (Colton Underwood) runner-up Hannah Godwin coached Season 24's (Peter Weber) Hannah Ann Sluss to her Ring Winner status.

If you make it through this initial series of phone or video conference interviews, next you will travel to Los Angeles to meet the casting Producers in person. This can be daunting, especially for players from smaller towns or players who haven't traveled extensively, but you've done your preseason work and you have nothing to worry about. Nonetheless, below are some common areas of concern surrounding the in-person interviews and methods to address them.

Dress and Makeup

Producers give the advice that you should dress "like you're going on a date." Your outfit should look good on-camera, convey your archetype, and be comfortable to limit the need to fidget or worry about it at all. Go for solid colors over distracting patterns, and leave any noisy, distracting, or political jewelry at home. And, of course, we recommend professional makeup and hair. The producers have met hundreds upon hundreds of players over the years and they can spot one who has the look of being ready for the game almost instantly. Make every attempt to create a look that could be seen on *The Bachelor* without any alteration.

Questions

At this point you've already answered hundreds of questions on applications and through phone and video interviews. It seems almost incomprehensible that the Producers would still have some lingering curiosities about various topics. And this is largely true. The questions they ask are very likely going to be ones you've already answered: What is your background? What is your family like? What have your dating experiences been like? What do you like to do for fun? They've designed this round of interrogation for the Producers to be able to see how you come across while answering. Prepare fun "off-the-cuff" anecdotes on each of these topics for this level of the casting process. If you don't have any crazy dating stories, make them up or, even better, borrow from a friend's life! It might have made your friend sad at the time but now her getting ghosted at the Cheesecake Factory by a magician who loves Crocs can help propel you to fame! Utilize the conversational tools of exaggeration, metaphors, and alliteration to help deal with Producers' lines of questioning.

Performance

Producers will scrutinize the tapes of these interviews well after the conversations have concluded, so render a strong performance. Ask the casting Producer where to look, either to the camera or to the Producer, and focus on the target as if you're having an intimate conversation with one person instead of an audience of Producers. Be as charismatic on-camera as possible.

Casting and Beyond

After the careful curation of all social media accounts and several rounds of interviews, Producers will call a lucky few to let them know they've been selected to compete on the upcoming season of *The Bachelor*. Congratulations, you've been cast! Now you need to complete an entirely new array of preparations, each equally important for setting up as deep a run into the game as possible.

Preparing Friends/Family for Hometowns

The Hometown round of the play-offs requires not only you to perform at the highest possible levels but your family as well. The MOTF (Meeting Of The Family) is generally the only part of the game in which your family makes an appearance, though in the case of single-parent players or leads, Producers sometimes orchestrate early MOTFs to facilitate the introduction of a child or two. And sometimes they arrange late familial appearances when a parent crashes a play-off round or the Crown makes a last-minute phone call to secure a Blessing before the proposal in the Finale. Do not take the MOTF event lightly; any family members or friends you select to take part in play-offs with you must know their pre-planned duties going into the date. Get them to read this book if you can.

Familial Walls

Just as you should prepare walls for the Bachelor to take down, so should your family prepare walls designed to come down in the Hometown round. The basic familial wall narrative involves one or more parents expressing skepticism at the process and thereby raising a wall that the Bachelor must overcome. At some point in a one-on-one conversation with one of the parents, have that parent convey that although they had their reservations, since meeting the Bachelor they can tell he's a good person. This should lead into the skeptical parent granting the Blessing, signaling the lowering of the familial walls. The relationship has progressed and the Bachelor has no overt reason to dismiss you.

Line of Questioning

In order to bolster the initial walls, members of your family can lightly interrogate the Bachelor with questions about his sincerity, his feelings for you, and his plans for the future. We go into more detail on this during the Hometowns chapter.

Colorful Family

Prepare your family to add color to your backstory and secure your brand. This can include family traditions (if none exist, you can manufacture them) such as traditional toasts, lighthearted games, a fun family-specific gift for the Bachelor (e.g., jersey for the family's annual Thanksgiving football game), and anything quirky that would likely make the edit. The other main area in which the family can enrich your story is by adding details to your PTC that you have already played. This will imbue the anecdotes with the power of 4TRR.

The Blessing

The Blessing is a time-honored prize won by the Bachelor and it can only be given by members of your family, traditionally your father, though others may step in to fulfill this role. The Blessing is a customary agreement between your parent and the Bachelor that your parent supports the idea of the Bachelor proposing to you. It is the most important play that your parent can make, it will almost always make the edit, and you both should time it to occur at the end of the Hometown MOTF portion, so that the Bachelor can leave your familial home with a sense of relief, feeling justified in his decision to move forward with you to Fantasy Suites.

Tying Up Loose Ends

Ideally, maintain good standing with all exes. Contact your exes before shooting begins so they can prepare to be contacted by the show and members of the *Bachelor* journalistic world as well as prepare their own social media for scrutiny. Agree on the historical timeline of the relationship (give at least three months since the end of the last relationship prior to going on the show). And if there are one or more exes whom you might not be on the best terms with . . . get ready to see them at the worst possible time in the game. Producers frequently bring in exes whom we started calling Skeletons to create drama. They flew Becca Kufrin's ex-boyfriend to Portugal to confront Kufrin and Arie Luyendyk Jr. right after they enjoyed Fantasy Suites on Season 22. And it's not just serious exes. In Season 24, they brought back a semi-one-night-stand of Victoria Fuller's, Chase Rice, as the musical guest during her 1O1 Date with Peter Weber. No one-night stand is safe, especially if they're a musician. Be ready, because the Producers are.

Brand Keeper

While the rules around social media keep changing, generally, once you are in-game, Producers prevent access to your phone and therefore you can't maintain your social media without the help of a trusted friend or even a professional social media manager. Ideally, this person is social media savvy, but if they are not, prepare them by having enough versatile material to push your brand remotely. In a worst-case scenario, you can use an app to schedule the release of your posts—though this can be risky should the post not gel well with timing of in-game or current world events.

IG Catalog

Prepare at least two months' worth of social media material to be used in conjunction with the airing of the season. Include pictures in every outfit that you will wear in-game in this catalog, each to be posted with its details tagged right after the episode airs. Ideally, monetize these posts (we detail fashion and makeup spon-con later in this chapter). This catalog can also feature emotional material, such as posts with more details about your PTCs, set to post in tandem with the episode airing during which you played the PTC.

The Deep Scrub

While you should perform a basic scrub before casting, after you've been cast, it is imperative that you perform a Deep Scrub properly. Follow up with any loose ends from your earlier scrub. Did you ask people to take down photos that they kept up? If the person is not a family member, take down any online ties with that person—by removing tagged photos together and unfollowing them. Next, turn to your family members. Bachelor Nation will heavily scrutinize all of these Instagrams. If your family member is not ready for that, have them put their Instagram on private and, most important, *not accept new followers until the season airs*. In terms of exes, direct them to go private if they are not prepared as well. Hopefully they will play ball in terms of removing any questionable content. Tread very carefully, though, as this can backfire. During the casting of Clare Crawley's sixteenth *Bachelorette* season, one potential player's ex-girlfriend posted a photo of her butt in response to her ex going on *The Bachelorette* and asking her to "clean up" her profile.

Go through all of your follows and be very intentional with political figures and groups that you keep on that list. Make sure that your follows are consistent with your brand and you would be OK if those follows became a news item. Follow any additional figures and groups that you think will help your brand before they announce casting. Rachael Kirkconnell on Matt James's twenty-fifth *Bachelor* season was caught following Black Lives Matter on Instagram only after news came out of her having liked problematic, racially insensitive IG photos. If you have decided to keep your original IG profile, go through *every single one of your likes* (and do the same on Twitter). Yes, likes can take down mountains. You can view all your liked IG photos in Settings and unlike around three hundred per day without getting banned by the app. There are some costly apps that will do this work for you. This process makes yet another argument for starting your Instagram from scratch. As far as Twitter goes, there is absolutely no benefit of keeping tweets older than a couple months, and players to this day are still getting in trouble for past combinations of 280 characters. There are free apps that will download and delete all your old tweets. The scrub is necessary and gets increasingly difficult as the game's fandom and scrutiny level up, but it will pay dividends for players who perform it well.

Physical Training

The Bachelor is a marathon, but it will also require sprints. Physical preparation ensures your ability to focus on the game as opposed to losing breath, getting tired, and being defeated by the various scenarios in which you might find yourself. And specifically there are several physically demanding date types on which you will drastically benefit from being in prime athletic condition. Players have put to use climbing, jumping, dodging, wrestling, punching, and bicycling skills season after season.

Getting in Shape

Prepare yourself and get in the best shape of your life. Hire a trainer if money allows. Almost every modern season features a relay race Group Date and the most physically fit person can win a PFT (Play For Time) competition. Be able to run short sprints for both GD athletic competitions and sprinting in order to greet the Bachelor first on any Group Date. Quit drinking and prepare yourself for remaining sober in-game. You'll need endurance, not just for dates that require hiking, running, sprinting, et cetera, but even for standing up in heels all night, as Cocktail Parties sometimes film through the night until the morning after.

Dance Yourself to Victory

If there is any one skill to focus on learning in the preseason, you should practice dancing. Because dancing is a visual gesture that can't be copyrighted, doesn't need to have perfect sound, can be done in any environment, and presents well on-camera, Producers often include it in the edit. It comes up in countless Group Dates. It comes up in countless 1O1s and at the private concerts after the 1O1 Rose is given out. This skill always makes for an interesting and chemistry-building mini-date activity and importantly requires no equipment. Slow dancing provides an easy Kiss Lead-In setup, as well as an opportunity to casually break the touch barrier. The more you kiss, the more screen time you will receive. Dancing can also help build your Second Audience game by bonding with the other players and frequently making the blooper reel or episode tags. And should you succeed and win the Ring or the Crown, you might have the opportunity to take those dancing skills to ABC's sister show, *Dancing with the Stars*, to continue dominating in the postseason.

Special Skills

While dancing and general cardio are important, take time to learn other skills that are the most common Group and 1O1 Date activities. These include learning how to: fight (wrestling, boxing, sumo, fighting with a stick), walk a runway, take a picture (should already be covered in pre-casting), skydive, bungee jump, climb, ride a horse, and throw a football. Football is one of the

best skills you can learn, as there are often collaborations with the NFL and the Bachelors are pleasantly surprised when players can perform this seemingly masculine skill.

Personal Talent

While learning skills just described keeps you generally prepared for most date types, specializing in a unique talent that can be used at will is a strategy that all but guarantees screen time. Your talent can be anything you are good at, but the best talents are easily and legally filmed and require no equipment. If you use brand names, those may be cut. If you do something that is too small to capture clearly on footage (for instance, dice, crossword puzzles, et cetera) or too cerebral and complicated to explain (quick large sum division), Producers may not air it. Ideally, your talent adapts well to any environment and is extremely visual (could be used silently with voice-over over the footage). Be prepared to perform it at a moment's notice. It's not the worst thing in the world if it requires a certain setting and prepared equipment if your talent is especially impressive, like fire dancing. Madison Prewett (Peter Weber—Season 24) created an entire personality out of her basketball talent and used her Hometown Date to put it on full, dominant display. Cassie Randolph (Colton Underwood—Season 23) taught Underwood some sign language in her first mini-date on Night One, a talent that was part of her Good Girl/Professional brand that utilized her speech pathologist vocation. Sharleen Joynt used her Professional talent spectacularly well in Season 18 by alluding to her job as an opera singer but not actually presenting the talent until the opportune 1O1 Date, building it up and using it as a reward for Juan Pablo Galavis. The best talents fit in with your brand, help paint a more colorful, cohesive narrative, and, most important, make the edit.

Face Play

Remember the *Bachelor* player who kept her face neutral the entire season? Neither does anyone. Face play is any kind of expression a person can make with their face without looking at the camera (though looking at the camera Jim Halpert–style is an interesting experimental strategy). Face play is one of the easiest skills to learn in the preseason and one of the most underutilized in-game but will reap rewards in the ancillary meme arena. Practice making faces in front of the mirror over and over. Film yourself doing it and know all of your best angles. Open your mouth wide, roll your tongue everywhere, open your eyes as wide as possible, and make it your own. Practice reacting big and often and pair it with a signature laugh. Study the infamous face-play work of Mykenna Dorn (Peter Weber—Season 24), known for her traveling tongue play, and Olivia Caridi (Ben Higgins—Season 20), known for her wide, open-mouth play, for inspiration. Caridi even eventually named her podcast after her extraordinary face play, *Mouthing Off*.

Crying Game

A player who can cry on command can make all of her stories more believable, seem more genuine, and sometimes get rewarding reactions from the Bachelor. Tears often equate to screen time and can even become your main personality trait.

Signature Gesture

Hand in hand with developing face play comes formulating a signature gesture, which can be a bold reaction to having your name read on the Date Card or even upon accepting a Rose. Perform a repetitive noise (squeal, squeak, grunt) and a gesture that conveys excitement. The Third Audience will be sure it makes the cut and the Fourth Audience might employ it for the meme cycle. Example: a player who fist-pumps and yells "Wowwiee!" whenever her name is called. Signature gestures allow you to capitalize on even the smallest increment of screen time. Demi Burnett (Colton Underwood—Season 23) was the prototype player for utilizing every second of time on-camera, and she came up with different, enthusiastic phrases every single time she accepted a Rose in order to steal the show.

Hujus

Any student of the game will already be familiar with a Huju, or Hug Jump. It is a signature physical move of the Bachelor Franchise whereby the female player runs toward the Bachelor, leaps into the air, clings to the Bachelor by wrapping her arms and legs around him, then often kisses him, and finally dismounts. While most perform this move during the play-offs, perform it at any time, including after you have sprinted faster than any other player to greet the Bachelor first on a Group Date. And you certainly don't want the first Huju you perform to be in-game. Find a willing friend who is at least six-two to be your target and relentlessly practice your Huju technique so when the time comes you can perform at an Olympic gymnastics level.

Prepared Written Material

Before heading into the game, brainstorm and memorize several different pieces of written material that can be applied to many different scenarios. Most often, you will utilize these prepared stories on Public Performance competition Group Dates (in the form of a song, stand-up, speech, and/or poetry), but you can modify them to meet other key moments in-game as well. When these are pre-written, you can focus on getting extra crucial 1O1 time with the Bachelor or celebrity guest host on the date, instead of on creating the original material on the spot.

The Trilogy

Prepare three different types of stories, all of which can be modified to meet whatever the date requirements are for written material. Make sure all three are on brand, include vivid details, and stir viewers' emotions. Practice on-camera and completely memorize all three. Test them on friends and family. The first story should be comedic and reveal an embarrassing moment, while painting a vivid picture of your life outside the game and illuminating at least one theme of your dynamic personality. Ultimately, the story should endear the player to all audiences, even if it paints you in a "bad" light (e.g., "I'm clumsy!" "I have a bad memory!" "I try and care *too* hard!"). Include subject matter universally liked by the Fourth Audience, such as pets, family, holidays, or food.

The second story should be dramatic and build to a crescendo by ultimately revealing a PTC. While ideally you should save your PTC for a 1O1 Date, sometimes you need to play it on a Group Date and you should never waste the opportunity! If you have mastered conjuring tears, sprinkle them in for 4TRR effect.

Make your third story emotional and center it around the Bachelor and the qualities you like about that person, highlighting specific events on your individual love journey. This is the only story that you can't completely prepare beforehand, as you might have to wait until filming/knowing who the Bachelor is in order to finish writing. As soon as you learn who the Bachelor is, write this third story in your journal, listing his positive qualities, combining heartfelt emotion with jokes. Document *everything* that happens in the relationship so that you can easily recall it back, should the need arise. Keep in mind that you will have to perform most of these stories in front of a large audience, possibly made up of other players not chosen for the Group Date, but your focus should be on the Bachelor. Ideally, include some sort of audience interaction with the Bachelor at a key moment, e.g., "and that was when we had our first kiss, which looked like *this*!"). Frequently, players who go the biggest, show the most enthusiasm, and/or go to the next level of incorporating the Bachelor into their performance get the GD win.

Listen to Your Heart

Come up with a bunch of different songs about the journey, especially if you are not a musician (which can beg questions of 4TWR). Make the songs very good and practice so they will seem even better "off-the-cuff." Compose songs about Cocktail Parties, a rivalry/the 2O1, and other parts of the game that you know are coming. Original songs help your Second Audience game—to bond with the other players and to secure a Colorful Narrator role, one of the most coveted positions in this game. You can even turn one of your unused Three Stories into a song for a Public Performance Group Date (poem, essay, stand-up) or into Mansion Free-Play Antics.

Catch Me if You Can

Come in with a catchphrase related to your brand. It can tie into your nickname, but it doesn't have to. Becca Kufrin (Arie Luyendyk Jr.—Season 22) entered the game Night One by making Bachelor Luyendyk repeat her catchphrase, "Are you ready to do the damn thing?," while fake proposing to her. She used the phrase again and again and it even became her mantra when she eventually wore the Crown. It was perfect for her brand because it was energetic, a little sassy, and a little dorky. It could be applied to many different scenarios and countless variations could be used by herself and others. Envision the ABC poster for your future season of *The Bachelorette* and what verbiage they would use as their tagline.

Brave Little Toaster

Prepare toasts for each step of the journey. They can overlap in content with your prepared songs and can be used in Mansion Free-Play Antics if you're not able to secure that week's toast position. The Bachelor gives toasts at the beginning of every Cocktail Party and GD After Party and after every Rose Ceremony. But you can also do these toasts. Example for early on: "Here's to that wild [insert Night One Curveball] and falling in love!" Example for mid-game: "Here's to vulnerability, [insert travel location], and Michelle's brave hat choice!" Play-offs: "Here's to putting the 'sweet' in Fantasy Suites and falling in love!" These can be generically funny, will often get screen time to bookend portions, and can also help establish a power position within the group.

Choosing Makeup

Perfect your makeup routines. Research and consult with experts who work in television who can tell you the right makeup for on-camera work, as this will be different from what looks best live. Keep a consistent signature makeup look so you can easily be identified, especially in the earlier rounds, when it is harder to stand out/differentiate players.

Five-Minute Face

Develop a quick version of your makeup routine that takes five minutes and ideally can be done with poor lighting anywhere. Practice the routine over and over. This is key prep if there's a Home Invasion–type date where the Bachelor or a previous player rips the player(s) out of bed at 4:00 am. You may not have slept and you're being forced onto a hot-air balloon at the crack of dawn, but you will look amazing!

Gold Level—Monetize It

Reach out to makeup brands before going on the show. This can help you keep on budget as well as earn some extra cash by preparing ads beforehand. Then you can have an ad prepared for the makeup look that either your Brand Keeper or you release concurrently when the specific episode with that look airs.

Choosing Wardrobe

The most important thing in choosing a wardrobe is comfort. Do not bring any clothes that make you itch, require constant adjusting, won't allow you to move freely and dance at a moment's notice, constrict your breath, create wardrobe malfunctions (unless you've prepared this story line ahead of time), make noise, et cetera. Problem clothes like this will get edited out and, most important, they won't permit you to be as present for this game of physical and emotional endurance, and you need any advantage possible. For this reason, wear all clothes you bring beforehand, ideally trying out some physical gestures and longevity in them. The second most important aspect of choosing a wardrobe is how it looks on-camera and how it reinforces your brand. For instance, if you choose a Good Girl strategy, leave the fishnets and chokers behind, unless part of your story arc you've created is a *Grease* reveal (dressing up as a vixen to surprise the Bachelor at some point in time). Film yourself in the clothes beforehand to make sure they appear well on-camera. Do not wear any visible brands or distracting patterns. You will need fashionable casual wear, swimwear, formal wear, activewear, winter wear, and maybe even a costume or two just in case.

Five-Minute Outfit

Just as with the makeup, prepare a go-to outfit for any type of activity in case there is a Home Invasion Date. The player who has her outfits ready to go can spend more time preparing mentally and less time worrying about putting together that day's look.

Gold Level—Monetize It

Reach out to clothing brands before going on the show. This will help you spend less money in the preseason as well as help start developing relationships with spon-con. You can also release details on the outfit with swipe-up links, concurrently with the episodes, ideally taking a cut of the profits.

Game of Time

Always wear a watch. Time is the most valuable commodity in the game and being able to track lengths of time or even generally what time of day it is will grant you a huge advantage. Tracking time allows you to give a certain amount of minutes before performing a Steal, to know when the Bachelor will likely finish his dates, and even to figure out if there is an opportunity for a Knock Knock. Players without any way to tell time will be at the whim of the Producers to construct their days.

What Else to Bring

Journal

This is the most important item to bring. Your journal gives you the ability to recount exactly what has happened in-game, specifically in your relationship with the Bachelor. It also allows you to track everything in-game, such as noting others' friendships, rivalries, et cetera. It also helps you memorize and improve your Three Stories.

Presents

Bring gifts for the Bachelor that tell a story of your brand, including food, physical trinkets, or photographs of loved ones to show them.

Special Talent Equipment

Pack anything you need for your prepared special talents: flamethrower sticks, ventriloquist mimes, et cetera. Do not rely on the Producers to provide anything.

With a good understanding of the game's structure and having done everything possible to achieve a strong preseason advantage, make your way into the game and put this knowledge and preparation to the test in the first round of play.

Chapter 3

NIGHT ONE:

SURVIVING THE SLAUGHTER

That's like the most important thing, is getting the First Impression Rose. I just want to like take it!

Corinne Olympios—Season 21 (Nick Viall), Night One

For most people the end of the year means trips to see their families for the holidays, giving and getting presents, willfully eating too much every day for a week straight, and breaking the promise you made to yourself not to get as drunk as you did last year on New Year's Eve. We do those things too. But, for us, all of the traditional merriment that surrounds the holiday season doesn't give us even a fraction of the pure, overwhelming, head-to-toe body high we get from the first Monday in January. Every year, this is the night when the long, dark off-season ends and our beloved game begins again with the unparalleled grandeur and spectacle of Night One.

We thought we knew a lot about Night One. We knew about the big Limo Exits throughout history. We knew how important the FIMP Rose was. We even knew Night One actually lasts well into the next morning, so it's more like a Night and Morning After One. But once we started going back through the data we collected during the Hyperbinge, it turns out we didn't know shit about Night One.

We learned there are eight specific types of Limo Exits, each with its own advantages. We learned that the FIMP Rose isn't all it's cracked up to be. And maybe most important, we learned that in the whole of the sporting world there is no moment, no endeavor, no event, no exotic purpose or single round of any game played on court or field more unforgiving and seemingly arbitrary in its cold brutality than Night One of *The Bachelor*.

Of the 676 players who have given it their all over the first twenty-five seasons, 239 of them have never received a single Rose. Known within the game as Night One Girls (N.O.G.), these sacrificial lambs are eliminated from play in the very first Rose Ceremony. This means without the influence of any other qualifiers, the moment you step out of the limo you are up against a 35.3 percent likelihood of being sent right back home before sunrise, or maybe a little after. These are the worst odds you'll face all season.

In this chapter we're going to break Night One down into its various elements and discuss some strategies for getting through this first, most difficult round of the game when any advantage, no matter how seemingly small, can mean the difference between survival and elimination without a single new IG follower.

A Night in Four Parts

Where other sports present both players and spectators with visible clocks that count down the finite resource of game time, *The Bachelor* offers nothing so simple. Instead, Night One measures itself through the course of four distinct but untimed rounds occurring in the same order each season with escalating tension and stakes as they proceed.

Round 1—the Limo Exit
Round 2—Cocktails First Half
Round 3—Cocktails Second Half
Round 4—the Rose Ceremony

Round 1—the Limo Exit

This is by far our favorite part of Night One. For us it's like the opening ceremony of the Olympics. The elegance, the pageantry, the farm animals . . . the Limo Exit has served as *The Bachelor*'s formal declaration of commencement every season all the way back to the game's premiere on March, 25, 2002, when an episode of *The Bachelor* was just an hour long and each of the players' Limo Exits were little more than quick hellos said through nervous smiles. But now, after nineteen years and twenty-five seasons of steadily growing fan engagement, the game's standard broadcasts have doubled in time. As a result, every element of the game has evolved into a more elaborate and intricate version of itself, including Limo Exits, which, in some cases, have even transcended the use of a limousine altogether.

Since the Paradise Era (which began in Season 19—Chris Soules), players have arrived in sports cars and police cars, ridden in on horses or other beasts of burden, and even been delivered zipped up tight inside of a piece of luggage waiting for the Bachelor's benevolent hand to release them from their self-inflicted prison of contortion. All of these strategies were efforts to accomplish the only true goal of the Limo Exit round—making a lasting impression on all four audiences simultaneously.

Once you're inside the Mansion your autonomy immediately gets stripped by the Producers and you have no control over your setting or circumstance. So your Limo Exit will be the last part of the game over which you have complete control. You have to treat it as much more than just the first time you're meeting the Bachelor—it's also the first and only moment the Fourth Audience (the viewers) is meeting you.

Over the course of twenty-five seasons there have been over six hundred Limo Exits and we watched every single one of them. To the untrained eye, the sheer volume can easily be misunderstood as a daunting variety of styles and strategies to choose from. But in reality we found that there are only eight types of Limo Exits:

1. *The Grand Entrance (or Grandy)*
2. *The Trick-Or-Treat (or TOT)*
3. *The Aloha*
4. *The Stand-Up (or Standy)*
5. *The Santa Claus (or Kringle)*
6. *The It Takes Two*
7. *The Sidecar*
8. *The Bland Entrance (or Blandy)*

The Grand Entrance (or Grandy)

This is the Cadillac of Limo Exits. Nothing demands attention and respect like the brazen ostentation and excessive spectacle of a Grandy. It requires you to discard the comfortable conformity of a limousine ride in order to make a strong, immediate impression on both the Bachelor and the other players alike with a bold entry in a luxury automobile or a law enforcement vehicle, accompanied by a marching band, or with some other nontraditional means of entry. The first-ever Grandy was performed by Lindzi Cox when she rode up to the Mansion on a horse in Season 16 (Ben Flajnik), and it has been a staple of Night One ever since. Due to the elaborate preproduction associated with the Grandy, the Producers only allow for a handful each season.

Grandies come in a wide variety of possible vehicles and accompanying flourishes, but the riskiest of all Grandy subcategories is the Live Animal Grandy, which requires either unmitigated bravery or madness in enough measure that you'll wager your first impression on the performance of a sub-sentient beast. In the best case, the animal conveys all the majesty and beauty of the natural world, conjuring an air of fantasy and adventure. But in the worst case, the Live Animal Grandy can yield unmitigated disaster in an embarrassing fall, the animal not cooperating or even, god forbid, turning the driveway in front of the Mansion into a toilet. And worse still, you run the risk of being upstaged by a mindless beast. Jenna Serrano knows all too well the bitter sting of being relegated to the shadows as a farm animal took her spotlight. For her Grandy in Season 24 (Peter Weber), Jenna ushered in a bovine that she named Ashley P, a reference to a former player. Ashley P was immortalized for all time, still appearing in memes today, while Serrano was cast aside, an N.O.G. whose name gathers dust in the footnotes of the game's records.

Possibly the most creative Grandy to date was performed by Kiarra Norman in Season 24, who put her flexibility on display as well as her tolerance for torture by zipping herself inside a piece of luggage that was deposited at the feet of then-Bachelor Peter Weber, forcing him to open it and discover her. Norman was eliminated in Week 4, but she established herself as the champion of Limo Exits by making the Producers give her over a minute and a half of screen time, more than any other player that season.

The Trick-Or-Treat (or TOT)

Halloween is widely understood to be the only twenty-four-hour period in which it is acceptable to don masks, regalia, costumes, and uniforms that would otherwise be disruptive to the regular flow of civilized public life. But for a lucky few, Night One offers an additional evening when flaunting disguises both comedic and horrifying is more than permissible. The TOT requires you to exit the limo in some form of costume, full or partial. The initial draw of a TOT is obvious, but it is important to keep in mind that while emerging from the limo in butterfly wings or a wizard robe might elicit an initial chuckle from the Bachelor or generate a week's worth of memes from the Fourth Audience, it renders you statistically locked out of Ring contention. It's true. The TOT has never produced a single Ring Winner.

The strong likelihood for the TOT's detrimental consequence lies in its inherent side effect of instantly marginalizing you in the eyes of the Bachelor. It is spectacle without the grandeur and awe of the Grandy. It is attention seeking that borders on farce. Where all other players wear stylish cocktail dresses that convey a level of seriousness and reverence for the game being played, the TOT can serve to make a joke of both you and the game and therefore the purpose of the entire night and subsequent weeks. A TOTing player runs the instantaneous risk of being perceived as more interested in putting on a performance than finding love—being there For The Wrong Reasons (4TWR)—a transgression for which there is only one penalty: dismissal.

The most successful TOTer in the game's history was Joelle "JoJo" Fletcher. She emerged from the limo wearing a unicorn head, which baffled Season 20's Bachelor, Ben Higgins. Then, once she was standing directly in front of him, in one precise move she removed the fantasy beast's head to reveal her true face, which dazzled Higgins with her stunning beauty. This minimal TOT using only a mask and only for a short time is recommended over a full-body TOT, which was employed in Season 21 (Nick Viall) by Alexis Waters, who arrived in a plush shark costume and claimed it was a dolphin despite the fact that she herself was an aspiring dolphin trainer and theoretically should have known the difference. Waters's TOT left such a lasting negative impression on the Second, Fourth, and First Audiences that she was forever and only known as Dolphin Girl for the remainder of her time

in-game. Although it earned her a brief appearance on *BIP*, the TOT is not recommended for players who want to convey that they take the process seriously.

The Aloha

This verbal greeting in a non-English language allows you to display your fluency in one of the many exotic tongues of the world or simply your ability to memorize a short phrase in a language other than English. Either way, the Aloha is short and sweet and quickly reveals something about your persona to the Bachelor—a possible ethnic heritage or academic linguistic pursuit or even a sense of humor depending on the phrase and its usage.

Very often, the Bachelor expresses pleasant surprise when he hears an Aloha and might ask you to teach him how to make the magical sounds coming out of your mouth. In this way the Aloha serves the double function of impressing the Bachelor with a display of perceived intellect as well as generating an anticipated mini-date activity of a language lesson later that night when you're granted 1O1 time with him.

Overall, the Aloha grants you a 65.21 percent chance of making it through Night One and the languages that tend to have the most favorable impact are Eastern European languages like Russian and Croatian. Spanish, Italian, and the Romance languages are also recommended. Nicole Lopez-Alvar spoke the Spanish version of "Half of my heart is in Havana, but hopefully the other part is with you" to Bachelor Colton Underwood in Season 23, which took her to Week 5 and eventually to a high sand placement with which she dominated her season of *BIP*. On the other hand, Chinese has proven to yield a lower success rate, as evidenced by Revian Chang's description of Colton Underwood as a "stud muffin" in Mandarin, which had her quickly saying, "Zàijiàn." (This is, of course, Mandarin for "Good-bye.") Vanessa Grimaldi is the only Ring Winner to have utilized the Aloha; DeAnna Pappas is the only Crown wearer to have started her journey with the Aloha.

The Stand-Up (or Standy)

If you're ready to put your entertainer skills on display, you might consider exiting the Limo with a Stand-Up, which requires you to deliver a solo performance upon meeting the Bachelor. The performance is usually an attempt at a comedic pre-scripted one-liner, but not always. Jokeless Stand-Ups include songs, dances, athletic flourishes, and monologues. The Stand-Up lets you show the Bachelor that you have a sense of humor while at the same time you give the Fourth Audience some material to make memes.

The quality of performance is very nearly irrelevant, as the Producers find value in the inclusion of footage of both well-delivered jokes and those that are poorly received. It should also be noted that while the Stand-Up most commonly takes the form of a simple joke or comedic anecdote, it also encompasses humorous musical performances, pratfalls, and other short-form pieces of physical comedy, as well as the use of comedic props.

Preparation is key when attempting a Stand-Up. You should definitely write and rehearse the exact joke and its delivery a dozen or more times by Night One so nerves are taken out of the equation and the performance goes according to plan.

Stand-Ups render a 66.34 percent likelihood of Night One survival. Past purveyors of the Stand-Up include Jillian Harris, who in Season 13 comedically exaggerated the importance of her potential mate's hot dog condiment preference when she greeted then-Bachelor Jason Mesnick. Jillian went on to wear the Crown of Bachelorette and she remains the only player from any of the pre-Paradise eras to have over 1 million IG followers. (See the appendix for descriptions of the various eras of our beloved game.)

The greatest postseason player of all time, Kaitlyn Bristowe, cunningly made use of the Season 19 Bachelor Chris Soules's Prince Farming moniker when she exited the limo and joked that he could plow her field anytime—a Stand-Up that was both charming and vulgar, guaranteeing further discussion from viewers. Kaitlyn, too, went on to wear the Crown. Demi Burnett in Season 23 began a flawless "Colorful Narrator" run with a negging joke to Bachelor Colton Underwood, "I have not dated a virgin since I was twelve, but I'm willing to give it another shot." She went on to recur in multiple *Bachelor* and *Bachelorette* seasons. She then made Bachelor Nation history as part of the first on-screen same-sex relationship in *BIP* Season 6 and soon accrued over 1 million IG followers. And all of her success began with an initial bawdy Stand-Up.

But you should exercise caution when attempting blue humor that could be potentially off-putting to the Fourth and/or First Audience. Katrina Badowski from Season 24 attempted a risqué Stand-Up when upon meeting Peter Weber she said, "You're going to love my hairless pussy," then revealed the punch line to her joke by producing a picture of her pet hairless cat. The joke fell flat and she was dismissed that night.

The Santa Claus (or Kringle)

Despite the incredible diversity of preference that exists in our species, there is not one among us who doesn't light up with excitement at the prospect of receiving a gift. This intrinsic human delight is what the Kringle attempts to exploit. Whether the gift is small or large, wrapped, hidden behind the back, or proudly carried with two hands in full view, all that is required to execute a standard Kringle is a gift. Nothing more.

The array of possible gifts is as big as your imagination. Small baubles and trinkets that can be easily tucked away inside the Bachelor's coat pocket work well to avoid the gift being discarded or handed over to Producers for "safekeeping." The Bachelor often appreciates foodstuffs, as sustenance is hard to come by during the shooting of the night's events. Gifts that hint at a romantically open attitude have had mixed reactions but always guarantee screen time. Season 22's Tia Booth gave Bachelor Arie Luyendyk Jr. a "tiny red wiener," while commenting that she hoped he didn't already have one, which set the tone for a run all the way to Hometowns.

An anecdote about the object's meaning, a request that the Bachelor keep the gift for a later use, and a suggestion that he is now obligated to give a return gift are all subtle ways you can attach more meaning to a Kringle and have a better chance of being remembered as the night wears on and even possibly trigger its true power—a recall.

At its best the Kringle creates the beginning moment of a story that can be revisited in a later round of the game. Alayah Benavidez in Season 24 delivered a letter written by her grandmother to then-Bachelor Peter Weber, then later opened and read the letter with Weber during her 101 time. This served the triple purpose of reminding the Bachelor of their earlier conversation, giving them an activity for their second encounter, and elevating the emotional significance of their 101 time. If the gift is meaningful and sincere enough, there is a high probability the Producers will bring it out again in a date scenario days or even weeks later.

Some other notable Kringles include Corinne Olympios's flawlessly executed hug token delivery on the twenty-first season, setting up a hug token redemption in her second conversation with Nick Viall, and Hannah Godwin's thoughtful presentation of a box to then-Bachelor Colton Underwood with the explanation that it contained his favorite underwear. When he opened it to find nothing at all, he was impressed that she did enough research to know he only wears underwear if he's sleeping with his dog. While she never got to confirm that information in the Fantasy Suite round of play-offs, she did get second place in her season and First Female Sand in *BIP*.

The It Takes Two

The Producers are tucked safely away inside the control truck watching events as they unfold on an array of screens, the host/s is/are relaxing in a greenroom until they're summoned to initiate the next round of the game, and even the Bachelor himself is rendered impotent, made to stand at the entrance of the Mansion and play the role of inert greeter to each of the players as they enter. It is at this moment that you can prod the Bachelor into action, forcing him to become a willing participant in any number of pre-planned mini-activities, or run the risk of seeming uptight or, even worse, afraid to fully give in to the process.

Whether it's coercing the Bachelor into becoming an awkward dance partner, a blindfolded taste tester, or an impromptu student of the Arkansas hog call, all you need to do to pull off a successful It Takes Two is engage the Bachelor in a brief activity that requires two people. These activities can range from comedic to overtly romantic in nature and everything in between.

The benefit of performing an It Takes Two is that you are forcing the Bachelor into a partnership with you. Almost a mini-date, the It Takes Two uses the known psychological phenomenon of enhanced memory creation related to shared experience, granting you a better chance of standing out among a field of twenty-five to thirty-five others.

Ideally, you'll have researched some of the Bachelor's preferences so you can tailor the activity to his strengths with something innocuous enough that there is no risk of accidentally upstaging him or inadvertently exposing one of his insecurities or other deficiencies.

Some notable It Takes Twos include Emily O'Brien's bold and forcible freshening of Ben Flajnik's breath with BYOB mouthwash in Season 16 as an entrée to kissing him before any of the other players had a chance. Leah Block brought a football and hiked it to Ben Higgins in Season 20, successfully exploiting the Bachelor's childlike love of football, letting him feel for a brief moment like the quarterback he never was. And who can forget Chantal O'Brien's "slap heard round the world," which she issued to the unsuspecting face of Brad Womack on his second turn as the Bachelor in Season 15.

The Sidecar

The rarest and most exotic of all Limo Exit strategies is beyond doubt the Sidecar. Only a handful have ever been attempted—and for good reason. Not only does this strategy require you to do some detailed planning, including getting assistance from the Producers, but also the Sidecar requires the active involvement of a third party from outside the game who comes in with you to greet the Bachelor.

This other participant could be anyone from a moderately well-known singer lending their crooning skills to create a soundtrack for your entrance to a family member you bring in to show how important familial bonds are to you. Whoever you bring, it's important to remember that a Sidecar has just as much chance of ending in disaster as it does of succeeding. Brittney Schreiner from Season 16 sent her grandmother as an emissary to greet Bachelor Ben Flajnik, switching places with the octogenarian at what she thought was the appropriate time. Schreiner then switched places once again, right out of the game during Week 3.

You can never be certain of a Bachelor's stance on a Sidecar or of his opinion of the selected additional participants. Some research about a Bachelor's favorite sport or musical artist can certainly be helpful when deciding who to bring, but ultimately there is always the possibility that a Bachelor might view the person as an interloper—an affront to him and the game itself.

In Season 21 Jasmine Goode exited the limo, said a few words to then-Bachelor Nick Viall, and then beckoned Neil Lane, the diamond dealer for the Bachelor Franchise, to emerge from the limo where he had been lying in wait. The play came across as equally comedic and reverential to the process, which granted her Sidecar instant immunity from scrutiny or dismissive doubt. It was proof positive that securing a third party who is closely related to the Bachelor or otherwise elevated by their obvious embodiment of the primary rule of the game—4TRR—is the right way to pull off a Sidecar.

It should be noted that in the event twin players are forced to exit the Limo simultaneously, the resulting qualification is an alternate version of the Sidecar known as the Gemini.

The Bland Entrance (or Blandy)

The Blandy is the easiest of all Limo Exits and well over half of all players do it. A Bland Entrance asks very little of you, only that you don elegant cocktail attire and deliver a pleasant formal greeting to the Bachelor with no attempt at humor or other conversational flourishes. Your physical engagement with the Bachelor can land anywhere in the range of handshake to brief hug and kiss on the cheek, stopping short of mouth kissing (open or closed). Both single and double hand holds are permitted during the introduction, which should include only your name, enthusiasm for the person selected as the Bachelor, and an assurance that you are looking forward to talking more inside the Mansion.

A Blandy's strength, if it has any at all, lies in its simplicity. You ground your identity in confidence and sincerity, conveying that you don't need the gimmick of a Grandy or the spectacle of a TOT to show the Bachelor that you are there 4TRR.

At a 69 percent Round Survival Rate the Blandy does boast the highest likelihood of safety of any Limo Exit type, but you have to remember that's due largely to the sheer volume of Blandies performed. There is no strong reason to perform a Blandy when all other options are available, but be warned—a purveyor of the Blandy is never to be underestimated, because what they may lack in initial panache or razzle-dazzle might be more than made up for with late-round strategies.

Combinations

In addition to these eight basic Limo Exits, you're always free to create combinations for augmented effect. Take for example Lacey Mark in Season 21, who rode into the Mansion on a camel, dismounted the creature, and said to then-Bachelor Nick Viall, "I hear you like a good hump. So do I." This flawless execution of a Live Animal Grandy punctuated with a Stand-Up produced a memorable *Grandy Standy* that was discussed by the other players that night with enough frequency and vigor that the Producers decided to dedicate a full thirty-second segment to it. With this combo Lacey was able to make at least some portion of the Limo Exit ceremony all about her and even raise the other players' nervous energy enough to possibly affect their ability to play a measured game as the night progressed.

No matter whether your Limo Exit is stunning or mundane, exotic or routine, dazzling or forgettable, a success or unmitigated disaster, once you've said your hello to the Bachelor, you are granted entry into one of the most hallowed buildings in the entirety of the sporting world—the Mansion.

Round 2—Cocktails First Half

You crushed your Limo Exit, your blood is pumping, Producers usher you into the Mansion, you see a few other players already inside, and you can feel your anxiety starting to creep up. Then as you round a corner into the main room, you see it—the open bar. The first half of Cocktails offers you the opportunity to take the edge off, to calm the nerves with whatever you want to drink. But this, of course, is a trap. The Producers will encourage you to loosen up with a glass of champagne or your favorite mixed drink, but nothing could be more detrimental than dulling your nerves and your reaction time in these first crucial moments of jockeying for position in the pack while you're simultaneously attempting to establish dominance, make friends, and avoid enemies.

Fake Drink Real Think

Commit this mantra to memory because it will serve you well from the first moment you step into the Mansion all the way to the Last Date with the Bachelor on the eve of the Final Rose Ceremony (FRC). Although indulging in drink can have obvious detrimental effects on your ability to make fast and correct decisions in a wide variety of situations, alcohol also shouldn't be avoided altogether. The only circumstance in which you should adopt overt and vocal sober strategy is if the Bachelor himself is also sober, which, to our knowledge, only has been the case with Juan Pablo Galavis.

So, how do you abstain while also giving the appearance of drinking in order to convey a fun-loving attitude free from behavioral restriction? With a tool that humanity has evolved over millions of years—deception. With a few easy-to-implement strategies outlined below, you can avoid the actual imbibing of alcoholic beverages to ensure a level head and clear judgment as the other players dull their wits and slow their reaction times.

The Sippy Cup

All you have to do is hold a drink and pretend to drink it. The greatest Night One player in the history of the game, Hannah Ann Sluss, was famously caught on-camera performing the Sippy Cup throughout the course of Night One in Season 24 (Peter Weber). Sluss opted to use a champagne flute, which she expertly tilted toward her mouth and then returned to level without ever parting her lips time and again. Her actions were as smooth and quick as a Las Vegas magician. All who beheld her open lie were fooled beyond doubt and it was only after the episode aired that further video scrutiny revealed the play, which astounded even expert members of the Fourth Audience.

Get-A-Drink-Leave-A-Drink (GADLAD)

Simplicity and elegance, the GADLAD requires you to do two things—get a drink from the open bar, then after a few minutes of meandering around leave the drink on a shelf or a table or hide it in a plant. Rinse and repeat. The GADLAD gives the impression that you're drinking far more than you actually are and can lead other players to perceive you as less of a threat.

The Bathroom Break

Over the course of the night you'll need to make multiple trips to the bathroom for a variety of reasons—makeup, wardrobe, urination, defecation, and crying. Bring your drink with you and pour out most or all of it into the toilet or sink. When you emerge to join the rest of the players it will appear as though you finished your drink and you're ready for another.

The Shirley Temple

One of the oldest fake drinking strategies ever devised, the Shirley Temple takes its name from the famous child actress who was served nonalcoholic versions of cocktails at Chasen's in Beverly Hills in the 1930s. To employ this strategy, just ask the bartender for a nonalcoholic version of any drink on the menu, making sure you're out of earshot of the other players when the request is made. The appearance of drinking alcohol is maintained and no one is the wiser except you.

The Oopsie

You have to have some acting skills to pull this one off, but it can be quite effective in not only selling the idea that you're drinking but also guaranteeing valuable screen time on the night when it's statistically hardest to get. The best Oopsies are performed with a tall, full glass of a brightly colored drink. With drink in hand, give a quick glance around the room to take account of camera positions, making sure that at least one is actively recording you. Then find a carpet or a step and trip as hard as you can on it. Eat shit in a glorious flourish of flailing arms and legs that sends your drink into the air and ultimately crashing to the floor. If you can execute a believable Oopsie the other players will think you're completely shit-faced and they'll write you off, making your progress through Night One that much easier.

Some cautionary tales of players who failed to employ fake drinking include Jordan Branch in Season 19, who drank to noticeable excess throughout the entirety of Night One, creating an unnecessary obstacle for herself. The stigma of her inebriation on a night that is meant to be taken seriously was too detrimental for even noted alcohol enthusiast and then-Bachelor Chris Soules to tolerate and she was dismissed in Week 2.

Never forget Ashley Palenkas in Season 17, who was so intoxicated that then-Bachelor Sean Lowe, who is the only Bachelor in the history of the game to give out twelve Night One FIMP Roses, sent her home before sunrise.

Alcohol is beyond doubt an important part of the game and you can use it as a tool to gain advantage wherever and whenever you can. Abstaining from merriment can be difficult, but if you can manage to win either the Ring or the Crown there will be ample time to drink deep from the waterfall of booze in the victors' circle.

Ready Player 1

If you are the first player to enter the Mansion you are given a very unique advantage. You alone will have the ability to scrutinize and catalog all other players as they enter the Mansion and not only witness but also influence their developing relationships with one another as the night progresses.

All players will be faced with the draining aftereffects of the Limo Exit adrenaline dump that accompanies their first moments in the Mansion, but as the first player, you are the only one afforded a moment of quiet introspection to practice any known meditative techniques, including deep breaths, visualization, calming reassurance, et cetera. Reenergized and refocused, you can get a drink from the bar and find the most comfortable seat in whichever room the Producers have directed you to. This perch should be central to the room, forcing all entering players to directly interact with you. The right position on the right piece of furniture will be invaluable in establishing early perceived dominance as well as allowing you much-needed physical comfort that later players may be denied due to the limited number of seats in the rooms where shooting occurs.

Even though being first to enter the Mansion might only give you a few moments more experience than all subsequent players, you're also going to be instinctively granted a de facto veteran status and therefore a slightly elevated ability to control the group's nascent social dynamic as new players enter and look to anyone who can help them. This is especially true of the first three to five players who can be convinced to forge an immediate and strong bond over their collective excitement, nervousness, and uncertainty about what's to come. As the group grows with each new arrival and tension mounts it is vitally important to maintain a clear head and not get rattled by any diversions the Producers might employ. Because while it is still a little too early for them to unveil their Curveball, they will, at this early stage of Night One, have designed some element of . . .

Crowd Control

Producers are going to try to get everyone's anxiety as high as possible as often as possible, and applying Crowd Control is one of the first tools they'll use to that end on Night One. Crowd Control can take a wide variety of specific forms, like multiple players wearing the same dress, having the same occupation, or even the same first name. In some cases, a player will arrive who has had some prior meeting or perhaps even a prior relationship with the Bachelor. And in other cases still, players themselves might have prior relationships that threaten the tranquility of the general player pool. Whatever the specifics might be, "Crowd Control" directly refers to the Producers' orchestrated use of some element of one or more players' identities to instill insecurity and doubt in as many other players as possible. Don't fall for it, especially if you find yourself among the affected group of players.

For example, if you find yourself wearing the same dress as another player, don't panic or even make mention of it. Pause, take a deep breath, and remind yourself that you are playing a game and this is just one element of it. If you don't react to their attempts to fluster you, then the Producers will have a harder time editing it into the episode and it will very likely fall by the wayside, which is exactly what Anna Redman and Alana Milne did on Season 25 (Matt James) when they found out the Producers separately convinced them to wear the exact same red cocktail dress.

Avoiding a Crowd Control trap might very well be your first test to find out exactly how susceptible you'll be to future Producer manipulations. Another fantastic way to avoid the negative psychological effects of Producer-orchestrated group social experiments is to surround yourself with like-minded players who are willing to work as a team.

Picking Teams

While the game is ultimately one that bestows the glory of victory on individuals, it is virtually impossible for you to make it to the final round without the support and strategic advantage that comes from belonging to a strong team. Whether you're engaged in actively building a team or simply trying to find the best existing team to join, you have to understand that not only will your team serve as an alliance to help you through the game, but also these other players will offer social media collaboration opportunities that will extend your viability as a personality in the culture of the game long after your playing days are done.

One of the most successful teams in the game's rich history was formed in the twenty-second season of *The Bachelor*, which ended in disgrace when then-Bachelor Arie Luyendyk Jr. reneged on his proposal to Becca Kufrin two months after the fact in favor of his second choice for wife, Lauren Burnham. The team, comprised of Bekah Martinez, Seinne Fleming, Kendall Long, Tia Booth, Caroline Lunny, and Kufrin herself, came together for a historical team play at that season's After The Final Rose (ATFR) when they all engaged in a prolonged group hug on the Hot Seat in a televised show of solidarity and support for the victimized Kufrin, who was the team's star player and anchor.

Alone, it's unlikely that any of these players would have been able to achieve what they did collectively after their season. But by appearing in one another's social media posts in the year that followed their season, they all went on to amass IG numbers in the six figures (some approaching the 1 million club), most had subsequent appearances on *BIP*, some have incredibly successful podcasts, some have cultivated relationships with other players from Bachelor Nation, and Kufrin went on to wear the Crown, one of only three players to ever achieve the Full Royale (winning both the Ring and the Crown), and she became the first and only Bachelorette to appear on *BIP*, further elevating the status of her team within the game's culture. This is the power of a good team.

So what makes a good team? As in any other sport, every successful team is anchored by a star player. Objectivity is paramount not only when determining who the star players are in any given season but also realizing that you may not be among them. This is especially difficult on Night One when very few indicators are apparent to hint at the Bachelor's top choice. You have to trust your instinct and gut feelings when you decide to partner up with other players on this first, critical night. Identifying players whom the Bachelor talks to multiple times, players who are lent his coat on a chilly night (a process called the Gentleman), certainly FIMP Rose and First Flower recipients, and players who have been trained by successful players are all safe bets for front-runners. The first player out of the limo is also a good choice for a teammate, as the Producers are likely trying to build a story around her.

And whether these first predictions bear out over the course of the season or not, the most important thing to keep in mind when picking a team on Night One is solidarity. Although it should never be openly stated to another player that the goal of team formation is progress through the game, at every opportunity you should implement language about having friends through this process and not going through it alone in order to strengthen the bond.

Just as important as conscripting star players for your team is cultivating the fine art of avoiding dead weight. Politely ignore players who exhibit erratic emotional behavior like excessive crying, laughing, or alcohol consumption, and players in costume. And certainly one player type to identify and invite into the group at all costs if you yourself don't claim this role as your own is the . . .

Colorful Narrator

Assuming the role of the Colorful Narrator guarantees massive amounts of screen time on Night One. As the night proceeds, you'll experience your first mandatory, direct-to-camera confessional interview, a process the Producers have named an ITM, or In The Moment. A Producer will pull you from the player pool and hustle you off into a side room where you will be forced to answer a series of questions and recite certain lines of dialogue as prompted by the Producers before you're permitted to join the general population again. Although the Producers certainly have an idea for narratives they've already begun to construct in the casting process, Night One is as much a feeling-out process for them as it is for you.

This first ITM grants you the opportunity to deliver a comedic recounting of the night's events or descriptions of the other players, which has become an intrinsic part of the Producers' editing strategy. They are actively looking for the funniest player who is the most concise in her delivery of necessary information.

On Night One most players are going to be too overwhelmed by the experience to realize this is even an opportunity. So coming in with some prepared, generic descriptions of different personality types and game-related events is time well spent in the preseason. To avoid a possible Villain Edit, these descriptions should never be derogatory and should instead comically celebrate any given personality type or the game itself.

Some examples of appropriate colorful descriptions:

A Loud Player:	"You never have to worry about her talking behind your back because you'll hear it if she does."
A Young Player:	"Pretty sure I have bras that are older than (Insert Young Player Name). But I can't be mad, every one of us wishes we were a few years younger. She actually is."
An Overtly Sexual Player:	"When she walked in wearing that dress . . . she was shaking what her momma AND her daddy gave her! And I don't know if she's got aunts and uncles, grandma, grandpa - whoever gave her what she was shaking, they gave her a whole lot of it."
A Drunk Player:	"You know what they say about booze, it's liquid courage! But in her case it's also liquid stumbling, liquid slurring, and liquid passing out."
An Intellectual Player:	"She's smarter than everybody in here. I mean not [insert Host's name], but everybody else."
A Foreign Player:	"That accent. It's like I can't really understand what she's saying, but I know it's hot."
A Single Mom:	"Being a single mom is just like the First Impression Rose. There's only one of you and you're very powerful."

A Player in Costume: "Say what you will about coming out of the limo to meet your potential future husband in a full-on witch's gown. At least the girl has pockets!"

A Player's Grandy: "If I would have known we could ride circus animals into the Mansion, I would have called up a few of my exes."

The Mansion: "I have only been in two buildings this fancy in my life and the other one was the Cheesecake Factory!"

The Bachelor: "He's the total package. Attractive, charming, and doesn't know about all my credit card debt!"

The Host Appears: "[The Host] is like my therapist—[he/she/they] gets paid a lot of money to make people cry."

The FIMP Rose Bestowing: "First Impression Rose, First Impression Rose—everybody's all worked up about the First Impression Rose. Sure, we all want it, but you know what I want even more, some first impression pizza! I'm starving."

The role of Colorful Narrator begins on Night One, but you can maintain it all season and well into subsequent appearances on *BIP* and even returning guest spots on *The Bachelor* and *The Bachelorette* if they should materialize. Demi Burnett is the most successful Colorful Narrator of all time and has raised the bar for all Colorful Narrators who will follow by amassing over 1.2 million IG followers and seemingly limitless appearances on every successive season of the game. The Producers valued her contribution to the legacy of the Colorful Narrator so much that they designed semi-scripted segments for her in both Season 15 of *The Bachelorette* and Season 24 of *The Bachelor*. "Demi's Detective Agency" and "Demi's

Extreme Pillow Fight Club" not only included her name on full display but also actually had some effect on the game itself, as Demi was used as a mouthpiece by the Producers to decide which players got to spend more time with the leads.

But if comedy doesn't come naturally to you, don't worry, there are other opportunities for screen time and attention in the next phase of the game. . . .

Round 3—Cocktails Second Half

Once everyone has delivered their wide variety of Limo Exits from Grand to Bland and you've all taken your places in the plush confines of the Mansion, the Bachelor will signify the start of the second half of Cocktails by crossing the threshold into the Inauguration Chamber to begin the Sisyphean task of engaging in thirty successive conversations with complete strangers. And the first possibility for a power play comes in this exact moment when you can establish yourself as . . .

The First Responder

This vaunted position is given to the player each season who snatches the first first impression by waiting patiently for the Bachelor's entrance, ready with his favorite drink in hand, which she delivers to him as soon as he appears. Then she stands silently beside him as he initiates the ceremonial toast that celebrates the start of an "incredible journey."

Although First Responders have had mixed results in later phases of the game, producing everything from Villains and Tattletales to FIMP Rose recipients and Ring Winners—they do have a better than 50 percent chance of surviving Night One.

This favorable bias is due in large part to two main First Responder elements. First, you convey invaluable caretaking capabilities in the subpsychology of the Bachelor, which not only soothes him on what is certainly a stressful night but also suggests that you possess all of the motherly qualities needed to successfully raise a family. Second, and even more important, being the First Responder grants you the opportunity to invite the Bachelor for his first 1O1 conversation before any of the other players can even react.

Corinne Olympios transitioned her First Responder play into the first conversation of the night so quickly in Season 21 that many other players audibly wondered if then-Bachelor Nick Viall vanished into thin air.

The first conversation carries multiple immense benefits. The first is time. The other players will initially be paralyzed by confusion and uncertainty about how and when to attempt the first Steal of the night. So whoever engages the Bachelor first almost always has the conversation most immune to interruption. Once the stealing begins, players become progressively bolder as the night goes on, mercilessly interrupting other conversations in shorter and shorter intervals. This will often leave a few of the less aggressive players without a chance to talk to the Bachelor during the second half of Cocktails at all.

As the First Responder you'll also leave a lasting impression on the Bachelor, as this will be his first real conversation of the night. His addled brain may not store the specific dialogue after fifteen hours of shooting, but he will associate you with a general pleasant start to his night, which may mean the difference between a Rose and dismissal due to getting lost in the shuffle.

The First Responder position is usually predetermined by the Producers based on little more than who seems most compliant, but there are strategies to increase your chances of manipulating the Producers into granting you this valuable role.

What's Your Poison?

This overt manipulation of the Producers is surprisingly simple to employ. At the end of your Limo Exit as you're letting the Bachelor know that you'll be waiting inside to talk more, you simply pause and say, "Oh, I have a question for you. What's your favorite drink?" When the Bachelor responds you smile and say, "I'll have one waiting for you when you come in—you're gonna need it!" This initiates a small but effective narrative that all but forces the Producers to bequeath the First Responder role to you if they don't already have machinations designed for a competitor.

Right Place, Right Time

Sometimes the Producers haven't selected a First Responder and they simply give the Bachelor's drink to whoever is standing in the correct position. This is always in the Inauguration Chamber where the Bachelor's entrance and inaugural toast will be shot, at the rightmost corner of the large pit group sofa. There is never any deviation from this pattern, so being there is a simple way to maximize First Responder potential.

A Special Moment (Experimental Strategy)

Now, it should be noted that throughout this book we will be mentioning some experimental strategies. These are things we've never actually seen put to use in the game, but we think they would work fantastically. So for this one, you have to know that the Producers love reinforcing patriarchal views of father/daughter relationships. Knowing this, once the ITM interview process starts you can tell the Producers a story about how you used to make your dad's favorite drink every day when he came home from work and that it was a sacred moment for you, a bonding moment, a celebration of the love between father and daughter. Then you convey a desire to do the same thing here, explaining that it's how you always imagined your love story would begin. The Producers will be salivating to include this in their edit.

But whether you're able to garner the First Responder role or not, you will have to procure and navigate a 1O1 conversation with the Bachelor in the next phase of the game. . . .

The Art of the Steal

If you want time with the Bachelor, you will have to steal him at some point in the night. We all know that. But something that dawned on us as we watched the Steal emerge over the course of the first few seasons was that if the Producers actually cared at all about helping anyone find love through this process, the Steal wouldn't exist at all. The show would be structured to give each player an equal amount of time with the Bachelor on Night One so that he would have an opportunity to form fair first impressions of each candidate in the dating pool. But, as anyone who has seen even one episode knows, this is not remotely the case. Instead, the Producers have designed Cocktail Parties to require you to engage in a series of hyperaggressive, cutthroat, kill-or-be-killed sabotaging of one another's attempts to build rapport with the Bachelor. It is survival of the fittest in a cocktail dress. It is every woman by herself, for herself. It is an overt display of competition that openly reveals the show to be a sport, and this round requires you to take what you want by force. This is the Steal.

Timing. Timing. Timing. It is the most important component of a good Steal. Performing too many Steals or stealing before another player has had a reasonable amount of time with the Bachelor can get you a one-way ticket to Villaintown. Catherine Agro in Season 23 learned this the hard way when she stole Colton Underwood a record four times, was quickly painted as the early Villain, and was dismissed in Week 3. But done properly, the Steal is a valuable part of your strategy not only on Night One but also as the game progresses, on any Group Date or at any Cocktail Party.

A Steal yields the obvious advantage of having 1O1 time with the Bachelor. But more than that, a high-level Steal can limit the amount of time another player gets with the Bachelor or even save the Bachelor from being subjected to unwanted time spent with an undesirable player.

Executing a good Steal requires patience and observation. Eavesdropping from behind a nearby shrub or curtain or even standing a few feet away in the shadows of the Mansion is always permissible. If the overheard conversation seems to be going well, steal now! If the conversation seems to be going bad, let it linger. The Bachelor is obligated, especially on Night One, to fully indulge conversation with each player. He is trapped. So let a bad conversation plummet to oblivion before finally swooping in with a Steal to save him from the awkward moment. A Benevolent Steal is imbued with the psychological benefit of the Bachelor projecting his sense of relief onto his rescuer.

Confidence, speed, and initiative should guide you while stealing, and always try to be in the first three players to perform a Steal on any given night. After this point Steal Fatigue sets in and results in diminishing returns. Once the pattern of Steal after Steal has been established and the novelty of the event has withered, players will find themselves being allowed less time before another Steal is attempted and will, therefore, be more forgettable to the Bachelor.

But even a shortened conversation is better than none at all. Players who are too ineffective at the Steal, considering themselves morally above it or perhaps relying on the traditional habit of waiting for the man to make the first move, are known within the game to be Turtling—a name derived from the metaphor of a frightened turtle hiding in its protective shell. Getting no time with the Bachelor on Night One is catastrophic and should be avoided at all costs.

Hindered by the misconception that fair allocation of time with the Bachelor should be the standard protocol, most players will only attempt a single Steal. But no matter if you're driven by bravery or maybe even desperation, you can choose to attempt multiple Steals on Night One. If performed properly, a Multi-Steal will impress the Bachelor with boldness. But you run the risk of possibly revealing a little too much of your hyper-competitive side, which can lead to accusations of you being there 4TWR. The Multi-Steal should be used only if the opportunity presents itself and if the Bachelor seems amenable, as it will surely have a detrimental effect on your Second Audience game and likely gain you a few unwanted enemies in the house.

Blocking

What do you do if a player is trying to steal from you? You don't let her. A well-executed block will nullify a Steal attempt and send the insurrectionist scurrying back into the shadows of the Mansion. A block can be counter-aggressive—you issue a hostility-tinged refusal to the stealing player, essentially daring the stealer to take it to the next level. A block can be pleading—you illustrate that you haven't gotten the proper amount of time and you really need to speak with the Bachelor. A block can even be friendly—you say you just need five more minutes and then the stealer can have him. But no matter what tone of block you use to defend a Steal, all good blocks require assertiveness, resolve, and unflinching confidence. Above all, you must maintain control of the 1O1 time with the Bachelor no matter what may come.

The Italian Steal

There is a special Steal in our beloved game that we named after the location and nationality of the two players who first performed it way back in Season 9. When local Roman players Agnese Polliza and Cosetta Blanca had then-Bachelor Lorenzo Borghese stolen by two American players, Lisa Blank and Erica Rose, they wasted no time marching over to them and stealing him right back. From that fateful moment forward, immediately stealing the Bachelor back from the initial stealing player(s) came to be known as the Italian Steal.

But no matter the quantity or style of your Steals, once you've successfully secured a secluded moment with the Bachelor a conversation immediately follows. This is potentially the most critical discourse you'll have with the Bachelor all season, because if it doesn't go well it will likely be your last. Luckily, we identified a tried-and-true pattern of Night One dialogue that has served as the foundation for successful players in every season.

Gift of Gab

There are a wide array of styles that work to execute a successful first conversation, but they all follow the basic formula of being light, upbeat, and innocuous. They rely on surface topics like how "crazy" everything is, how relieved you are that the specific Bachelor was selected for the role, and how excited you are for the next time you'll be able to see the Bachelor. If you've done proper preseason research you can easily fill time by bonding with the Bachelor over similar interests or life circumstances whether they are real or not. Remain engaged with a growing amount of surprise at how much you actually like the Bachelor now that you've gotten a chance to talk to him. Convey an unbridled amount of romantic interest in him that is bubbling just under the surface, barely able to be contained. And by the end of the conversation, your skepticism for the process should be replaced by excitement for your newfound curiosity about its potential success.

And always remember, the Bachelor has almost nothing to do with deciding who stays on Night One. Other than his top one or two players, the Producers are deciding on the rest of the player pool by watching how you perform on-camera in this conversation. So you want to seem as 4TRR as possible. The Producers are looking for their Villains, their Fools, and their Weirdos to weave into narratives that can sustain the regular season, but they're also looking for their Top 4.

WARNING: Never, under any circumstances play your PTC on Night One. It's invaluable in later stages of the game and a complete waste to play it this early. Revealing too much too soon or becoming too overly emotional usually leads to an awkward moment, which can be all the Producers need to send you packing.

You want to be remembered as a willing and beneficial addition to the dating pool who presents no outward signs of future problematic behavior for the Bachelor while at the same time giving Producers enough to want to build stories around you.

And once you've turned in a stellar first conversation, punctuate it with a kiss.

The First Kiss

The kiss is one of the most sacred human endeavors, linking two people in a moment of passion, intimacy, and connection that is often indescribable and transcendent. And ever since Kelly Jo Kuharski made history as the first Night One kisser in Season 4 (Bob Guiney), it's also given players a 95 percent likelihood of making it through to the next round. Our data is all derived from the formal document—the episodes of the show. So we can't ever be sure if there are kisses that didn't make the final edit, but of the twenty Night One kissers featured in the edits, only one has been sent home on Night One.

It can be hard to go in for a first kiss in regular circumstances, let alone while a dozen camera people are watching you and a team of Producers is making bets on whether or not they can get you to cry by the end of the night. But worry not, we found that the most successful players all follow the same basic pattern of behavior for their first kiss.

They start out sitting close enough to the Bachelor that he is enticed to make the first move. And after a few minutes of enticing banter, you are primed to raise your Love Level for the first time. A simple "I didn't know what to expect, but I like you" or "I know we just met but I'm feeling something. Are you feeling it?" are perfect ways to hit LL1 and lead straight into a Night One kiss.

Hannah Ann Sluss, the only player in history to pull off three Night One kisses, used the giving of a gift to get Peter Weber to move closer to her. And when he did she engaged in a textbook Night One kiss that began with trepidation and nervousness. Uncertainty was still the motivating emotion, but after a few exploratory moments the nervousness melted away and in its place an overwhelming sense of uncontrollable chemistry blossomed.

Successful first kissers often end the performance with a small flourish—a wide-eyed expression that conveys a dazed state as though the experience took her senses from her. A sigh followed by an exclamation like "Wow!" or "My god!" helps to convey the staggering effect of the kiss. And finally, saying a phrase like "We have to do that again sometime" to convey you're romantically very interested in the Bachelor is the cherry on top. Preparing a charming and seemingly improvisational tagline to punctuate your first kiss is highly recommended, for the benefit of both the Bachelor and the Producers. In addition to a strong first kiss, you can level up your first 101 conversation by using the Producers to help you create a mini-date.

The Mini-Date

The conversation and potentially the first kiss can happen anywhere on the grounds of the Mansion. Some players opt for a simple, straightforward strategy of sitting on a cushioned bench in the backyard or a secluded anteroom separate from the main group of mingling players. But the mini-date offers you the chance to show the Bachelor a different side of your personality through pre-planned activities, settings, gifts, and other elements of augmentation that can transform the conversation into an event.

Similar to Limo Exits, there are a wide variety of styles of mini-dates and the degree of complexity and pre-planning is directly commensurate to the level of Producer involvement required to facilitate them.

For example, a language lesson as performed by Cassie Randolph in Season 23 required no more than Randolph casually teaching then-Bachelor Colton Underwood how to say the word "kiss" in sign language. This led to the perfect opportunity for a Night One kiss, which she executed well enough to get a Rose that night and start what would ultimately become a dominant run all the way to the end of her season, where she eventually claimed the Ring.

In that same season Tayshia Adams went to the other end of the producorial engagement spectrum by conscripting them to build a scaled-down carnival called Tayshialand in the driveway of the Mansion. In the grand tradition of some of Hollywood's most iconic endeavors, Tayshialand required stage direction, lighting, and even custom props to be manufactured. Tayshialand simultaneously built her name recognition, made it harder for another player to steal Colton, and provided a natural excuse for breaking the physical touch barrier when Tayshia demanded Colton give her a human "pony ride" around the driveway. She went on to place third that season, secured first-day entry on *BIP* the following season, and eventually went on to wear the seventeenth *Bachelorette* Crown in the second half of *Bachelorette* Season 16.

Mini-dates offer a slight advantage where screen time is concerned and any advantage you can get must be exercised on Night One in an effort to have any chance of winning one of two most important prizes the grueling event has to offer. . . .

A Tale of Two Roses

The FIMP Rose—there's only one (except in the case of Season 7, which had two, and Season 17, which had an overwhelming twelve), it's delivered on a special tray by the host, and whoever gets it is immediately safe in the most difficult round of the game. Most people think the FIMP is the most important Rose of the night. We certainly did, right up until we started going through the numbers we generated during the Hyperbinge. We were shocked to learn that although the FIMP Rose is definitely an incredible prize, in recent years there's another Rose that's even more statistically valuable—the First Flower. This is what we came to call the often-overlooked Rose given to the first player in the Night One Rose Ceremony. It yields even greater advantages than its high-profile counterpart.

Since the start of the Paradise Era (Season 19—Chris Soules), the First Flower boasts an incredible average finish of 3.28th place to the FIMP's 5.21st place. And going all the way back to the beginning of the game, the First Flower has produced three Crowns to the FIMP's one and four Ring Winners to the FIMP's one.

The FIMP Rose

This isn't to say that the FIMP Rose isn't a valuable prize. It most definitely is. If you can get it, you're guaranteed early advancement to the next round of the game while the other players are left to fight for the remaining spots. Even more important than the obvious benefit of immunity from elimination on Night One, the FIMP boasts an incredible statistical advantage that extends through the entirety of the season, second only to the First Flower. Fifty-three percent of FIMP Rose recipients have progressed to the Hometown round or further and only one of the twenty-one honored players has gone home the following week. In plain terms, securing the FIMP Rose very decidedly means you're all but guaranteed a deep run in the season.

If the Producers (Third Audience) are responsible for giving you the FIMP, it means they have plans to orchestrate a deep run through the season for you. If the Bachelor (First Audience) was allowed to make the choice, then the psychological phenomenon of Confirmation Bias will be largely responsible for the FIMP effect. Once the Bachelor has made his first decision, it will take an overwhelming amount of counter-evidence to convince him that this first impression was incorrect. He will continuously interpret new information as confirming his previous beliefs about you and this will translate into a string of Roses that require very little effort.

Receiving the FIMP Rose also means you're immediately unburdened by the need to engage in the tense game of constant emotional manipulation to which the other players will be obligated daily. Avoiding the need to overtly express aggressive interest or desperation, you can instead engage in a slow-burn play style. Always be happy to see the Bachelor but never disappointed or frustrated if he should fail to find adequate 1O1 time with you over the first few weeks.

The early investment of the FIMP Rose will never be forgotten by the Bachelor, yielding multiple Roses in the weeks to follow without your doing anything more than conveying a growing romantic interest in the Bachelor and a trust in the confidence he has for your relationship. Become the Bachelor's constant, his rock, unwavering and resolute in your willingness to endure the entirety of the process to be with him.

And then as the play-offs approach and a Hometown Rose is secured, you will have laid fertile ground on which you can turn the tables. When the Bachelor asks how you're feeling later in the season, this is the opportune moment to reveal that the pressure is beginning to become overwhelming. It's simply harder than you thought it would be to see him going on dates with other women. Claim that you need some show of faith from the Bachelor in order to keep persisting through the final rounds. All great FIMP Rose recipients erect walls at this point, forcing the onus back on the Bachelor. This demand reinvigorates his interest, motivated by fear of loss, which is especially effective if you've successfully conveyed your loyalty.

Past recipients of the FIMP Rose have garnered the award with a wide array of strategies, making it impossible to generate a single winning formula. Some have kissed the Bachelor; some have not. Some have performed Grandies, some Blandies. Some have set up elaborate mini-dates; some have done little more than repeatedly remark how "crazy" everything is while compulsively blinking their eyes. But regardless of how you decide to approach the puzzle of the FIMP, always be aware that it's not necessarily the Bachelor who makes the decision. The Producers can have incredible influence over this important Rose, which is why your Third Audience game must always be on point. So no matter what may be happening in the house or what sinister schemes the Producers may be cooking up, if you can convey to the Bachelor that you are 4TRR and extremely romantically interested in him while simultaneously conveying to the Producers that you'll play ball and give them a strong anchor around which they can build stories and drama, you have as good a chance as any to walk away with the FIMP Rose.

No Sitting in the FIMP Room

Although this has no bearing on actual game mechanics, we couldn't help but notice something that seemed to repeat every season. If you're looking to save yourself a little psychological anguish, never sit in the room where the FIMP Rose is on the table. Not only does staring at the FIMP Rose produce unnecessary levels of anxiety, but also the FIMP Rose is almost never given to a player sitting in that room. The Producers craft this environment each season specifically to get a shot of the Bachelor entering the room to retrieve the FIMP Rose before leaving to bestow it upon a player not present as those who remain wither in disappointment. Simply avoiding that room before the FIMP Rose is bequeathed is a simple way to save a little peace of mind.

The First Flower

This completely overlooked Rose is simply the first one given out at any Rose Ceremony. The First Flower on Night One carries with it enormous value even beyond the FIMP Rose. As stated earlier in this chapter, First

Flower recipients enjoy deeper runs on average than FIMP Rose recipients and they are granted both the Ring and the Crown more often than FIMP Rose recipients. While there is little that can be overtly done to qualify for this precious bloom, as it is decided almost completely by the Producers, strong 101 time strategies like familial discussion, kissing, and hinting at Love Level 1 are all encouraged. Avoiding controversy and drama of any kind is also helpful. Above all, if you don't get the FIMP Rose, stay calm and remember the First Flower yet remains.

But you shouldn't get too distracted chasing the FIMP Rose, the First Flower, or any single goal for that matter, because the Producers will certainly attempt to derail both the Bachelor and players alike with a Night One Curve-ball.

SEASON	BACHELOR
19	Chris Soules
20	Ben Higgins
21	Nick Viall
22	Arie Luyendyk Jr.
23	Colton Underwood
24	Peter Weber
25	Matt James

FIMP	PLACE	FIRST FLOWER	PLACE
Britt Nilsson	6th	Kaitlyn Bristowe	3rd 11th Bachelorette
Olivia Caridi	8th	Lauren Bushnell	Ring Winner
Rachel Lindsay	3rd 13th Bachelorette	Vanessa Grimaldi	Ring Winner
Chelsea Roy	8th	Becca Kufrin	Ring Winner 14th Bachelorette
Hannah Godwin	2nd	Caelynn Miller-Keyes	4th
Hannah Ann Sluss	Ring Winner	Victoria Paul	7th
Abigail Heringer	8th	Bri Springs	3rd

Night One Curveball

The first Night One Curveball was in Season 4. Bachelor Bob Guiney's mom showed up at the Mansion to chat with some of the players and make sure her son was doing all right. It was cute and sweet and the only person made nervous by her supposed surprise visit was maybe Guiney himself. But in recent years the Night One Curveball has taken on a much more sinister tone. The Producers seem to pride themselves on inserting some catastrophically disruptive element into the game on Night One. And just like the Steal, the Night One Curveball is clear evidence that the Producers' goal is not to foster burgeoning romantic relationships but instead to control a series of game rounds designed to produce as much psychological distress as possible.

With the contemporary Night One Curveball, their specific aim is to destroy any progress any players have made with the Bachelor and sow the seeds of doubt in as many minds as they can. Jeannette Pawula summed it up best in Season 9 when the Night One Curveball took the form of two new Italian players joining the Cocktail Party halfway through. She said, "Gorgeous Italian women walk in. That makes me feel nervous, intimidated, scared, more competitive, everything, because I want to get a Rose tonight." In Season 24 the Producers arranged for Hannah Brown, the prior season's Bachelorette and then-Bachelor Peter Weber's ex-girlfriend, to crash the Mansion. Many of the players were so flustered by her arrival they gave in to anxious, erratic play, hindering what were, up to that point, some very well-played Night Ones.

To avoid this reaction to the inevitable Night One Curveball, you have to be ready for anything. Expect something to happen or some element to be introduced to the game that seemingly serves to invalidate the entire premise of the show itself. And no matter what form the Night One Curveball takes, support the Bachelor and outwardly concern yourself with his reaction to and feelings about this unexpected event, expressing no panic or dread yourself. Be totally fine with something like the Bachelor's last serious girlfriend crashing your first date with the Bachelor. Never be rattled by jealousy or insecurity—in fact, express only that you are thriving! This is a strong indicator to the Bachelor that you'll be able to make it through the various upcoming psychological minefields inherent in the game and eventually be able to handle your boyfriend potentially having sex with other women in the play-offs.

Confidence in the face of adversity is what he will be looking for here, and although the Night One Curveball is meant as a direct attempt to disable players' strategies, it can serve as a valuable opportunity to shine one last time before the night's conclusion.

Round 4—the Rose Ceremony

As the sun slowly crawls up from the other side of the world, the dark curtain of the night's sky begins to brighten and the host emerges from the shadows once again. Three shrill notes cut through the chill of the early morning air as a silver knife is brought to a crystal champagne flute in a series of quick strikes. *TING-TING-TING*—*The Bachelor*'s version of a buzzer when the game clock hits zero, signifying the end of standard play and the beginning of the first iteration of the most sacred event in the game: the Rose Ceremony.

You will be made to stand along with all thirty players on risers in a large room and remain silent and still until the Bachelor, who stands beside a pedestal with a neat pile of Roses on top, calls you each by name. Prepare yourself. The Rose Ceremony might only take up ten minutes in the course of an episode, but the shooting of this process takes hours. The Bachelor can't be expected to remember all 30+ players' names let alone the order the Producers have decided their names should be called out. So in almost every season, the Bachelor delivers three Roses and then retreats to a deliberation room where the Producers will tell him the next three players' names to be called. He will return, call those names, and then head back to the deliberation room to be told the next three names. The process repeats until all Roses have been dispensed.

If you hear your name, give a brief smile, then politely maneuver around the other players toward the pedestal.

Since the first Rose was given to Amanda Marsh in 2002 at the culmination of the very first Night One, the Bachelor has been required to say this exact phrase: "[Player], will you accept this Rose?" You have some leeway in response, but this only serves as a flourish to what is already a win in receiving a Rose. Replies can vary from the innocuous "Yes, I will" and "Of course" to the more lively "A thousand percent," or the southern flair of "Darn right I will." But be warned, making too much of this moment can instantly land the player in 4TWR territory, so select any embellishments carefully and execute them as genuinely as possible.

Many players feel a great deal of anxiety as the Rose Ceremony approaches, but this is wasted energy. Once official play is over, there is nothing left to be done. This is the time to breathe a sigh of relief and take a moment to feel confident about what was hopefully a quality Night One performance. If ever there was a time to allow for alcoholic indulgence it's once the Rose Ceremony has been announced and the Producers have separated the Bachelor from the player pool.

If you're feeling like it's unlikely you're getting a Rose on Night One, it is possible to attempt a Hail Mary. In all nineteen years of the game, a Night One Hail Mary has never achieved its goal. Thus far it has only served to add desperation to the list of qualities that both the Bachelor and the Producers have already identified as unworthy of remaining in the Mansion. That said, there is always a first player to break new ground, to write her name in the record book, to make history. Might as well give it a shot.

Once all players are standing on the risers and the Rose Ceremony is in progress, be aware that cameras are rolling even if the Bachelor might not be standing at the pedestal. Any facial expressions, corrections of posture, scratching, or other impure bodily functions will be captured and could potentially be included in the final edit out of context to produce whatever effect the Producers desire. Mykenna Dorn learned this the hard way when her wandering tongue searching and probing her own gum line and lips became the go-to reaction shot for many key moments in Season 24 (Peter Weber). She should've taken a lesson from Season 20's notorious Villain, Olivia Caridi, whose impossibly large gaping mouth was the tag shot on practically every scene. While this might offer a small chance to get a few more seconds of screen time, it more often lends itself to inadvertent bad footage, and the Producers don't tend to give the outlandish behavioral edits to front-runners.

If you receive a Rose you should be respectful of those who did not and say your good-byes to them in a quick, orderly, and sincere fashion. It is impossible to predict who among them might be admitted to Paradise, so it behooves you to be cordial to every other player. Make note of which other players have left the game and what these choices indicate about the Bachelor's and Producers' preferences. Who got First Flower? This is often a front-runner. Who were the final names called? These are often the players the next week's story arc will have been built around, and quite often the last name called is a Villain saved until the end to build a dramatic conclusion into the episode.

Take a moment to enjoy the victory. You've survived the statistically most difficult round of the entire season and you will have at least some IG gains waiting for you when the Producers allow you contact with the outside world again.

A Night One exit is of little consequence. Whether you decide to praise the process and give thanks to the Producers for the opportunity or burst into a hysterical fit of tears and complaints makes little difference statistically. A handful of N.O.G.s have been granted access to Paradise, but their exits played no part in those decisions. Unfortunately, leaving on Night One means a virtual 0 percent increase in IG followers, in-game standing, or likelihood of return to the game.

With the N.O.G.s gone, the Bachelor raises a glass and leads you and the remaining players in a toast to starting a new journey together. With this final shot of glasses clinking and all players cheering in unison as they surround the Bachelor, the Producers temporarily discontinue their abuses and finally allow you to sleep.

Budget your sleep time wisely, because getting as much rest as possible is paramount in being ready for the trials ahead—and there will be many. They will be both exhilarating and terrifying, empowering and degrading, astonishing and mundane. Over the course of the next eight weeks you will be subjected to the ultimate game of attrition and manipulation. The regular season has begun.

Chapter 4

REGULAR SEASON PART 1:

HOUSE LIFE

When I think of all the amazing things that have come from being on* The Bachelor, *my very FAVORITE one is YOU! Thanks for being my best friend! I love you!* 👭 *@joelle_fletcher

Becca Tilley, both a runner-up (Season 19—Chris Soules) and fifth-place finisher (Season 20—Ben Higgins)

We both remembered Season 20 primarily for Ben Higgins setting off an emotional atom bomb by telling both of his finalists that he loved them in the Fantasy Suite round. But when we went back during the Hyperbinge we saw that this season had so much more. One of the most important events that took place was an incredibly beautiful story of friendship that neither of us remembered. Tilley wrote this chapter's opening quote on an IG post in 2017, dedicated to her best friend from the game, her Dynamic Duo partner, the runner-up from Season 20, and the twelfth Bachelorette, Joelle "JoJo" Fletcher.

The pair befriended each other during Season 20 and continued their friendship in the postseason, attending music festivals and holidays together, with Fletcher even asking Tilley to be a bridesmaid in her wedding to her Ring Winner, Jordan Rodgers. Fletcher has gone on to become one of only four players currently to have over 2 million IG followers and she has used that parasocial clout to help Tilley amass over 1 million of her own.

The Bachelor may seem like a show about dates, but their friendship didn't start on a date. It started in the house where you're going to be spending the majority of your time developing your own relationship with the Second Audience. Since Season 11, traditionally, the "house" has been "Villa de la Vina," aka the "*Bachelor* Mansion," a ten-thousand-square-foot palace sitting on ten acres in the Santa Monica Mountains of Malibu. Players are packed into a few rooms filled with bunk beds, perfect for sparking friendships and drama. Most *Bachelor* and *Bachelorette* players live there for at least the first few weeks of every season, until the travel round begins. Rachel Lindsay (Season 21—Nick Viall; thirteenth Bachelorette) described the *Bachelor* Mansion in a 2021 Vulture article, saying:

> *"I hated it. I always tell people it was the dirtiest place ever. Think the movie* The Money Pit. *Once you get inside, you see the cracks in the foundation. Appliances don't work; the backyard is not complete. (This in addition to 22 women living in three rooms.) By the time we left, my eyes were puffy. I had an allergic reaction from the lack of sleep, drinking too much, and feeling dehydrated."*

To our knowledge, ABC has not commented on her depiction of the Mansion. Lindsay survived the boozy pressure cooker and went on to be one of the most successful players of all time, hosting multiple TV shows and podcasts and penning a book.

"The house" has been presented in many forms, from a giant Borghese palace in Rome, to the sprawling grounds of the Nemacolin resort in Pennsylvania for a COVID season, to any hotel players have stayed at while traveling, or even jumbo RVs, as was the case on Ben Flajnik's sixteenth season. For the purposes of simplicity, whatever the home base of filming is is what we shall refer to as "the house," where Producers sequester all players not on dates and force them into various "Girl Chat" segments designed to drive manufactured narratives about rivalries and friendships. We'll cover strategies to help you get the most out of your non-date time, a key component of any strong four-audience game.

You Are Here to Make Friends

In the year 2000, the runner-up of *Survivor*, Kelly Wiglesworth, uttered the phrase "I'm not here to make friends" for what we believe to be the first time on reality TV. Since that moment, many reality stars have repeated these six powerful words. The first-ever Villain Edit recipient, Rhonda Rittenhouse (Season 1—Alex Michel), was the first player to utilize it in our beloved game and it's now taken on a life of its own in this franchise, conjured up by countless players to justify competitive behavior. While it's gained immense popularity, the sentiment has never been more misguided than in the current era. You may get to go on as many as ten dates with the Bachelor over the course of nine weeks. Ali Fedotowsky (Season 14—Jake Pavelka; sixth Bachelorette) wrote on her E! blog: "You don't really know the person when you're on the show. You spend about a total of 12 hours together in the first two months of the show and it's under very strange circumstances." You will spend the majority of your time with the other players. Cultivating relationships with them may not seem like the primary focus, but friendships are actually extremely important for benefiting your relationship with all four audiences.

Develop a flawless Second Audience game to make it less likely that other players will initiate Tattle attacks to the Bachelor (First Audience), to make the Producers want to highlight your friendships with screen time (Third Audience), and to make you more likable to Bachelor Nation (Fourth Audience). The Fourth Audience loves to "ship" friendships from the show and players often post on social media about finding a "different form of love" than they had expected going in.

One of the most important benefits of a strong Second Audience game, however, is how you can continue using these relationships in the postseason parasocial game. In order to maximize IG gains, make friends with any and all other players, especially the ones you know have, or predict will have, the largest social media followings. Making friends will enable you to post group IG photos and TikToks, plan trips together, and bolster each other's following. So if you don't make it to the Final Four, which is statistically very likely (88.63 percent), but one of your friends does, you can still benefit by getting some IG follower runoff long after your time in the game has concluded.

Making friends is a key component of house life, but so, too, is presenting yourself as an individual by putting your chosen archetype on full display even and especially in the house.

The Twelve Archetypes

Producers use the players to fill certain roles in the show—roles they have designed. While you can stand out in your Limo Exit and perhaps even make the edit of the featured mini-dates on Night One, Week 1 is where you start creating your own character, story, and brand—or else you inadvertently let Producers choose each of these elements for you.

Cultivate your own chosen archetype (refer to page 26 for the master list of the twelve archetypes), but also observe which roles your peers are falling into or Producers force them into. Develop a strong knowledge of each of the roles so you know when you're being coaxed into them and you can perform the necessary defensive maneuvers. For instance, when you're assigned the singular humiliating costume on a Group Date, stealthily switch it out or refuse to wear it in order to avoid the archetype of the Fool.

Producers will attempt to position you as a certain archetype as early as the filming of your intro package. If they ask for footage that is goofy, could paint you in a bad light, or could paint you in a different light than you want for your brand, politely decline and suggest footage that is more germane to your plan. Always try to figure out their story lines and constantly gather info in the house. Pay special attention to what questions are asked of you and who you are being asked to talk about while filming ITMs, but simultaneously maintain the illusion of blissful ignorance to the Producers' machinations.

They want to create a compelling TV show, no matter the personal cost. They cast Lee Garrett, who had openly racist tweets, on the first Black Bachelorette Rachel Lindsay's season and then focused on his altercations with Black men on the show. While this is among the more nefarious of their choices, they do similar things on all seasons—from bringing in ex-girlfriend Skeletons, to encouraging contestants to sabotage other players' mini-dates (a la the #Champagnegate disaster of Season 24), to bringing in five new players halfway through Season 25 in an attempt to destroy as many players' relationships as possible. They manipulate everything. Thus, paying attention and observing will help you in many ways, including allowing you to distance yourself from someone who is getting a Villain Edit, the first archetype.

The Villain

The Villain is the most important archetype for the Producers in our beloved game. They don't have a show without one, and once a Villain is eliminated they will immediately find a new player on whom to bestow this archetype. Whether the Villain's game style is subtle and manipulative or wild and bombastic, the common traits among Villain archetypes are a terrible Second and Fourth Audience game. Producers create story lines and edit the show to portray Villains in a negative light, and fellow players often accuse them of being 4TWR. The strongest Villains are able to compensate with terrific First Audience games. Often, a few different players will play into this archetype throughout the season, though generally one Lead Villain emerges from several candidates. The Lead Villain of a season comes in approximately 6.88th place. We don't recommend playing into this role if your ultimate goal is the Ring or the Crown, but if you think you're out of the running for those, this strategy works to gain screen time and a following during the main game, ultimately securing an invitation to *BIP*. It should be noted that the IG gains for Villains have declined in recent seasons.

Playing the Villain role is the ultimate Faustian bargain. The Producers will give the Villain the screen time she desires, but they will also destroy that player for the pleasure of the Fourth Audience. If you embrace this role successfully you must be prepared for an avalanche of internet blowback, bullying by the Fourth Audience, and to be known as a *Bachelor* Villain for the rest of your life, but you may be able to find a redemptive story line in Paradise. You can also win other prizes. Some Villains have hundreds of thousands of IG followers and two Villains have won the Ring. However, no Villain has ever won the Crown.

Courtney Robertson and Vienna Girardi were the two most successful Villains of the Modern Era, the sole Villain Ring Winners. They played before Instagram existed and therefore have modest numbers. Robertson ultimately penned a book, *I Didn't Come Here to Make Friends*, and sits at 47.4K. Girardi has 19K, even after a traumatic on-screen breakup with Jake Pavelka. Michelle Money (Season 15—Brad Womack) was also a successful pre-IG Villain. After her season she competed on *Bachelor Pad* Season 2 and accrued a respectable 305K, making her the most successful female Villain from the time before Instagram.

As Instagram began to influence the game more and more, one Lead Villain, Corinne Olympios (Season 21—Nick Viall), flourished, and any player considering a Villain strategy should look to Olympios as a Hero Player. She took over her season by mastering a variety of strategies and played to her strengths: a colorful backstory, comedic energy, and a strong chemistry game. This propelled her all the way to the first round of play-offs (Hometowns). She relied on ABF (Always Be Funny) to produce her own highly entertaining show, including very strong face play and repeating colorful catchphrases like discussing her "platinum vagine," all of which ensured her screen time. She also performed Mansion Free-Play Antics in the house, where she was always napping, which not only provoked the rest of the players but also garnered a lot of screen time, even when she was unconscious. She created a colorful backstory of being an adult with a nanny, which arguably made her a Hometowns shoo-in, where we eventually met the nanny in question—Raquel.

Olympios performed a historic voluntary nudity play on a photo-shoot Group Date, coaxing Viall to fondle her in a pool in front of the other players, throwing them off their game as well as dominating the story line of that episode. She also played into a strong rivalry by antagonizing Taylor Nolan, ensuring more screen time, including a hostile-environment 201 Date in which Olympios vanquished Nolan, and she continued that rivalry into Paradise. In the postseason Olympios has more IG followers than any other Villain in history, 713K. She appeared on multiple talk shows and Sacha Baron Cohen pranked her in *Who Is America?*

The second most successful Villain player in the Paradise Era was Krystal Nielson. She was a fairly standard Villain during her main game with a lacking Second Audience game, giffable catchphrases, and producing and starring in her own melodrama. However, she pivoted during *BIP*, attaching herself to a solid Floater, Chris "Goose" Randone. ABC paid for their wedding and made them an integral part of the following *BIP* season. While they were the first couple to divorce from the franchise after almost eight months of marriage, Nielson ultimately walked away with 652K IG followers, many lucrative spon-con deals, and a successful Total Body Guide fitness program.

Other notable Lead Villains include face player extraordinaire Olivia Caridi (Season 20—Ben Higgins), IFI (Injury Fear Illness) champion Tierra LiCausi (Season 17—Sean Lowe), and infamous "Sanderson Poe" PTC player Kelsey Poe (Season 19—Chris Soules). A notable footnote Villain, Rozlyn Papa (Season 14—Jake Pavelka), was kicked off early in her season in a franchise first, for allegedly engaging in romantic activity with one of the Producers. In an interview with *Entertainment Tonight* in 2010, when asked if she had sex with the producer, Papa denied the allegation by saying, "No, absolutely not. It seems they want the ratings. This seeps into my personal life. I have a seven-year-old little boy at home that I want to look up to me, and to have this blatant lie out there perpetuated by the show itself, it's hurtful. It's scary to think what my son will think of me."

The Fool

In a common modern use of this archetype, some intentionally choose the Fool route on Night One by donning an animal costume and performing a memorable full-body TOT out of the limo. If your main goal is making it to *BIP* and you don't think you have a chance of staying past the first few Rose Ceremonies, choose this splashy path. While you will forever be known as Shark Girl or The Sloth, you will be known.

But be warned, this strategy will negate you from most long game play and dashes most chances of ending up in the IG Eden of the Final Four. Exceptions include JoJo Fletcher (wore a unicorn head and went on to wear the Crown), Clare Crawley (wore a fake baby bump and also went on to wear the Crown), and Lindsay Yenter (wore a wedding dress and achieved runner-up). Producers and/or editors can drag you into this archetype completely unaware. You might not even realize you've been turned into a Fool until the show airs. Watch out for obvious signs like Producers assigning you a ridiculous costume on a Group Date (e.g., the "Elderly Lunch Lady" role while everyone else gets "Sex Kitten" or "Princess" on the Professional Wrestling Group Date [Season 22—Arie Luyendyk Jr.]).

One of the most successful Fools from recent seasons was Alexis Waters (Nick Viall's twenty-first season). She wore a shark costume for her TOT Limo Exit on Night One, repeatedly insisted it was a dolphin, and despite being eliminated in Week 5 was guaranteed a spot in Paradise. She employed the ABF strategy to a T, creating many giffable moments that allowed her to rake in 320K followers despite only a brief stint on *BIP*.

One of the other most successful Fools in the IG Era was Annaliese Puccini (Season 22—Arie Luyendyk Jr.). While she did choose to enter the game with a TOT, exiting the limo wearing a mask to mock Luyendyk for his nickname the Kissing Bandit, her route to the Fool's Edit appeared unintentional.

Puccini detailed a traumatic childhood experience with bumper cars, which was immediately exploited by the Producers. They put her on the Bumper Cars Group Date and they constructed silly, poorly reenacted flashback montages of her trauma. She was subsequently eliminated in Week 3. Producers continued to put together fake, mocking flashbacks of her childhood on two consecutive *BIP* seasons, where she was repeatedly victimized by male players but also got a lot of screen time for her phobias and her tears. She was publicly humiliated on her first *BIP* reunion by Kamil Nicalek and garnered a lot of sympathy from Bachelor Nation. But for bearing the Fool's burden for all of her time in-game, the Nation rewarded her with a solid 154K IG followers.

The Foreigner

Players don't usually choose the Foreigner archetype. It chooses them because they all share one attribute: They are not from the United States. So if you hail from a non-American country, you qualify for the Foreigner archetype, and although you can layer in another archetype, the Foreigner will be your default. You can highlight your exotic background via language, dress, references, and Kringles. You might want to choose the Aloha Limo Exit to demonstrate your knowledge of another language and make yourself easily distinguishable from the rest of the player pool.

One of the most successful Foreigner players was Kristina Schulman (Season 21—Nick Viall), in part because of her intense backstory. She told Viall one of the darkest PTCs in our beloved game's history, that she grew up food poor in Russia with an abusive mother, including detailing an incident in which she ate lipstick, until she got adopted from an orphanage and moved to the United States. She elaborated on the deeply sad PTC during the WTA, saying that a teacher had insinuated she would need to go into sex work if she didn't choose to get adopted and go to America. Schulman was able to beautifully weave her role of Foreigner into an American dream narrative that Producers exploited multiple times throughout her career. While she was eliminated in the Round of Six (the round just before Hometowns when six players are left) she went on to dominate Seasons 4 and 6 of *BIP* and now stands at a solid 701K IG followers.

In the most recent *Bachelor*, Season 25, Magi Tareke stood out from the field by telling her story. She grew up in a small town in Ethiopia and only moved to the United States on a diversity lotto visa. She ran a nonprofit that provided shoes to girls in her hometown and campaigned heavily for disaster relief for the war in Tigray. She came off extremely 4TRR through all of this work and ended up with 49.7K IG followers.

Technically, players don't necessarily need to be from another country if they choose to pretend to be this archetype, as one player, Bri Barnes (Season 23—Colton Underwood), did experimentally. She faked an Australian accent to try to stand out to Underwood in her Limo Exit, but she didn't last much longer after her ruse came to light.

The Professional

Players with the Professional archetype know how to get the job done. If you have a non-influencer job already, which you possibly even have to quit to play the game, you just might be a Professional. You can even use the fact that you had to leave your important job as a play, called the Sabbatical. The Sabbatical garners players a high-level certification of 4TRR and they are quite often Crown contenders, as they represent the modern woman looking for love. If you make a deep run as a Professional, you can also use the Sabbatical dilemma about resignation to urge the Bachelor into action, possibly even to clinch a high-value Rose.

Rachel Lindsay (Season 21—Nick Viall) portrayed the pinnacle of a Professional Hero Player. She got the first intro package, showing her working as an attorney as well as dancing with a vacuum cleaner. She could do it all! She was the first Black player to get the FIMP Rose, to make it to both Hometowns and Fantasy Suites, and to wear the Crown. She married her Ring Winner, now hosts multiple podcasts and shows, and has just under a million IG followers (940K).

The Good Girl

If playing a hard-line 4TRR strategy sounds appealing, then the Good Girl might be for you. Generally representing themselves as sweet, "Here to Make Friends," and innocent, Good Girls often perform Blandy Limo Exits to convey simplicity and authenticity. You don't have to be a virgin to adopt the Good Girl archetype, but plenty of players have. And *Bachelor* virginity doesn't necessarily mean literal virginity, but you can use it to exaggerate your naïvety in either physical or emotional experiences in the following subtypes: Kiss Virgin, Born-Again Virgin, Never Been in Love, Never Had a Boyfriend, Never Experienced Climax, et cetera. Good Girl archetypes can often pull a Ring win or possibly First Sand in Paradise. Playing a PVC (Personal Virginity Card) sets up a very clear story for the Fourth Audience to follow. Will we watch this player experience this thing in-game that they've never experienced before?

The most successful player to utilize the Good Girl archetype was Madison Prewett (Season 24—Peter Weber). She curated two main tenets of her brand: Christianity and an unrelenting competitive nature, especially in the realm of basketball. She discussed her virginity and her faith throughout the season and the Producers included several sequences of Prewett stroking a curtain while wearing a promise ring to bring this narrative to visual life. Her strong play earned her the early MOTF 1O1 Date, during which she attended Weber's parents' vows renewal. She used a series of walls, always kept a lower Love Level than Weber, and ultimately played an infamous Fantasy Suite Ultimatum, in which she told Weber that she wouldn't be able to get engaged if he was intimate with other women during this round of play. She was one of only twenty-four players in the history of the game to self-eliminate, though she briefly reunited with Weber at the ATFR episode of that season. Prewett gained the most IG followers for a player who never wore the Crown (1.7M). She also pulled the most TikTok followers of *any* player in the game's history (2M).

Another Good Girl who never wore the Crown but still gained over a million followers on Instagram was Becca Tilley (Season 19—Chris Soules). Tilley loaded her PVC (Personal Virginity Card) in Episode 4 to the Fourth Audience but didn't play it to Soules until Fantasy Suites week. He told her he respected her decision and she made it to the finals. She finished the season as runner-up and was so well liked that she was allowed to return for a Second Tour (Season 20—Ben Higgins), where she placed fifth.

One of the other most successful players who used the Good Girl archetype is Ashley Iaconetti. Producers consistently humiliated her again and again by obsessively focusing on both her virginity and her propensity for tear play, generating entire montages from footage of her sobbing throughout the season. Soules sent her home on an infamous double-elimination 2O1 Date with Kelsey Poe and she should've faded into obscurity like many other players before Instagram came to prominence. Instead, her meme-able tears and virgin story line, as well as an obsession with Jared Haibon, a player who constantly kept her in the friend zone, propelled her into Bachelor Nation infamy. She reigned in Paradise and successfully stayed relevant in the postseason with her podcast, *The Ben and Ashley I Almost Famous Podcast*. With 1.2M followers and by finally marrying Jared Haibon, Ashley I has become one of the most successful players in *Bachelor* history, despite never being the Bachelorette or a Ring Winner, a rare feat.

The Free Spirit

Whether crafting outrageous sexually charged Standy Limo Exits or performing full voluntary nudity plays on Group Dates, the one quality all Free Spirits share is that they defy conventions of all kinds and can be somewhat of a wild card. Often, Free Spirits will have a strong Second Audience game as they encourage the rest of the house to party and/or engage in any of the Mansion Free-Play Antics they initiate. Adopting the Free Spirit archetype can sometimes get you accused of playing the game 4TWR or not being serious or ready for an engagement, but focusing on your genuine brand and being vocal about staying true to who you are can successfully deflect these attacks by reinforcing your sincerity as a Free Spirit.

The most successful Free Spirit in the history of our beloved game and a Hero Player for *all* future players to consider was Canadian Kaitlyn Bristowe (Season 19—Chris Soules). She entered the game with a raunchy, topical one-liner Standy ("you can plow the fuck out of my field any day") and played her whole season with a cavalier wildness that stood in stark contrast to more measured players, which attracted both Soules and Bachelor Nation. She jumped in on toasts with her own jokes, jumped into a lake naked on a Group Date, and got all four audiences to fall in love with her. She placed third in her season and was immediately rewarded with the Crown. She became the first Bachelorette to have sex before Fantasy Suites and continues to prove that this is Bristowe's world and everyone else is just living in it. She now has a successful podcast, a scrunchie line, a wine line, and friendships with multiple Bachelor Nation power couples; she's won *Dancing with the Stars* and has 1.9M IG followers. She also co-hosted Seasons 17 and 18 of *The Bachelorette* with Tayshia Adams and got engaged to fellow third-place player Jason Tartick in 2021. Bristowe is beyond doubt a constant fixture in the conversation about the greatest player of all time.

The most successful Free Spirit in the Professional Era has been Katie Thurston. She entered Matt James's historic season carrying a vibrator—a prop-Standy first in the history of our beloved game. She played an extremely strong 4TRR Second and Fourth Audience Game, befriending even the new players who "crashed" that season, and committed to her sex-positive brand in all of her parasocial play. She went on to wear the Crown, despite only placing eleventh in her season, a record in itself.

The Single Mother

If you don't have a child, this will be an impossible archetype to employ. If you do have a child, this will be your only choice for an archetype, which is not a bad thing at all. While the Single Mother has both advantages and disadvantages, it is beyond doubt iconic and oft repeated. The benefits include being the only player who is able to have contact with the outside world. While all other players are separated from everyone they love, the Producers will allow you to Facetime your offspring as long as it's on-camera. And this conversation with your child or children renders a powerful advantage in that it has the emotional resonance of a PTC. You will garner a lot of sympathy and an implication that you're there 4TRR because you've left your kid(s) in order to find love. When you reveal your motherhood status to the Bachelor, this play is called a Package Deal. We don't recommend playing a PD Night One unless you feel very worried about leaving, as it generally guarantees a player at least one more week. However, you should play it during Week 1 to avoid looking like you hid it from the Bachelor.

While kids statistically hurt players' chances of winning a Ring, with only one player in history winning the Ring with kids (Emily Maynard [Season 15—Brad Womack]), they can propel you far in the game. The Bachelor always outwardly takes his relationship with the Single Mother more seriously, as she will be seen as "sacrificing" more than the other players to be there. This also results in earlier exits sometimes if the Bachelor hasn't selected her as a Ring Winner, on the grounds of knowing she needs to get back to her child/ren. That easy out for the Bachelor is baked into this archetype.

Emily Maynard was the most successful Single Mother in our beloved game and broke many records. She had a very intense PTC that coordinated with her PD play—that her race car driver husband was killed in a small plane crash and then she found out she was pregnant with his child. She came off extremely 4TRR with her own tear play and even inspired tear play by other players. She was the clear front-runner and Ring Winner. When she and Womack broke up she went on to wear the Crown. She was the only Single-Mother Ring Winner as well as the only Single-Mother Crown.

Chelsea Roy (Arie Luyendyk Jr.—Season 22) is another Single Mother you should study if you're playing this archetype. She was the first Single Mother to win the FIMP Rose and she was able to pivot away from a Villain Edit by using her PD 4TRR defense as well as playing a heartbreak PTC to traverse her season, ultimately going home during the sixth Rose Ceremony. She has 141K IG followers.

Amanda Stanton (Ben Higgins—Season 20) also sits in the pantheon of successful Single Mothers. She garnered massive attention for herself and her kids during her season and then two subsequent *BIP* seasons. Her kids even accompanied her on dates in Higgins's season, where she went home after Hometowns. She has 1.1 million IG followers, despite never being the Bachelorette, and her kids have 28.3K and 29.3K. They are both under ten years old.

The Bumpkin

Just because you're from the Continental United States doesn't mean you can't re-create some of the allure of the Foreigner's exotic appeal! That's where the Bumpkin archetype comes in. To be a Bumpkin you simply choose to play up aspects of the region of the country you call home. Traditionally, players from rural towns in the South choose this archetype, but you can hail from any part of the country and still be a Bumpkin. Just lean hard into your region through accent, customs, dress, and phrases. You'll have an elevated chance to nab the Colorful Narrator role by incorporating and exaggerating your regionalisms into ITM descriptions of all things happening in-game.

The prototypical Bumpkin players are Raven Gates (Nick Viall—Season 21) and the player she trained, Tia Booth (Arie Luyendyk Jr.—Season 22). Gates hailed from Hoxie, Arkansas, and she played that up from her very first onscreen moment, her It Takes Two Limo Exit, when she made Viall "call the hogs" by yelling, "Woo Pig Souie!" She also performed a What I Do for Fun Hometown Date by taking Nick Viall muddin'. Ultimately, Gates made it to the finals and went on to have an extremely successful *BIP* run in which she met and later got married to Floater Adam Gottschalk. Today Gates has 1.1M IG followers.

Tia Booth was Gates's protégé. She entered the game with a spicy food-themed Kringle, handing Luyendyk a tiny hot dog, adding, "Please tell me you don't already have one," to not only represent that she was from a rural town in Arkansas called Wiener but also challenge Luyendyk's masculinity and initiate a subtle chemistry play. During her Hometown Date Booth took Luyendyk to a racetrack, keeping on theme. While Luyendyk eliminated Booth after that date, leaving her in tears, she went on to dominate the story line on her first *BIP* season by attempting to attach herself to Bachelor-to-be Colton Underwood. And she came back for a second season of *BIP* on which she was granted star status by the Producers, who gave her a bullet-proof hero edit. Today Booth has 1.1M IG followers.

The Weirdo

Possibly the easiest comedic persona to adopt is the Weirdo. There are a wide variety of behaviors you can employ to build this persona. This can range from abnormal pre-show hobbies or careers to new quirks picked up in the house. Examples include: talking to things that aren't there, performing experimental face play, getting in the tub with your clothes on, creating a friendship with a pool animal, mispronouncing a word repeatedly, making up a nonsensical song, working out in a bizarre way, always asking if it's raining, doing a signature dance, starting each morning with a primal scream, or even assuring the other players that you have accurate premonitions about everything from natural disasters to who the Bachelor is going to take to Fantasy Suites.

The most successful player to employ the Weirdo archetype was Kendall Long (Season 22—Arie Luyendyk Jr.). Her intro video featured her singing and playing the ukulele, as well as showcasing her taxidermy hobby, which was featured again and again throughout the season. This culminated in a Hometown Date during which she showed Luyendyk her full collection of dead animal friends. She and Luyendyk then created their own diorama of rats in costumes, representing their own love story if they traveled to Paris. While she was dismissed after Fantasy Suites, she went on to dominate five weeks of *BIP* Season 5, teaming up with the most successful Night One Guy of all time, Joe Amabile; and the she returned to *BIP* Season 7 for another round of screen time as Producers attempted to use her to break up Amabile's new relationship with Serena Pitt.

Another iconic player who fell into the Weirdo archetype was Ashley Salter (Season 19—Chris Soules). She was known for her Mansion Free-Play Antics, including obsessing over an onion that was actually a pomegranate, befriending a stray cat, as well as talking to things that weren't seemingly there. She also took on a bizarre approach to a paintball Group Date, becoming aggressively competitive and behaving as though the fake zombie narrative was, in fact, real. Although she went home after the fourth Rose Ceremony, she was the first player to ever receive an on-camera invitation to *BIP* from then-host Chris Harrison at the WTA.

Another notable player who received the Weirdo Edit was Shawntel Newton (Brad Womack—Season 15). Her intro depicted her job as a funeral director, and Producers played this occupation for laughs her entire season. She performed a Take Your Bachelor To Work (TYBTW) Hometown Date during which she showed the Nation her family business funeral home but was ultimately thwarted by her own family questioning her plan to leave the business and move to Texas with Womack. She was eliminated before Fantasy Suites and made a brief attempt at a second tour on Season 16.

The Pageant Queen

There is perhaps no greater preparation for a Bachelor player than a background in pageants. If you have competed in this ancillary competition you are often well prepared in giving media-trained answers to questions, navigating all-female competition, always being camera ready, and being prepared for whatever is thrown at you in a competitive gauntlet. In our beloved game Pageant Queens frequently enter with sash TOT Limo Exits to display their greatest pageant victory and routinely perform better than other players who do not have this extremely helpful experience under their belt.

The most successful Pageant Queen players in the history of the game were no doubt the rivalry turned Dynamic Duo of Hannah Brown and Caelynn Miller-Keyes (Season 23—Colton Underwood). Brown was Miss Alabama 2018 and wore a pageant crown in her intro package, although she entered the game with a Blandy. Miller-Keyes was Miss North Carolina 2018. She entered the game wearing her Miss North Carolina sash, performed a flawless TOT Standy, telling Underwood, "Hopefully I can get another title," while revealing the back part of the sash to say: "Miss Underwood." Brown and Miller-Keyes played up their dramatic pageant rivalry for half of their season, ultimately and skillfully squashing it before they could be forced into a 2O1 Date. While Brown placed seventh in her season, she went on to wear the Crown and become the most successful IG player in history (2.5M). Miller-Keyes was eliminated after Hometowns but went on to team up with IG powerhouse and *BIP* veteran Dean Unglert, for *BIP* Season 6, where they dominated and became a very successful IG couple. Miller-Keyes has 1.4M and Unglert has 1.3M IG followers.

Another notable Pageant Queen was Mandy Jaye Jeffreys (Season 5—Jesse Palmer). During her Hometown Date in Austin, Texas, her mother showed off their Pageant Room, a haunting chamber filled with ribbons and awards, solely dedicated to Jeffreys's achievements in pageantry. Her mother described how her daughter would make a great "NFL wife" because her pageants prepared her. Jeffreys's stepfather spent his 101 time with Palmer by exclusively discussing pageants and his disappointment that Jeffreys never won Miss Texas. Jeffreys placed third in Palmer's season and likely further disappointed her pageant-centric family.

The Princess

At first glance, the Princess archetype might seem very similar to the Pageant archetype because they both focus on an outward aesthetic, but they are actually very different. If you're an attention seeker who feels most comfortable in the spotlight and you've elevated brand-name shopping to a lifestyle then the Princess might be the archetype for you. While Pageant players are more likely to play a 4TRR game, the Princess is "not here to make friends" and will frequently sacrifice her Second Audience game with attention-seeking behaviors. A Princess will quite often happily trade a possible Villain Edit for screen time.

The most successful Princess Hero Player in our beloved game is, of course, Corinne Olympios (Nick Viall—Season 21). While she utilized the Villain archetype, her second archetype of Princess was just as important. Right out of the gate, she began her Princess branding with an intro video shot in the style of Elle Woods from the film *Legally Blonde*. Olympios also used the day portion of her Hometown Date to do a reverse *Pretty Woman* Date, taking Bachelor Nick Viall on a shopping spree at her favorite stores in Miami, creating a film-style montage. She had one of the strongest First Audience games of any Villain and consistently created scenarios in which she could shine, including approaching Viall in a trench coat and making him eat whipped cream off her for a mini-date, as well as napping through a Rose Ceremony.

The most recent successful Princess player was Victoria Larson (Season 25—Matt James), who was also a notorious Villain. She entered the game with a Queen-themed TOT, wearing a crown and carrying a scepter. She continued to play up her Queen branding, including physically removing a TOT crown from a Pageant Queen named Catalina Morales when she entered the game late. Her Not Here To Make Friends strategy garnered her one of the highest levels of screen time in the game, despite her going home at the fourth Rose Ceremony. She then evolved her archetype by giving her title a promotion to "Goddess" when she entered *Bachelor in Paradise* Season 7, with a new and bigger headpiece TOT, which she made sure to tell people was "expensive."

The Dynamic Duo

One of the best archetypes for a 4TRR Second and Fourth Audience game is the Dynamic Duo. It requires you to pair up with another player in order to exponentially benefit along with your counterpart. You can team up for GD challenges, create Mansion Free-Play Antics together, and combine your social media followings in the postseason parasocial game. Duos have taken bubble baths together, worked out together, and even held hands while competing in an Obstacle Course. The best Dynamic Duos spend as much time together as possible in order to maximize the chance that Producers will use them as a C-plot story line, often appearing together in tags.

The most successful Dynamic Duo was JoJo Fletcher and Becca Tilley (Season 20—Ben Higgins). It was Tilley's second season after coming in second on Chris Soules's Season 19 and perhaps she was more easily able to spot a front-runner in Fletcher due to her experience. The two bonded over McDonald's and teamed up, always competing together on Group Dates. The sincerity in their friendship conveyed extreme 4TRR, even during the competition dates when they seemed like they were just having fun with each other. They also bonded in the house. Even when Fletcher wore the Crown the two stayed close and continued to post IG photos of their best friendship still today. Matching Halloween costumes, hitting the concert circuit together, and even doing joint spon-con are all parasocial plays they've made since their time in-game.

Another notable Dynamic Duo was Ashley Spivey and Ashley Hebert (Brad Womack—Season 15). They struck up a quick comradery and for the first time in the show's history the Producers punished a team-up by pitting the two against each other on the 2O1 date that season. Hebert got the Rose and eventually third place, while Spivey went home between the fourth and fifth Rose Ceremonies. Hebert went on to wear the Crown, marry, and have kids with her Ring Winner, J. P. Rosenbaum, and Spivey was a bridesmaid in their wedding. Hebert and Rosenbaum divorced in 2021 and Spivey became an important voice in the progressive Bachelor Nation space. She and Hebert are still friends today.

The first Dynamic Duo featured in the history of our beloved game was in Season 10 (Andy Baldwin). Two blond innovators, Erin Parker and Susan Anderson, became best friends on-camera and their friendship earned them special screen time. During an Athletic Activity Triathlon Group Date, the two performed their own version of a protest by walking and swimming slowly through each leg together, holding hands for the duration and openly mocking the competitive element of the date. Baldwin himself questioned whether the two even wanted to spend time with him, given how much they liked each other. This Duo was short-lived unfortunately, as Anderson went home during the second Rose Ceremony and Parker the third.

House Strategy

No matter which of the twelve archetypes you wind up representing, you must develop a sound strategy for navigating life in the house. And while yours will be slightly different from all other players', a style tailored to your own selected brands and character identities, there are some universal truths about living in the house to remember at all times.

They Are Always Listening

Never forget that anything you say or do is being recorded and analyzed by the Producers in order to determine the best ways to exploit you. Be aware and on your toes at all times. You don't necessarily need to always be truthful or even nice. As long as you have a game plan, the fact that the Producers are always listening and watching you can actually be turned against them. You can devise a game within the larger game and trap the producers into playing it.

Take control by initiating a well-thought-out misinformation campaign if you should see the opportunity. When you're alone, pretend like you don't know there are mics and cameras on you. Say something out loud to yourself, about a feeling or attitude you have regarding another player or even the Bachelor himself. Whatever you say, the Producers will attempt to use it in the construction of a plot. This is an invaluable technique in creating a rivalry you design instead of letting the Producers do it, delivering information to the Bachelor without having to say it to them, because whatever you say will be reported back to him by the Producers if it's salacious or interesting enough for them to build a plot around.

You can even garner audience sympathy with a fake expression of sorrow or doubt at the entire process. Living in a state of constant surveillance can produce high levels of anxiety and negatively affect your judgment and performance. Jillian Harris (Season 13—Jason Mesnick) wrote in a blog for *Parade*: "To never be alone with your thoughts, and to be away from phones, computers, magazines, and the news, is difficult, so having someone to chat with is PARAMOUNT!" But repositioning the context of the situation can be helpful. Think of the cameras as a conduit to the Producers instead of their unfeeling, all-seeing, all-hearing eyes and ears, and turn an objectively terrifying circumstance into what amounts to a delayed conversation with slightly strange parameters.

Be a Producer

Although you're always at the whim of the Producers, you certainly don't have to wait for them to spur you into action. You have full rein in the house while you're sequestered. You can devise a plot and orchestrate any situation you want, especially given that you have so many hours of downtime between dates. Never be bored. Use the time you have with the other players in the house to build your brand, to use your catchphrases, to do your dance—whatever your identifying characteristic might be, exploit it. And use the time to fold the other contestants into your story. Create your own cliffhangers. Think of all activities in terms of producible segments like the ones that are in every season. You can build dramatic tension that demands resolution but that may take a few episodes to resolve. Generating a fake rivalry with another player, a new friendship, and an unorthodox morning routine are all simple stories that you can control, assuring yourself more screen time.

ABL—Always Be Listening

Part of being your own Producer means you need as much information as possible. Journal constantly but not about your feelings. Use the journal to keep charts and diagrams of the other players' movements, alliances, weaknesses, and progress through the game. Try to figure out where they are on the Love Level chart. If you're going on a Group Date, attempt to figure out what PTCs the other players plan to play. If someone has planned an unbeatable PTC, save your own. If there's one you think you can beat, play it on that Group Date. But this information has more than just personal value. In some cases you can trade information directly to Producers in exchange for things like extra sleep or additional 1O1 time with the Bachelor. Tia Booth recently revealed via social media an image of a page from the notebook she kept while she played. In it, she detailed the alliances in the house and each remaining player's attitude toward the various groups. Booth explained that she made a deal with the Producers to divulge this information in exchange for an extra hour of sleep. As in war and prison, information is power.

Peeping Tom

Hand in hand with Always Be Listening is the Peeping Tom. Study the house's layout to find places where you can hang out to overhear and oversee other conversations and behaviors. Perform Peeping Toms to keep track of which other players have kissed the Bachelor or played their PTC, as well as to see if the player you spy on tells the truth about their 1O1 time.

Sometimes the Producers will set up Peeping Tom scenarios for the housebound players while the Bachelor is on a 1O1 Date in order to create as much jealousy and frenzied animosity as possible toward the player on the date and to make the experience of not being on a date as stressful as possible so that you are more likely to do outrageous things when you do get time. Producers have forced all the remaining players outside to hang by the pool while the Bachelor and his date fly by in an airplane over the Mansion. They have supplied binoculars to players in their hotel room and forced them to witness another player on a parasailing date. In recent seasons they have frequently made players go out onto the balcony just in time to witness nearby fireworks, which studied players know means their competitor has had a successful 101 Date, is probably engaged in strong chemistry play, and probably already has a Rose in hand. During Season 25, the players openly acknowledged that the fireworks indicated this information while Bri Springs was on her 101 Date with Matt James, signifying a concrete raising of the bar where general knowledge of game mechanics is concerned.

Mansion Free-Play Antics

When you are not on a date with the Bachelor, work on your Second, Third, and Fourth Audience games. Prepare games involving all the players that Producers will film and maybe include in the edit. Tie the game to your brand or other identifying characteristic, like a job, which will help you shine. Make up songs about anything and everything that is going on and even encourage other players to sing along with you. Do not perform popular songs that the show would have to license to include in the edit. Try creating makeshift drums from objects in the house. Dance with animals. Dance with other players or camera operators. Dance with inanimate objects.

Mansion Free-Play Antics don't even necessarily need to involve other players, though that is preferred. Corinne Olympios (Season 21) napped as part of her MFPA strategy. She even slept through a Rose Ceremony. Because MFPA tactics are so unique to your particular brand, you can experiment. For example, if you've chosen a Free Spirit archetype, attuned to your own wellness and inner peace, bring a special meditation cushion and then insist on meditating during fights or while everyone is in the pool, et cetera. You could even repeat some sort of mantra or affirmation or even a noise. Producers could always cut away to your comedy bit while everyone else engages in an agitated argument. And you could even call this back with a few deep breaths with closed eyes at the Rose Ceremony.

Gold Level: During Chris Soules's nineteenth season, Ashley Iaconetti didn't get the Princess/*Pretty Woman* Date. While Jade Roper was on the date, Iaconetti wore the sparkly dress that she planned to wear if she would've received this honor. She pranced around the house in her gown and performed strong tear play as she sadly ate corn on the cob. For professional players, it doesn't matter if you're on the date or not; you can turn downtime in the house into screen time, assuring that you don't waste a second of game play.

ABF—Always Be Funny

Producers usually identify one player as comic relief. If you can make this happen, the Producers will grant you more screen time than most others, especially in early rounds of the game. They will use your confessional ITM footage as commentary in virtually every group and individual situation. And it's a safe bet they will highlight you in the humorous tag at the end of each episode. Be incompetent! Hannah Brown made the Season 23 blooper reel by repeatedly struggling to open the house microwave. Be competent! Kaitlyn Bristowe (Season 19—Chris Soules) used her sense of humor deftly in her four-audience game. Many of her toasts and ITMs made the edit and Producers gifted her the celebrity 101 Date to go toe-to-toe with Jimmy Kimmel. She ultimately won the Bachelorette Crown.

A good way to be funny is to focus on your prep work in the preseason. If you've already written a bunch of funny toasts, ITM metaphors, and a comedic story as one of your Three Stories, you don't need to come up with them in the house. You just need to focus on your delivery and timing. If you're not a naturally funny person, don't worry, as there are several easy methods by which you can enhance your comedic value to the Producers. These include pre-planned strange food aversions or preferences, phobias of innocuous animals and items, and all manner of non-threatening behavioral quirks. Quirks can include hiccups, a funny-sounding laugh, or even an occasional display of a double-jointed shoulder or thumb to do the trick.

Colorful Narrator

The Producers' ultimate job is to tell a series of captivating small stories that add up to a riveting season-long journey, designed to deliver the highest ratings possible. And despite shooting almost twenty-four hours a day, they still need interstitial pieces of narration that help drive the stories they've created. Generally, they don't use Producers on-camera in order to achieve this, although they've included occasional big-moment conversations with Producers. They prefer players to deliver this narration, most often through confessional interviews or ITMs. One of the most successful ways to dominate the ITMs is to take on the role of the Colorful Narrator, which most professional players do in order to maximize screen time.

To be a successful Colorful Narrator you have to use all the tools at your disposal to create compelling ITMs that the Producers will want to include in every single edit. Use vivid metaphors to describe other players and situations, as well as descriptive language to break down your own emotional moments on your love journey. If you have an accent, indulge in the beautiful harmonies of your native cadence and rhythm to accentuate kitschy colloquialisms from your hometown or even make them up. No one will know. Create and repeat a catchphrase over and over, and combine it with strong face play to guarantee you to serve as a meme muse for the Fourth Audience.

Raven Gates (Nick Viall—Season 21) is the prototype for a Colorful Narrator. She never let anyone forget that she was born and raised in Hoxie, Arkansas. In her ITMs, she leaned deep into her southern accent and southern phrases to describe the various dates and other players. When a group volleyball date became a drunken disaster, complete with violence and tear-stained sand, Gates took to her ITMs to sum up another player, Jasmine Goode: "If Jasmine were a vegetable, she would be a turnip because she's turned all the way up!" Gates, whose innocent southern charm and wide-eyed enthusiasm for the experience endeared her to Bachelor Nation, placed second in her season, and Producers gifted her a very high sand placement (this refers to the order in which players appear on the beach) on the subsequent season of *BIP*, which ultimately resulted in an engagement to Adam Gottschalk. You can come up with memorable phrases like that for many situations, before you even enter the game.

Demi Burnett (Colton Underwood—Season 23) was another Colorful Narrator luminary. She constantly talked about people in funny ways, made silly faces, and eventually she even teamed up with another skillful Colorful Narrator, Jordan Kimball, in *BIP* to form an expert-level Colorful Narrator Dynamic Duo. It should be noted that catchphrases and colorful narration are ideal to use in ITMs, but use them more sparingly with the Bachelor. If you overuse your catchphrase with the Bachelor or even the other players you may earn yourself an early exit on the accusation of being 4TWR. Tammy Ly (Season

24—Peter Weber) accused Mykenna Dorn of being 4TWR for discussing her set of hashtags she had prepared.

Evade! Evade! Evade!

Learn to recognize the telltale signs of rising tensions in the player pool that can lead to an argument or even an outright fight. If you have the sense that an altercation is brewing, *get out!* Remove yourself from the situation immediately—this is especially true if you find yourself a possible participant in the event. You can even do this if you've caused the problem. Victoria Paul (Season 24—Peter Weber) expertly dropped small bombs into conversations and then immediately left the scene, seemingly vanishing into the background, Homer Simpson–style, to let the other players fight among themselves.

With rare exception, the Bachelor never looks kindly on witnessing or even being told secondhand that a player has been any part of a negative event, usually described as "drama," during his immaculate journey to find love. If you find yourself in such a situation, calmly turn on the balls of your feet, face the opposite direction from the source of the conflict, and silently disappear into the shadows. There is no need to fire a parting remark or even to make sure the other players understand what you're doing. Simply turn and walk to the nearest bathroom where the cameras can't follow. Vanish, vaporize, become a ghost, and leave the fighting to players who aren't skilled enough to evade its dark allure.

Rivalries

If you want to ensure screen time and have a high tolerance for risk, develop a rivalry with another player. Often, Producers pick rivals for the high-risk/high-reward 2O1 Date, which guarantees that at least two full episodes will devote significant time to both members of the rivalry. The Producers love nothing more than to put rivals on this date who supposedly hate each other for the maximum humiliation when the Bachelor sends one or both home.

Infamous rivals Ashley Iaconetti and Kelsey Poe went head-to-head on Season 19's 2O1 date in the Badlands of South Dakota. Iaconetti, Poe, and Chris Soules flew in a "romantic" helicopter ride over Mount Rushmore on their way to the showdown. Chris Soules described the trip in his blog as "probably the most uncomfortable ride I have experienced in my entire life" and called it a "steamy chopper full of hate."

Both Iaconetti and Poe threw each other under the bus in epic fashion. Iaconetti said, "I'm Glenda the Good Witch; she's the Wicked Witch of the West; when I come home we're going to toast to ding-dong the witch is dead," but Soules eliminated her first, leaving her sobbing in the desert. Poe, who played up their rivalry with equal flair, described the date: "I just got thrown under the bus. This is a game to her. She's a Kardashian who didn't get to go on a Princess Date, who has way too much makeup on to be genuine." Both players were eliminated immediately after their mutual attacks against one another, and Soules choppered away from the devastated pair, enveloping them in his dust and presumably leaving them to ding-dong die together.

A major benefit of a rivalry strategy is that the Third Audience loves it. Producers will savor the dynamic and will often stoke the aggression between the players again for more screen time at the WTA, and then again on sand on the following season of *BIP*. The ideal handling of a rivalry is to openly discuss it with the other player involved and negotiate how the 2O1 will go down off-camera, almost like a pro wrestling match. However, getting that off-the-grid time can be next to impossible.

Phobias

Producers will often exploit your fears for comedic purposes, which sounds bad until you realize that means screen time. Players have utilized phobias of every kind, from birds to fish and even bumper cars. Manufacture your own harmless phobia and enact overly horrified reactions when confronted with the source of your false terror. Bugs, heights, cats, and any other innocuous thing a player might encounter in the house are good options. Kaitlyn Bristowe indulged her fear of birds in a performance that was so well remembered, host Chris Harrison referenced it in the Season 25 WTA, six years after she wore the Crown.

These moves can be small. Nicole Lopez Alvar made the Season 23 blooper reel by arming herself with a broom in order to try to get an errant bird out of the house. Bugs are a pretty universally accepted *Bachelor* phobia, so feel free to indulge in your reaction. Scream, run away, knock over objects, cling to other players, throw your drink, or do anything else you can think of to get away from the bugs and cause a huge scene. You could also manufacture an exotic phobia like caviar, coins, or feathers. While it seems unlikely that you would encounter these things, rest assured, if the Producers know you have a phobia they will create a scenario specifically to exploit it. Afraid of feathers? Get ready for a pillow fight!

Foodie

The house is the only place you actually get to eat when you want to, so comically indulging in a passion for a certain food or for all foods can garner more screen time. Many players have used this very relatable prop play to delve into their archetypes, delighting the Second and Fourth Audiences. Some have used obsessions with pizza, cold cuts, chicken nuggets, and even scallops to add to their personas.

Demi Burnett (Season 23—Colton Underwood) made the bloopers by shoving an entire roll of cut-up salami into her mouth and then playing with the meat mass. Producers generate subplots around various players' interactions with foods as a mainstay of the game. Constantly ask for a certain food, talk to your food as you eat it, or get ingredients to make a certain food for the rest of the house to introduce your comedic identity. If you use food to bond with the other players you can even escalate things to a food fight, which will surely at least make the blooper reel. You can even call out a use of food in dialogue to tie it to your emotional story. For instance, you could reveal in an ITM, "I only eat chocolate when I am having an emotional breakdown." Then comedically stuff your face with chocolate after using some tear play or when the house is in shambles, something the Producers could use as a comedic callback.

You can even use food sparingly to further your First Audience game by Kringling the Bachelor with some delectable treat in the middle of a Cocktail Party, which he will surely appreciate. If you tie yourself to a specific food often enough, you can even use it in the postseason to sell spon-con. Kelsey Weier (Season 24—Peter Weber) starred in a champagne incident with Hannah Ann Sluss and Weier used champagne in many social media posts after her time in-game. Ashley Iaconetti even gifted her a giant bottle of champagne at the WTA in another food callback and Weier entered *Bachelor in Paradise* Season 7 carrying a bottle of champagne.

Experimental strategy: Declare an obsession with a certain type of food, for instance charcuterie, and then constantly serve it to other players as if you are the house cook. Put on a makeshift apron or fun hat to demonstrate this chef character.

The Tattletale

Once you're in the house getting to know the other players, personalities will invariably rub each other the wrong way and the Producers will strongly encourage any antagonistic relationships that might be brewing or create them from thin air. They might even cast someone you knew outside the game specifically to build a rivalry plot as they did with Hannah Brown and Caelynn Miller-Keyes.

Keep in mind that no matter how badly you dislike another player and no matter how much it seems like exposing that person as being there for the "wrong reasons" seems like a good move, it never is. Being the Tattletale is almost always a no-win proposition. It might pad out a rivalry plot for another episode or two, but even if you're successful in taking out your target with a well-worded plea to the Bachelor about her improper motives or personality shifts for the cameras, being the Tattletale will *always* get you sent home soon as well.

The Shoulder To Cry On (STCO)

As the rivalries start developing, jealous tensions naturally rise as the game escalates and the Producers prod all players toward the edge of nervous breakdowns. Players are bound to start unintentionally crying and emotionally collapsing. This may seem like a bad thing, but one player's breakdown is your opportunity for screen time as the STCO. Provide a Shoulder To Cry On is an extremely 4TRR move. It can be a one-off, or you can adapt the STCO as a prolonged character trait like a House Mom. Renée Oteri (Season 18—Juan Pablo Galavis) played this permanent STCO role expertly for the entirety of her season. The benefits of this move are that you initially build a strong Second Audience game, but you also end up looking very 4TRR for the Fourth Audience.

Katie Thurston (Season 25—Matt James) performed an expert series of STCOs for several of five late-entry players when they were bullied by the original players. In rare cases, you can even play the STCO on the Bachelor himself. When Colton Underwood broke up with Tayshia Adams (Season 23) after their Fantasy Suite round, she performed an STCO for him and it came off extremely 4TRR. She landed high sand placement and eventually wore the Crown.

I Love Cleveland

When house life moves to hotel life, expect to be forced to perform advertisements for the various hotels and locations you visit, all of which pay the production entities to be featured in the program. This staple of house life takes its name from Season 24 when the players traveled to Cleveland, where they were forced to pretend as though Cleveland was Paris, New York, and Dubai all rolled into one.

To begin this performance of false enthusiasm, as soon as the host or the Bachelor announces the new city to which you will all be traveling, react with hysterical excitement. Whatever the destination, convey that it is your favorite place on planet Earth, a city that has been the focal point of your travel obsession since you were a child. Spout fun facts about the city during that conversation or during the week you're in that city (these facts do not even need to be true). Entering the hotel room is the second part of the I Love Cleveland. Enter the hotel room with wide eyes, mouth agape, a high-pitched shriek, and an immediate jump onto the nearest bed. Perform this movement bigger and more enthusiastically than everyone else. Add a new twist such as pretending to make out with a pillow while the other players jump on the bed or make fake phone calls to room service on the rotary phone. Perform the "happy baby" yoga pose on the bed. Use your Dynamic Duo to perform a two-person excited gesture, such as a fist bump, a chest bump, or a special, visually interesting handshake.

Experimental strategy for a Free Spirit: When the Producers make everyone yell, "I love [insert city or insert Bachelor's name]!" off a balcony, perform a voluntary nudity play by flashing the entire city.

House life is obviously a crucial component of our beloved game and mastery of Second Audience development is a virtue. But finding a way to navigate the social dynamic with the other players is only the first step of survival. To truly excel at the game you will have to use the relationships you build in the house in what will very likely be your first post–Night One test with the Bachelor . . . the Group Date.

Chapter 5

REGULAR SEASON PART 2:

GROUP DATES

Um, so it's a Group Date, right, and I don't know if you guys know this, but they're kinda weird.

Nick Viall, the twenty-first Bachelor, upon commencing the first Group Date of his season

We've gotten to a point where we can tell people about the Hyperbinge in a way that doesn't immediately fill them with panic or fear. "We challenged ourselves just to see if we could do it and we actually watched every episode of *The Bachelor* back to back, in order, on 2X speed!" That might get a "Wow! Crazy!" or a "That's dedication." Sometimes we even get a laugh or two. But when you start to dig a little deeper beyond the comically quirky idea that we're just obsessed superfans who did a marathon-style binge, when you start to see what that really means, the unhinged nature of what we managed to do becomes impossible to hide.

We didn't just watch every season of *The Bachelor*. We watched 164 Group Dates over the course of two and a half months and we are forever changed. The Group Date is among the most difficult challenges you'll face in the regular season and statistically it is most likely to be the very first challenge you'll encounter after Night One. Since the Paradise Era began in Season 19, each season has an average of 8.71 Group Dates, and Producers put the vast majority of players to the test in this competitive setting before they will grant you time alone with the Bachelor. And virtually no one avoids finding themselves on a Group Date. Front-runners and Turtles alike must test their mettle in these events that can include anywhere from twelve to eighteen players in early rounds and may involve a wide variety of physical, psychological, and emotional tests designed specifically to push you to your breaking point.

But the Group Date wasn't always defined by its unmitigated brutality. Much like all life on this tiny planet, it has evolved through the years after a series of trial-and-error additions and subtractions by the Producers to arrive at its current form, honed to bring out the most vicious competitor in every player.

The History of the Group Date

The very first Group Date took place in the second episode of Season 1 and it went by a different name. Chris Harrison appeared before the players who survived the first Night One and described what he called "the Fantasy Dates." These first ancestors of the modern Group Date were lavish, extravagant, fun, and most astounding of all they were fair. Producers split the fifteen remaining players into three groups of five and sent them on separate Group Dates, giving everyone an equal opportunity for time with Alex Michel.

The first Group Dates were celebrated occasions, initiated by the delivery of a Date Card along with an entire Date Box that contained not only the list of players who would be attending but also knickknacks and trinkets to give the players an idea of what the date might entail. Trista Rehn, who went on to secure second place that season and then wore the first *Bachelorette* Crown, was granted the honor of retrieving the first Date Box from the porch to open in front of the remaining players and begin the first Group Date in history.

Poker chips and playing cards revealed a trip to Las Vegas that would set the standard for all Group Dates to follow and the five players who marched into history as the first Group Daters were Kristina Jenkins, Shannon Oliver, Angelique Madrid, LaNease Adams, and Katie (last name lost to time).

The show treated them to a luxury penthouse, dinner at a five-star restaurant, and a blackjack competition that turned out to be the first-ever PFT (a game mechanic that allows one or more players to get extra time with the Bachelor as a prize for winning a mini-game within the Group Date). LaNease Adams won this first PFT and was rewarded with a gondola ride through the canals of the Venetian Hotel and Casino with Bachelor Alex Michel. The gondola pilot informed Michel and Adams that it was tradition for couples to kiss as they floated under the bridges crisscrossing the canal and LaNease Adams secured the first kiss in *Bachelor* history.

The other Group Dates included a day trip to a spa (complete with a mud bath and massages) and a day of sporting clays and champagne on the back of a yacht. Producers did not weave humiliation, forced nudity, forced violence, and all manner of designed torment into the fabric of the Group Date for many, many years. They also didn't bring in one of the most crucial elements of modern Group Dates—the GDR.

Group Dates in the first three seasons allowed players to attempt to connect with the Bachelor without the ever-present threat of competition that is embodied by the GDR lying on a table for all to see. The style of these early Group Dates was much more relaxed and players got to develop a slower-paced First Audience game, much different from the breakneck speed of Steals, Love Level raises, Tattles, and PTCs we see today.

The first GDRs didn't appear until Season 4 and they were an experimental version of what exists in today's game, almost an inverse of the current GDR. On his first Group Date of the season, Producers tasked Bachelor Bob Guiney with dispensing white Roses to four of the five players attending, thereby eliminating the player who did not receive one. The Producers quickly realized that this negative reinforcement did little to stoke the players' competitive drives, an oversight they remedied in Season 7, during which they gave Bachelor Charlie O'Connell the awesome power of bestowing contemporary GDRs on two players per Group Date. The first two players to ever receive GDRs were Kindle Martin and Anitra Mohl, who impressed O'Connell with their pool-playing skills in a New York City dive bar. Including GDRs that granted the winners immunity from elimination stoked their competitive fire, and the Producers have included them every season since.

Through the years the Group Date has seen many forms, including one of the most reviled events in the entire game—the 2O1. Season 5 ushered in the first-ever 2O1, pitting that season's most notorious Villain and FIMP Rose recipient, Trish Schneider, against eventual Top 4 finisher Mandy Jaye Jeffreys. The duo faced off for Jesse Palmer's attention on top of a double-decker bus and then later in a spa. There was no Rose up for grabs in this first iteration. It was merely time spent locked in binary one-upmanship that ultimately garnered each of these historic players Roses at the Rose Ceremony later that night.

It wasn't until Season 8 that the 201 Date Card featured the phrase "One rose, one goes," which would come to be used on almost all other 201 Dates. Travis Stork granted the first 201 Rose to Sarah Blondin on a camping date, eliminating Jennifer Tammaro. Notably, Blondin was also that season's FIMP Rose recipient. In the more recent seasons of the Paradise Era Producers have molded 201s into aggressively competitive grudge matches, usually between a Villain and her rival and set in hyperhostile environments like deserts or swamps. And even more recently the Producers have transmogrified the 201 into a more exotic GD type, the Three-on-One.

As of this text's creation, only nine players have been forced into this manufactured three-way competition, which has produced five total Roses. Season 20 spawned the first Three-on-One during the Round of Six and it featured star players Caila Quinn, Becca Tilley, and Amanda Stanton, playing for a single Rose. Stanton pulled off the first Three-on-One Rose, but Quinn received a Rose at the next Rose Ceremony, where Tilley was eliminated. The second Three-on-One took place in Season 22 (Arie Luyendyk Jr.), also in the Round of Six, and offered two Roses to be won. Kendall Long took home the first Rose, leaving Bekah Martinez and Tia Booth to head into dinner in a pared down 201. Booth pulled off a successful "too-young-to-be-serious" attack and sent Martinez packing. And the most recent Three-on-One occurred in Season 24's (Peter Weber) Round of Six, forcing Kelley Flanagan, Hannah Ann Sluss, and Victoria Fuller to vie for two available Roses. After Producers gave Flanagan a brutal Villain Edit, Weber dismissed her, leaving Sluss and Fuller with a straight run into the final four.

Group Dates can be daunting, especially early in any given season when fighting for time with the Bachelor is a seemingly insurmountable task as upward of a dozen other players are putting in their best efforts as well. In almost every case there is only one Rose available and you're forced into situations that require a high degree of skilled First, Second, and, as always, Third Audience play. Of course, you should always use a general strategy of blind optimism and excitement about whatever the date might entail, but the best preparation for Group Dates is to study the most statistically common situations you're going to encounter.

GD Types and Elements

Producers build each Group Date around one central activity or location that defines the day portion of the date. This is the date's type. In addition to the type, each Group Date can also feature a variety of secondary elements that augment the competitive nature or offer some extra level of torment designed to stoke the player pool's group anxiety or traumatic emotional response. Here we've listed the various types and elements of all Group Dates since the beginning of the game in 2002.

GD TYPES/OCCURRENCES (164 GDS)

Adventure (8)
Amusement Park (3)
Animal Husbandry (7)
Aquatic (5)
Artistic Activity (26)
Athletic Activity (30)
Bar (3)
Beach/Lake (5)
Boat/Yacht (11)
Botanical Garden (1)
Child Play (1)
Club/Dancing (1)
Concert (2)
Cultural Appropriation (2)
Exotic Cuisine (1)
Gambling (7)
Hay Wagon (1)
Hot-Air Balloon (1)
Karaoke (1)
Manual Labor (1)
Obstacle Course (9)
Outdoor Activity (1)
Paid Advertisement (1)
Pajama Party (1)
Picnic (4)
Plane/Sea Plane (2)
Pool Party (17)
Public Performance (15)
Roughing It (9)
Snow Inner Tubing (1)
Spa (5)
Sporting Event (1)
Tractor Race (1)
Train (1)
When In Rome/ Tourism (3)
Wine Tasting/ Champagnery (3)

GD ELEMENTS

Celebrity
Charity
Fear Factor
Forced Nudity
Forced Violence
GTTC (Get To The Chopper)
Home Invasion
Hot Tub
Overnight
Pretty Woman

Over the course of twenty-five seasons Producers have implemented a wide array of activities, locations, and components in what has been an ongoing effort to maximize the dramatic function of the Group Date within the larger context of the game. As an incoming player in the Professional Era, you cannot adequately prepare for every possible scenario, and thankfully there is no need. Despite the large field of potential GD types through history, four types occur much more frequently than any others and it is all but guaranteed that you're going to be subjected to at least one of them during the course of your season of play.

The Athletic Activity

Of the 164 Group Dates Producers have constructed, thirty of them have been Athletic Activities. Accounting for roughly 18 percent of all Group Dates, the Athletic Activity is the most common type and has been featured at least once, in some cases multiple times, in every season of the Paradise and Professional eras. Producers have used casual sports like tennis, volleyball, and bowling. They've also forced players to engage in violent sports like rugby and tackle football and even combat sports like wrestling and boxing. And general Athletic Activities like rock climbing, skiing, and working out have also served as the scheduled events on these dates. But no matter the sport, an Athletic Activity Group Date falls into one of three possible competitive structures—team sport, individual sport, or subjective sport—and each has their own best strategy.

Team sports like bowling, tackle football, volleyball, and Roller Derby have all set the stage for past Group Dates that see the players split into two teams, forced into no-holds-barred competition. And not always but very often these can be Plays For Time, and only the victorious team earns a ticket to the After Party. So winning is obviously incredibly important, but it's still secondary to the main goal of all Group Dates—the acquisition of the GDR. And while we recommend obvious tactics like aligning with the most athletic players and those most knowledgeable or skilled in the specific sport, the most important element of strategy on an Athletic Activity Group Date is to maintain a positive attitude and convey unbridled enthusiasm for the event even if the opposite is true, especially if you wind up on the losing team.

The Producers have increasingly used the false threat of early dismissal for the losing team to stoke baseless anxiety, only to have the Bachelor invite the defeated players to the After Party after all. This was true in Season 22 when the Producers decided to let the losing bowlers attend the After Party, much to the dismay of Krystal Nielson, who was a front-runner right up until the moment she became a sore winner, pouting in her room and refusing to attend the After Party because the losers were allowed to join. While this pity party did garner her a check-in with Luyendyk, it ultimately reversed what had been a solid First Audience game up to that point and proved to be the beginning of Nielson's demise. This exact same scenario played out again in Season 25 when the losing team, again in a bowling competition, was made to return back to the hotel only to receive a Date Card reinviting them to the After Party. Remember that losing isn't the end. You might still be going to that After Party. And probably more important, winning doesn't necessarily mean you're going to have the Bachelor all to yourself. Whether you win or lose, keep a cool head and save yourself unnecessary mental and emotional anguish so you can really shine at the After Party.

Individual sports present a slightly different competitive arrangement. They've taken the form of Season 25's Battle for the Bachelor boxing match that forced players to face off in brutal physical combat against one another or have materialized in Season 24's Extreme Pillow Fight Club, which was a single-elimination tournament with several rounds. Much like the team sport, the most important tactic here is to convey willingness, enthusiasm, and excitement for whatever the activity is, no matter how debasing, physically traumatic, or painful. Keeping spirits high broadcasts a willingness to engage in the larger game to not only the Bachelor but the all-important Third Audience of the Producers as well. Certainly attempt to secure a victory in the chosen sport, especially in the case of a PFT, but be aware of how aggressive you seem as you compete. There are limits to the degree of effort you can put in without causing a possible rift with the Second Audience. If the sport is violent, for example, injuring another player can result in a costly Villain turn. If you're just a lot better in a sport than the other players, a blowout performance can land you in the role of a show-off. You have to walk this line in order to produce a victory that is believably difficult to achieve without being too merciless on the battlefield. And by all means, extend a hand to help your defeated opponent up off the ground once you've secured the W.

And finally, subjective sports do not allow for the determination of a clear-cut winner based on scores or other objective measures. Producers have included working out, ice skating, and professional wrestling as the subjective sports on Group Dates. The main function of the subjective sport is to allow the Producers to decide "winners" and "losers" to suit their narrative machinations. If you find yourself on one of these dates, approach it with high energy and enthusiasm for the task at hand and use the notion of learning the sport (which is a staple of these types of dates) as an opportunity to seek 1O1 time with the Bachelor. A bashful "Can you show me how to do it?" is usually enough to get a smile and some extra time from the Bachelor, who will be more than happy to put his expertise on display whether real or imagined. And in the end, Producers sometimes present the winner of these challenges with a prize or trophy, but the subjective sports are rarely PFTs, so winning them is far less important than the other two types.

It's always a good idea in the preseason to learn some basic athletic skills that will help in a wide array of Athletic Activities. We recommend preparatory strategies of playing catch with a football and learning how to throw one properly, going to a batting cage to learn how to hit a baseball, and even taking a class in a combat sport like jiujitsu or kickboxing.

The Artistic Activity

The second most commonly occurring Group Date type is the Artistic Activity. It accounts for 26 of the 164 Group Dates or roughly 15.85 percent. Artistic Activities have included modeling, sculpting, singing, acting, dancing, and even delivering monologues, both serious and comedic.

Just as with the Athletic Activity, if you have an artistic background you'll have a definite advantage, but because Producers can only judge the Artistic Activity subjectively, literally anyone can win one of these Group Dates regardless of skill level, and indeed in many cases the most skilled player might defer victory to the player who makes the biggest show of her attempt, through either comedy or outright audacity. Take for example the first Group Date of Season 21 when Producers made the players wear themed wedding dresses for a photo shoot with Bachelor Nick Viall. The players were on equal footing until Corinne Olympios set a new bar by initiating a voluntary nudity play when she took her top off and forced Viall to cup her bare breasts. This brazen move demanded extra screen time, extra attention from Viall himself, and ultimately secured her the victory, a PFT GD win, as well as the GDR later at the After Party.

Take an improv class, write a short story or poetry, watch a few vocal-training videos on YouTube, and of course test out some dance moves on TikTok to brush up on an array of artistic skills. And if the talent necessary for one of the Group Dates is beyond reach, make up for it with unbridled enthusiasm and sincerity in the attempt. No matter how terrible you might be at the selected skill, this might very well lead to a comedic moment that garners screen time and possibly even the victory.

The Pool Party

The elegant simplicity of the Pool Party makes it the third most frequently occurring Group Date. There have been seventeen pool parties over the past twenty-five seasons, it accounts for approximately 10.36 percent of all Group Dates. Because it requires no special equipment and no locations other than the Mansion, the Pool Party is extremely versatile and Producers use it as an emergency fallback at virtually any time, including in lieu of a formal Cocktail Party before a Rose Ceremony, in which case it becomes a specialized Group Date known as an All-Player Date, which allows all players to attend.

The benefit of the Pool Party is that it requires virtually no psychological preparation and there is no overt competition outside the mandatory ceremonial chicken fights. Unlike other GD types, the Pool Party allows you to indulge in a more casual and social atmosphere that's much more conducive to getting meaningful 1O1 time with the Bachelor than, say, a day of being forced to engage in full-contact combat or eat bugs. It eliminates all of the time spent learning a new skill, competing against one another, or even interacting with celebrity guest hosts. So if you're lucky enough to find yourself on a Pool Party Group Date, do as much as you can to capitalize.

Isolate the Bachelor away from the rest of the group to assure a more private conversation and to make engaging in chemistry play more natural. The harder it is for the other players to find you, the more alone time you're going to get. Assume the role of First Responder by always having a drink ready for the Bachelor as a simple way for you to anchor yourself to him at the beginning of the Pool Party. And the opposite strategy can also work—establish a more dominant role by asking the Bachelor to bring you a drink.

Ultimately, the Pool Party is a welcome reprieve from the physical and psychological brutality that most other GD types rely on, but don't mistake that for a reason to relax. Exactly the opposite is true, because this will likely be what most other players are doing and it could very well be the perfect opportunity to bypass them with keen adherence to a game plan.

The Public Performance

Rounding out the most common GD types is the Public Performance. There have been fifteen of these celebrations of anxiety in the history of the game, accounting for roughly 10 percent of all Group Dates. This type requires you to engage in a performance, usually of the artistic variety, in an extremely public venue. It can require all players on the date to appear in front of a screaming audience, as was the case on a Week 3 Group Date in Season 18, when Juan Pablo Galavis dragged six of the remaining players onto a stage where they were made to dance alongside the world-famous K-pop group 2NE1 in a shopping mall. Or the Public Performance can be a reward for the sole winner of the Artistic Endeavor portion of the Group Date, as was the case in Season 22 when Bekah Martinez won the GD challenge at the Moulin Rouge in Paris and was awarded extra time with Bachelor Arie Luyendyk Jr. as they took the stage alongside professional dancers during what was presented as an actual cabaret show performed for a paying audience.

In either case, the Public Performance will test your skill, your confidence, and your ability to adapt to the pressure of being in the spotlight. These dates are less about securing a victory, if one is even offered, and more about mitigating the anxiety and nervousness that can arise as the result of performing in front of hundreds, if not thousands, of people. A solid performance at the After Party is still your primary goal, so avoid any negative psychological or emotional effects at all costs.

Take a class in public speaking, perform stand-up comedy at an open mic, or even go to a public thoroughfare and break into a dance routine while onlookers stop and stare for excellent off-season practice to help you acclimate to the feeling of being the center of public attention before you are thrust into a similar scenario for the first time in-game. Develop and rehearse the Three Stories you created during the preseason so you can focus on adding flourishes, like getting the Bachelor's audience participation, rather than on the written material.

The Obstacle Course

Although the Obstacle Course is not technically one of the most occurring GD types, this is only because it is a relatively new addition to the game. But it is absolutely a dominant GD type in the Paradise and Professional eras, appearing nine times in the past seven seasons, comprising almost 15 percent of all Group Dates in those seasons. Astoundingly, Producers have incorporated this test of will and endurance twice in multiple seasons since it was introduced in Season 17 (Sean Lowe), and only Season 22 (Arie Luyendyk Jr.) did not feature at least one. At its core the Obstacle Course is a race, but it is much more than that.

The very first Obstacle Course set the tone for all that would follow, including elements of both physicality and humiliation. Eight players faced the first Obstacle Course: Selma Alameri, AshLee Frazier, Desiree Hartsock, Catherine Giudici, Sarah Herron, Lesley Murphy, Robyn Howard, and Daniella McBride. Producers split them into two teams, pitted against each other in a PFT that forced them to pilot kayaks across a lake, drag bales of hay across an open field, manually saw logs, and finally milk a goat. But the true humiliation came when, in order to win, Desiree Hartsock willingly drank a mason jar full of warm, unpasteurized goat milk as Bachelor Sean Lowe laughed from a few feet away, entertained by the horrific sight of viscous off-white liquid pouring down Hartsock's chin and neck.

Just as with the Athletic Activity, the Obstacle Course is not always a team game. In Season 24 Producers made Courtney Perry, Jasmine Nguyen, Deandra Kanu, Shiann Lewis, Victoria Paul, Tammy Ly, Kelley Flanagan, Victoria Fuller, and Hannah Ann Sluss face off against one another in a winner-take-all individual PFT airplane-themed Obstacle Course that proved to be one of the most important moments in pushing Obstacle Course strategy forward.

After the players spun themselves dizzy in swivel chairs, put on inflatable life vests, slid down grease-covered inflatable ramps, walked against the pressure of giant wind turbines, and changed their clothes in porta-potties while Peter Weber laughed at their folly from inches away in some cases, the two players in the lead and therefore the only two allowed to continue were Tammy Ly and Kelley Flanagan. The final leg of this Obstacle Course required each of them to mount a tricycle with airplane wings attached and pilot it through a series of cones laid out on the ground.

What Flanagan did here would rewrite the Obstacle Course playbook for all time. Instead of following the curved path laid out before her, Flanagan opted for a straight line, cutting through the cones and making a path of her own. It was blatant cheating recognized by everyone who beheld it, including Ly, who openly yelled out, alerting everyone to Flanagan's transgression. But it simply didn't matter. Flanagan crossed the finish line first and was awarded the PFT prize of extra time with Weber on a private flight. Despite the obvious cheating, all that mattered was that she completed the course first.

This is an important lesson. The rules of the Obstacle Course don't actually matter. The rules of the larger game are what you must maintain and, in this case, Flanagan was only bound by the same rule that governs the game as a whole—4TRR. Yes, she cheated, but only because she wanted to spend time with Weber. This is unassailable reasoning and has therefore proven that cheating in an Obstacle Course is not only permissible; it is recommended.

Of course, blatant cheating and malicious cheating can be detrimental and possibly result in a Villain Edit, but nonchalant and even believably accidental cheating are valid strategies for this GD type. And even the openly malicious type of cheating is permissible if it can be done without being caught, as Anna Redman accomplished in Season 25's squirrel-themed Obstacle Course when she hid a specific nut from Victoria Larson, who was stalled at the nut-digging event of the Obstacle Course for the duration.

Elements

Most elements included on a Group Date are innocuous and some are even enjoyable. Group Dates have included celebrity guests, charity work, helicopter rides, and even on rare occasion material gain via a *Pretty Woman* element that gifts a player clothing and/or jewelry. None of these elements require preparation or strategy, but there are others for which players in past seasons have been utterly unprepared and they have paid the price.

The Fear Factor

Producers have forced players to wrestle greased pigs in the mud, shovel the manure of barnyard animals, and even eat live bugs. The preparation required to withstand the purposefully crafted discomfort of the Fear Factor element is primarily psychological. But remember, while fully engaging in these repulsive acts will certainly yield screen time, it isn't always necessary. In Season 23 Bachelor Colton Underwood took eleven players deep into the jungles of Thailand for a Roughing It Group Date on which they met a survival instructor who showed them where to find worms they could eat for protein and how to drink water from the stalks of native vines. Hannah Brown did eat a worm during this portion of the Group Date, but later, after the eleven players were split into smaller teams and sent into the surrounding jungle on a scavenger hunt for bugs and plant water, star players Hannah Godwin, Hannah Brown, and Demi Burnett flexed their incredible Third Audience game to convince the Producers to let them return to the hotel and come back to the group with champagne and hamburgers in stark contrast to the other players' piles of grubs and dirty water. Underwood happily bit into a burger and these three players were the focus of the Group Date, proving that you can override the Fear Factor element. So if you find yourself staring down a plate of roaches or a pile of dung, remember you can find a creative way to get out of the situation and get screen time nonetheless.

The Home Invasion

Technically, the first inkling of the Home Invasion element occurred in Season 7 when Producers woke all of the players from slumber in the wee hours of the morning on Night One and told them they had five minutes to get ready to meet Bachelor Charlie O'Connell. But in its modern form, the Home Invasion GD element is even more Machiavellian, as it involves the Bachelor himself entering the room where the Group Daters are sleeping to deprive them of much-needed rest through rude awakening. And in the case of Season 17, Producers armed Bachelor Sean Lowe with a Polaroid camera, which he wielded with reckless abandon, chuckling and popping flashes in the players' unsuspecting faces as their minds were still coming to consciousness. To adequately prepare for the possibility of being the victim of a Home Invasion, practice your five-minute routine until it is down to a science. You have to be able to do complete makeup, hair, wardrobe, and styling in the allotted time. Although going to sleep in full makeup is certainly not required, Britt Nilsson employed this tactic perfectly in Season 19. On a 101 Date that included a Home Invasion element, Chris Soules showed up to stand over her bed as she slept before forcing her awake for their date. But because her hair and makeup were done the night before, she rolled out of bed camera ready and the Producers' attempt to catch her off guard failed miserably.

Forced Nudity

One of the most intimidating GD elements, forced nudity requires one or more players on a Group Date to engage in partial or full nudity in service of the GD type. The first time we saw this was in Season 13 when Bachelor Jason Mesnick took eight players, including that season's Ring Winner, Melissa Rycroft, on an Artistic Activity Group Date that required the players to make plaster molds of their nude breasts for a breast cancer charity. All of the players that season were seemingly willful participants, but this has historically not been the case. Often, Producers will cloak the forced nudity element in the guise of a charity end goal.

In Season 15, second-time Bachelor Brad Womack started off a Group Date with a Home Invasion that quickly turned into an Artistic Activity, requiring the players to model swimsuits on the beach. Producers coerced both Chantal O'Brien and Ashley Hebert into removing their bathing suit tops despite their initial protests. Then again in Season 18, Juan Pablo Galavis took thirteen players on an Artistic Activity Group Date that required them all to pose in various costumes for a photo shoot that would benefit an animal-related charity. Producers assigned some players humorous costumes while they singled out Elise Mosca and Andi Dorfman to pose nude. Neither player wanted to oblige. Dorfman finally acquiesced while Mosca eventually traded her "outfit" with another player, Lucy Aragon, who had already performed several voluntary nudity plays that season. In Season 19 Producers forced players to wear bikinis for a tractor race in downtown Los Angeles. And in Season 22 Producers required players on a Group Date in Paris to don risqué clothing and perform onstage at the Moulin Rouge.

While the pressure to give in to the Producers and even possibly the lead can be great, remember that you're never under any true obligation to do so. You can always utilize the power of 4TRR in a forced nudity situation in order to override the Group Date itself. Simply tell the Bachelor that you're not ready for him to see you naked just yet, that you want to build a connection with him before you take your clothes off. The Producers won't like it and you will run the risk of some form of their petty retribution, but this 4TRR defense is unassailable, as it is the primary rule of the game.

Forced Violence

The genesis of this element occurred in Season 17 when Producers split eight players into two teams on an Athletic Activity Group Date that forced them to survive a match of Roller Derby. Despite the date starting out lighthearted with skating lessons from some local Roller Derby players, once they introduced the element of violence to the date Sarah Herron broke down into tears, citing her fear that having lost one of her arms at birth would make

this task extremely difficult. And as the match was underway, Amanda Meyer sustained a violence-related injury when her jaw smashed into the track, requiring medics to tend to her, and ultimately Sean Lowe put a benevolent end to the proceedings. Season 22 saw the return of the forced violence element on two separate Group Dates. One required a group of players to engage in a demolition derby, which resulted in Brittane Johnson becoming injured so badly that she had to be taken away for medical treatment before returning to the After Party later that night. And the other required a group of players to engage in several professional wrestling matches after aggressive training with some former GLOW stars. The endeavor proved too traumatic for Bibiana Julian and Tia Booth, who both consoled each other through tears in a darkened corner of the room where they enjoyed the illusion of privacy. Then in Season 23, after receiving a GD Card that read: "Are you ready to fight for love?," eight players joined Colton Underwood at a martial arts center in Vietnam to learn the Vovinam fighting style. Skilled player Hannah Brown embraced the task wholeheartedly and even pretended to fight the cameraman with a bamboo stick, a flourish that made the blooper reel. After their lesson, for the first time in the game's history, Producers made the players engage in hand-to-hand combat against each other. Just as in Season 17 when Sean Lowe wielded his First Audience power to end the brutality of Roller Derby, so, too, did Colton Underwood end the fights after witnessing Demi Burnett sustain a beating from Katie Morton. And of course Producers brought back the forced violence element in Season 25 when they made several players train in boxing before being paired off to slug it out in an actual boxing ring as entertainment for the players not on the date. And once again, Bachelor Matt James ended the proceedings early when he witnessed Serena Pitt endure a crushing blow to the nose that required medical attention.

There are two basic strategies you can employ in the face of forced violence. The first is casual participation and projected enthusiasm. Although all of these dates result in one or more injuries, most players are able to engage in the dictated Athletic Activity and seem properly upbeat about doing so without incurring bodily harm. But if you want to avoid participation in the forced violence element of any Group Date, or any element or activity on any date for that matter, you can always play an "IFI."

IFI

The IFI play should be familiar to anyone who has ever used the excuse of a malady (real or imagined) to avoid attending work, school, or a social gathering. This standard counter-play involves using the excuse of an injury, fear, or illness as the basis to exempt yourself from whatever the activity at hand might happen to be. When used properly on a Group Date the IFI can not only save a player from the potentially costly results of physical or psychological trauma, but it can also generate 1O1 time with the Bachelor himself.

It should also be noted that the IFI is not exclusive to Group Dates. It can be used on 1O1s, at Cocktail Parties, or really any time you see an opportunity. And even leads have used this powerful technique to invalidate preplanned date activities, like former player Hannah Brown did when she wore the Crown on Season 15 of *The Bachelorette*. Brown contracted an illness that rendered her unable to comply with the plans of her 1O1 Date with Connor Saeli, who was then forced to forgo helicopter rides and hot tubs in favor of spending the day with her as she lay sick in bed.

Twenty-five-year-old Hooters waitress from Avondale, Arizona, Angela (last name lost to time) performed the first IFI in history in Season 1. She incurred an eye injury on her Group Date to a spa that required medical treatment. The next day when Bachelor Alex Michel was on the road with five other players on their way to a Group Date on a luxury yacht, he took the time to call Angela back at the Mansion to see how she was feeling. This first IFI established a very important behavioral response that has held true to the most recent season of the game—the Bachelor must check on a player who initiates an IFI and he must accept her injury, fear, or illness to be real. In the case of Angela and her history-making IFI, the injury was genuine, but through the course of the game's evolution many players have used deceptive IFIs to their advantage.

Perhaps the greatest IFI strategist in history was a twenty-four-year-old leasing consultant from Denver, Colorado, in Season 17 named Tierra LiCausi. Her first IFI would change the game forever in that it was not on a Group Date. It was not on a 1O1. In fact, it was played at a time when LiCausi should not have had any screen time at all. Bachelor Sean Lowe was on his way to the Mansion to pick up AshLee Frazier for a 1O1 and LiCausi was able to shift attention from Frazier to herself by initiating a planned fall down the stairs followed by an incredible performance of acting dazed by the spill. Despite all other players seeing through the ruse, Lowe himself was obligated to check on her for several minutes when he arrived at the Mansion. It earned LiCausi screen time and psychologically thwarted Frazier. The Bachelor will always be forced to take an IFI at face value because there is simply no benefit in him ever questioning the validity of the claim. Imagine if after learning that LiCausi claimed to have fallen down the stairs Lowe would have dismissed it with a laugh and proceeded on his date with Frazier without checking on LiCausi. He would be perceived as the worst Villain lead of all time.

Later in the season LiCausi found herself on an Adventure Group Date that required the players to take a polar bear plunge into almost-freezing water. Although most of the players expressed some hesitation, they all performed the action without injury or complication. All except LiCausi. When she emerged from the icy waters, she immediately began exaggerated shivering and once again displayed signs of being dazed. Medical personnel tended to her, wrapped her in a thermal blanket, and whisked her off to her hotel room, where Lowe was then obligated to appear to check on her once again. Not only did she completely steal the focus of the entire Group Date; she also was able to isolate Lowe for valuable 1O1 time away from the other players. It was a master class in the effectiveness of IFI play, especially the deceptive variety.

An IFI can also have other incredibly beneficial psychological effects on the lead if it is played in the context of a more complex narrative. Take for example Victoria Paul's expert use of an IFI in Season 24. She was forced into a gravity simulator gyroscope machine on a Group Date early in the season despite actively objecting to participating. Weber laughed at her as she screamed to be set free from the torturous device. Then two weeks later when Paul found herself on an Athletic Activity Group Date with a forced violence element, she delivered her stunning IFI play. As the other players were suiting up for a game of tackle football, Paul took Weber aside and told him that her back still hurt from the gyroscope and she wasn't able to participate in the scheduled gladiatorial events of the day. Weber had no choice but to honor her IFI as legitimate and allow her to stand on the sidelines with him. Not only did she successfully exempt herself from the possibility of further physical injury, which several of the other players incurred as a result of the tackle football game, but she also manufactured 1O1 time with the Bachelor that included a shoulder massage, which Weber gave her right in front of every other player.

There is truly no incorrect time to play an IFI, but you should be aware that it can have diminishing returns. LiCausi, for example, was eliminated shortly after her second IFI with an explanation from Lowe that he didn't want to see her suffer anymore. The best IFIs are those that come with visual evidence of their legitimacy—blood, a cast, a bruise, and a believable limp are all excellent flourishes that will leave no doubts in any audience's mind that the IFI is real and therefore so will be the sympathy it generates. Just ask Vanessa Grimaldi, Season 21's Ring Winner, who in part solidified her victory by vomiting into a bag in zero G with then-Bachelor Nick Viall. We saw echoes of LiCausi's IFI strategy during Season 25, when Sarah Trott, who already had a Rose in hand, fell off the risers in the middle of the second Rose Ceremony. She not only garnered 1O1 time with Bachelor Matt James, but she also constructed an entire episode's cliffhanger with this play, whether the fainting was real or not.

The After Party (AP)

No matter what happened during the day, eventually night must fall, and as the sun melts away behind the horizon, drinks will be poured for the second and the most important half of any Group Date—the After Party. This is where you get a final opportunity to make plays that might influence the Bachelor and/or the Producers to grant you the true goal of any and all Group Dates, the GDR.

Think of the After Party as a scaled-down version of a Cocktail Party (which will be discussed later in this chapter). Getting private, intimate time with the Bachelor that was not possible during the day activity is crucial and the same array of strategies used at a Cocktail Party apply here in addition to a few new ones. Avoid Turtling with First Responder tactics, Steals, and isolation techniques. But because all players have had time to acclimate to one another in the house and to some degree the Bachelor, to form group dynamics and possibly even to analyze one another's play styles, some bigger plays are now on the table.

Love Levels

As outlined in the fundamentals chapter, you have four Love Levels at your disposal to illustrate your escalating emotional attachment to the Bachelor. If you're on a Group Date, this automatically means that the Producers are not giving you a chance for a 1O1 Date that week. So After Parties are the perfect place to raise a Love Level. Although you should reserve the higher Love Levels (3 and 4) for 1O1 Dates if possible, you might find yourself with time running out if you're on a Group Date late in the season and have no choice but to deploy a high Love Level raise. As with the use of all tools, pacing and timing are crucial. Gauge where the other players are in their Love Level increases. Getting left behind can lead to a plausible dismissal from the Bachelor on the grounds of other relationships progressing faster. And raising your Love Level too high too fast runs the risk of overstepping the comfortable building of an emotional connection. But being the first or only player to raise a Love Level or raising it to a level higher than all other players on a Group Date will almost certainly guarantee a GDR win. Tread lightly with the use of this powerful tool at an After Party and make sure you've properly isolated the Bachelor to avoid interruption, but don't wait too long to use it.

PTCs

One of the only tools that can override another player's use of a Love Level raise at an After Party is the PTC. And just like the raising of a Love Level, you can play the PTC any time you have 1O1 time with the Bachelor; but unlike the raising of a Love Level, in most cases you'll only be able to use your PTC once throughout the entirety of a season. You must critically plan the exact moment you play a PTC and execute it to gain maximum value. And it's likely that your first real opportunity to use this powerful tool will be at an After Party.

Playing a PTC will almost guarantee screen time and if no other players have played a PTC on a Group Date it will be a virtual lock for the GDR. But you have to gauge the likelihood of being granted a 1O1 Date in later rounds as well. If you think a 1O1 Date is in your future, it might be wise to hold the use of the PTC for a moment when you don't face direct competition for a Rose. But ultimately there are no guarantees in our beloved game and one of the worst errors you can make is being eliminated from the game without playing your PTC. The PTC, if used correctly, will generate a situation that makes it almost impossible for the Bachelor to justifiably dismiss a player. So even if another player outranks your PTC or raises a Love Level to counteract your PTC play, it's more than likely that you're at least going to get a Rose at that week's Rose Ceremony.

In some of the more recent seasons, Producers have designed Group Dates specifically around getting as many PTCs out of the players as possible, through Artistic Endeavors and Public Performances. Ideally, play a lesser PTC in this forced group scenario and play the complete version when you have time alone with the Bachelor. Opening up in a more intimate conversation carries more weight.

Never play a PTC on Night One, and it is perfectly fine to hold a PTC back in the first week of play, but if you're on a Group Date with the third Rose Ceremony coming up, play your PTC with the intent of building one of two narrative strategies:

The Better Person Narrative

This narrative illustrates how any past trauma has taught you something and helped you to see the world in a different way. The tragedy has made you stronger, more ready for love, and/or clearer about what you truly want from life. The pattern of conversation when delivering this PTC follows a basic three-act structure. The first act details the traumatic incident. The second act details the aftermath. And the third details the positive effect that resulted from the healing that occurred after the event. The purpose of this narrative is to show that you've experienced adversity in life and used it to become a better person who is ready to move on.

The Walls Narrative

This is a slightly more complex PTC strategy but highly effective. After you divulge the traumatic event, explain that there is still a lasting emotional or psychological effect that makes it hard or even impossible for you to open up. You gain sympathy for the trauma while at the same time erecting an obstacle that must be overcome in your next interaction with the Bachelor, a wall. Then, when that wall finally does come down, the Bachelor gets to experience firsthand the final act of this PTC narrative as you seem to overcome the final effects of your trauma not only right in front of him but also because of him.

Tattling

The riskiest of all After Party strategies, Tattling requires you to reveal some incriminating information about another player to the Bachelor in private. You can also use this strategy at a Cocktail Party, but in that environment you run the risk of derailing the entire evening for all other players, which can quickly escalate into a Villain Edit and a ruined Second Audience game.

The type of information that qualifies for a Tattle runs a wide variety of perceived transgressions. Everything from revealing another player's true age to accusations of a player's 4TWR status is admissible fodder for a Tattle strategy. In Season 25 we saw a flawless preemptive Tattle when Anna Redman was building a standard Tattle strategy around a false rumor that Brittany Galvin was a sex worker. But before Redman could get a moment alone with Bachelor Matt James, Katie Thurston initiated the preemptive Tattle by leaving a Cocktail Party to find James outside and tell him that rumors were starting to swirl that could ruin someone's life. Tattling is an incredibly difficult strategy to pull off without the Tattling player ultimately being eliminated herself as a result of her proximity to the perceived drama. Thurston, however, was able to keep her distance by offering no specific names or details about the rumor. She expertly planted the idea in James's mind that a situation had arisen that needed his attention and then she left the rest up to him.

Vague Tattling is the best possible style of Tattling if you're going to attempt Tattling at all. But in some cases you will be forced into Tattling by the Bachelor himself. The forced Tattle is most likely to occur at a GD After Party at which all players involved in the drama are present. If you're forced to divulge information, remain as vague as possible. But if the Bachelor demands names and details, never, that is *never*, return to the group and reveal to them that you have Tattled. This allows the target of the Tattle time to prepare for the interrogation by the Bachelor that is soon to follow. Convey ignorance about every aspect of the Tattle at all times in order to avoid a revenge play by the target of the Tattle.

The 201

There is another type of Group Date that distills down the nature of competition to its purest form by reducing the size of the dating pool to two players. Producers force the pair to go head-to-head after their names are called on a Date Card that invariably contains the phrase "Two Women, One Rose, One Stays, One Goes." This kill-or-be-killed, all-or-nothing matchup is called the 201, garnering its name from the numerical description of the date's participants—two players and one Bachelor.

201 History

The 201 has not always been a part of our beloved game. The Producers first toyed with this mechanic back in Season 5, when the first iteration of the 201 had no Roses up for grabs on the actual date and allowed both players to attend the following Rose Ceremony, where they each received a Rose.

Then in Season 6 the Producers used the 2O1 to further experiment with the game structure by sending Bachelor Byron Velvick to meet two mystery players in a bar. It was not only the first time Producers introduced new players to the player pool after a season had already started, but it was also the first time they brought back players from prior seasons for a second tour. Producers allowed Heather Cranford, who made it to Week 4 in Season 2, and Mary Delgado, who made it to third place in Season 4, to make their case for why Velvick should give each of them a Rose at that night's ceremony. Although Cranford was denied reentry, Delgado went on to win the Season 6 Ring.

It wouldn't be until Season 8 that Producers introduced the unforgiving 2O1 Rose or Goes mechanic to the game, which resulted in Bachelor Travis Stork dismissing Jennifer Tammaro in favor of keeping Sarah Blondin for some private time on a camping date. Season 14 saw a strange step backward in the evolution of the 2O1 in that no Rose was awarded. Instead, Jake Pavelka presented both Vienna Girardi, that season's Ring Winner, and Gia Allemand Roses in that week's Rose Ceremony. But the Rose or Goes mechanic made a strong comeback the following season when Brad Womack used his second tour as Bachelor to pit the Dynamic Duo of two Ashleys, Hebert and Spivey, against each other in a performance competition with Cirque du Soleil. Hebert walked away with the Rose and got to perform in front of a live audience with Womack later that evening.

Chris Soules's Season 19 saw both Iaconetti and Poe eliminated in the first double dismissal in 2O1 history. Season 20 brought with it the first sister versus sister 2O1 as Bachelor Ben Higgins accompanied the Ferguson twins to their hometown in Las Vegas and not only met their mother but also eliminated Haley Ferguson in her own living room. Season 20 was also the first double 2O1 season, when Producers forced Emily Ferguson to participate in a second 2O1 against Olivia Caridi and impressively she walked away with another Rose, the only player to have survived two 2O1s.

And most recently in Season 25, which was shot in the COVID bubble of the Nemacolin resort, Producers forced Jessenia Cruz and MJ Snyder into a makeshift 2O1 conversation with Bachelor Matt James to discuss the bullying and toxicity of the house. Cruz snatched the Rose and James sent MJ packing.

201s at a Glance

PLAYERS	SEASON
Trish Schneider vs. Mandy Jaye Jeffreys	Season 5 (Jesse Palmer)
Mary Delgado vs. Heather Cranford	Season 6 (Byron Velvick)
Sarah Blondin vs. Jennifer Tammaro	Season 8 (Travis Stork)
Erica Rose vs. Agnese Polliza	Season 9 (Lorenzo Borghese)
Peyton Wright vs. Tessa Horst	Season 10 (Andy Baldwin)
DeAnna Pappas vs. Jade Beazley	Season 11 (Brad Womack)
Holly Durst vs. Marshanna Ritchie	Season 12 (Matt Grant)
Stephanie Hogan vs. Nikki Kaapke	Season 13 (Jason Mesnick)
Vienna Girardi vs. Gia Allemand	Season 14 (Jake Pavelka)
Ella Nolan vs. Kathryn Sherlock	Season 14 (Jake Pavelka)
Ashley Spivey vs. Ashley Hebert	Season 15 (Brad Womack)

OUTCOME	FINAL PLACEMENT
No Rose available—both players received roses at that week's Rose Ceremony	Schneider—4th place, Jeffreys—3rd place
No Rose available—Delgado received a Rose at that week's Rose Ceremony, Cranford did not	Delgado—Ring Winner
Blondin gets the first Two-On-One Rose, Tammaro eliminated	Blondin—4th place
Polliza wins the Rose	Polliza—4th place
Horst wins the Rose	Horst—Ring Winner
Pappas wins the Rose	Pappas—Finalist/ Bachelorette
Ritchie wins the Rose	Ritchie—5th place
Hogan wins the Rose	Hogan—5th place
Girardi wins the Rose	Girardi—Ring Winner
Both eliminated (first double elim)	N/A
Hebert wins the Rose	Hebert—3rd place

PLAYERS	SEASON
Blakeley Jones vs. Rachel Truehart	Season 16 (Ben Flajnick)
Tierra LiCausi vs. Jackie Parr	Season 17 (Sean Lowe)
Ashley Iaconetti vs. Kelsey Poe	Season 19 (Chris Soules)
Emily Ferguson vs. Haley Ferguson	Season 20 (Ben Higgins)
Olivia Caridi vs. Emily Ferguson	Season 20 (Ben Higgins)
Corinne Olympios vs. Taylor Nolan	Season 21 (Nick Viall)
Danielle Lombard vs. Whitney Fransway	Season 21 (Nick Viall)
Kendall Long vs. Krystal Nielson	Season 22 (Arie Luyendyk Jr.)
Tammy Ly vs. Mykenna Dorn	Season 24 (Peter Weber)
Jessenia Cruz vs. MJ Snyder	Season 25 (Matt James)

OUTCOME	FINAL PLACEMENT
Truehart wins the Rose	Truehart—6th place
LiCausi wins the Rose	LiCausi—6th place
Both eliminated	N/A
Emily Ferguson wins the Rose	Emily Ferguson—5th place
Ferguson wins the Rose	Ferguson—5th place
Olympios wins the Rose	Olympios—4th place
Both eliminated	N/A
Long wins the Rose	Long—3rd place
Ly eliminated, Dorn advances to Rose Ceremony but gets eliminated	N/A
Cruz gets the Rose	Cruz—6th place

201s by the Numbers

The Nation has long regarded the 201 as the worst possible date on which you might find yourself, but the statistics tell a different story. There have been twenty-one 201 Dates, two of which did not include a Rose or Goes mechanic and four of which resulted in double eliminations. Bachelors have awarded fifteen total 201 Roses and the average finish for a 201 survivor is 3.93rd, a better standing than FIMP Rose recipients. The 201 has produced four Ring Winners and one Crown in DeAnna Pappas, as compared to the First Flower's three Crowns and four Ring Winners and the FIMP's one Ring Winner and one Crown.

201 Strategy

It's easy to get overwhelmed by dread and fear when you hear your name read on a 201 Date Card, based on the idea that you have a fifty-fifty chance of elimination. While this is true, the 201 also gives you the only fifty-fifty chance in the entire season to acquire a Rose outside the Rose Ceremony other than the Final Rose itself. And in most cases all you have to do to win it is engineer a scenario in which the other player can falter. The 201 is daunting to be sure, but by applying a few basic strategies you can maximize your likelihood of success:

Never Too Late to Apologize

In almost all cases in the most recent seasons, 201s were the culmination of a Producer-manufactured rivalry between two players. So if Producers escort you into what they call a Girl Chat (a forced conversation between two or more players usually about one or more other players), be aware of the fact that they're likely grooming you for a role in a rivalry. It will become increasingly apparent if you're forced into one-on-one conversations with another player that are contentious from the beginning. And it will be irrefutable when you hear your name read on that 201 Date Card. In this case, the first and best play is an immediate and sincere apology to whoever the other player in the rivalry might be. Diminish the Producers' ability to use perceived hostility against both of you and ultimately turn the 201 into a civil affair, allowing you to rely on more traditional tools like Love Levels, PTCs, walls, or a chemistry game, which will make the date more akin to a 101 Date as opposed to a battle of Tattling.

4TRR Attack/Defense

In many cases both players rely on a 4TRR attack that involves a heightened Tattle, resulting in the outright accusation of the other player being 4TWR. The basis of these accusations is usually centered around the notion that living in the house has given you the chance to observe insincere behavior or attitudes from your opponent of which the Bachelor is not yet aware. The danger in this style of 4TRR attack is that it comes off like a last-ditch effort to sink the other player. To avoid this outcome, always preface the 4TRR attack with a few words to explain that the Bachelor's emotions and the sanctity of the process are your only concerns. And then for that reason, commence the accusation. This attack should never seem like it's based on personal dislike for the other player or have any petty elements. Elevate it to a protective tone to help solidify its proper effect.

Similarly, if you're the target of such an attack, the best defense is a counter-4TRR attack. Accuse the accuser of the exact same thing and deny every allegation conjured against you, or at the very least explain them away by assuring the Bachelor that words have been twisted and taken out of context. Tell him that the rest of the players will back you up. And above all remain calm. Too often, players are overwhelmed by the grand stage of the 2O1 and they allow their emotions to run wild, clouding their judgment and overriding any possible chance to stick to a game plan.

The Three-on-One

This is by far the most exotic Group Date subtype, having occurred technically only twice over the course of twenty-five seasons, and its formal inclusion in the game is relatively recent. Group Dates with only three players have been in the game since Season 2, but the modern Rose or Goes mechanic that is now a hallmark of the Three-on-One wasn't introduced until Season 22. Arie Luyendyk Jr. took Tia Booth, Kendall Long, and Bekah Martinez to a private estate where he handed a Rose to Long, leaving Booth and Martinez to join him on an impromptu 2O1 dinner that night. Booth successfully employed a "too young to be serious" attack on Martinez and grabbed the Rose, sending Martinez home.

And the only other official Three-on-One occurred in Season 24 when Peter

Weber took Hannah Ann Sluss, Kelley Flanagan, and Victoria Fuller to an estate much like the location of Luyendyk's Three-on-One. And in a similar paring down he issued Victoria Fuller the first of two Roses, leaving Sluss and Flanagan to duke it out on an implied 2O1. Flanagan's overconfidence was her undoing, as Sluss took the last remaining 301R.

If your season includes a Three-on-One it will always be the last Group Date before Hometowns, and so far the odds may be even better for getting a Rose than on a 2O1. With the only Three-on-Ones presenting an opportunity for two players to get a Rose, it seems the best strategy might simply be to avoid conflict. If Producers set up a rivalry between two of the three players on the date, the Bachelor will be forced to choose between the two players involved. So if you can position yourself as the third player, outside the drama of whatever rivalry might exist, that makes the Bachelor's choice for the first Rose very easy. This is what both Kendall Long and Victoria Fuller did expertly. Fuller pulled it off so well that even despite her misplaying her First Audience game into what had become a contentious relationship with Bachelor Peter Weber, he and the Producers still found her to be an easier choice than Sluss or Flanagan, who were forced into a squabbling match.

As the Three-on-One occurs more over the coming years, new data will yield a more precise picture of how best to approach this specialized contest.

The Cocktail Party (CP)

No matter what happens on a Group Date, you'll have one more chance to convince the Producers and the Bachelor that you deserve a Rose. There are two scenarios as you enter the Cocktail Party after a GD appearance. You either won the GDR or you didn't.

Rose in Hand

If you won the GDR, the Cocktail Party may seem like little more than a formality, a bit of ceremonial protocol with which you don't have to concern yourself because you're safe. Nothing could be further from the truth. Capitalize on any and every opportunity to accrue more time with the Bachelor no matter your Rose status. To keep your Second Audience game strong, make sure your Steals aren't egregious or too frequent. And once you get 1O1 time with the Bachelor keep it light and fun and lean into your chemistry game. Comment on how incredible the Group Date was and how much closer you feel to the Bachelor because of the time you spent together. There is no need to use a PTC or raise a Love Level at the Cocktail Party if you have a Rose in hand. These plays are best used to secure a Rose on a future Group Date or 101 and using them in this situation is a waste.

Empty Hand

If you survived a Group Date but walked away empty-handed, the Cocktail Party is an extension of the After Party. Employ every strategy here in order to secure a Rose, including possible use of PTCs and Love Level raises if you haven't already used these strategies at the After Party. If you did, reiterate the Love Level raise or thank the Bachelor for being understanding about the PTC to get any and all remaining value out of the play. And of course, as always, *never* Turtle. Find time with the Bachelor by any means necessary.

In order to make it to the play-offs, you'll have to find a way to survive three or four Group Dates. It is not an easy task, but with preparedness and sound strategy you can turn Group Dates into Roses and use them to progress your narrative of love with the Bachelor even when you're surrounded by other players. But the more concentrated work you have to do in order to advance into the later rounds of the game must ultimately take place on . . . a 101 Date.

Chapter 6

REGULAR SEASON PART 3:

ONE-ON-ONE DATES

The One-On-One is everything and if I get this far without having a One-On-One it sucks. Then it just leaves you with a big "what if?"

Serena Chew (Season 25—Matt James)

The idea of the 1O1 Date didn't really strike us as odd until we were forced to hear the phrase "One-On-One Date" repeated again and again and again during the Hyperbinge. Players said it; leads said it; hosts said it; even guest celebrities said it on occasion. And the more we heard it the more it dawned on us . . . the 1O1 Date is just . . . a regular date. Through the process of the Hyperbinge and the writing of this book, we talked with each other every day, certainly about *The Bachelor* but also about every aspect of our lives. At no point did either of us ever hop on a morning Zoom call and say, "I went on a pretty good One-On-One Date last night." The addition of those three words, "One-On-One," started to take on a whole new meaning for us. It became evidence of the acknowledgment by the Producers and the players alike that *The Bachelor* was indeed a game with its own formal terminology. And now not only have we expanded that list of terms to be a language of its own (see the lexicon at the back of this book), but we also have been sucked so deep into the fandom of this show that we exclusively speak this language when discussing anything and almost none of our friends can understand what we're saying.

Anyway . . . Serena Chew perfectly encapsulated the importance of this staple of our beloved game, just before Producers passed her over for a 1O1 Date once more during Week 5 of Season 25. And just as Chew feared, she never got the chance to prove her mettle on a 1O1, as Matt James sent her packing shortly after in the Round of Six, leaving her to wonder, *What if?*

Unlike the manufactured competitive environment of the Group Date, the 1O1 offers a situation most similar to what you experience in standard, real-world dating. Producers set up a daytime activity of some sort followed by a dinner at which you have the opportunity to get to know the Bachelor better and vice versa. Since the start of the Paradise Era, each season has averaged 10.6 1O1 Dates, and Season 21 was the only one with fewer than 10. In the current era it's not uncommon for Producers to bestow multiple players each season with two 1O1 Dates, so the chance of any single player landing one of these coveted opportunities is only around 23 percent. Although a small handful of players progress to the play-offs without receiving a 1O1, all Ring Winners and Crowns have had at least one. It is *everything*. Of all game elements that have evolved through time, the 1O1 is perhaps the most stable of them. You can barely distinguish the 1O1 today from its inception back in 2002.

The History of the 1O1

Amanda Marsh, Season 1's Ring Winner, received the first 1O1 of all time. Producers designed an incredibly simple date—a dinner at a nice restaurant followed by a massage at a spa. Marsh initiated a strong chemistry game on her 1O1 that propelled her to final victory. While we had assumed before our Hyperbinge that 1O1 Roses blossomed into existence simultaneously with the game's origin, at the end of the first 1O1 Date Bachelor Alex Michel handed Marsh nothing. Marsh pulled out her best First Audience game and the Producers still forced her to endure a Rose Ceremony later that night in order to get a Rose.

Producers didn't include Roses on 1O1 Dates until the Experimental Era in Season 7, when they bestowed the opportunity to win the very first 1O1 Rose upon a player named Megan (last name lost to time). Unfortunately for Megan, Bachelor Charlie O'Connell decided to deny her the Rose. O'Connell also granted her a rare honor, with her becoming one of only two players in the history of the game to endure elimination on the first 101 of the season. The 101 Rose opportunity also inspired the creation of two additional game tropes: the first forced bag-packing and the first appearance of the Grim Reaper. Producers coined the phrase "Grim Reaper" to describe a person who is usually a Production Assistant dressed in all black, whom they send into the house to remove the eliminated player's luggage as the remaining players watch, mouths agape. Cameras always film the Grim Reaper's dark task, as well as the other players' reactions. Depending on the cut player's Second Audience game, the waiting players' reactions range from uncontrollable tear play at the loss of a close friend to champagne-popping, dance party celebrations when the Bachelor eliminates a Villain.

Since the addition of the 101 Rose, it beckons tauntingly on the dinner table of nearly every 101 Date. Producers have kept the daytime portions of 101 dates largely the same since the beginning, ranging from athletic and adventurous activities to relaxing time on boats or at spas. Unlike the competitive spectacle of a Group Date, Producers design the 101 for the player to maximize her opportunity to develop her First Audience game.

As time moved forward and the network added more episodes, bolstering a standard season from six to ten or twelve, including a WTA and an ATFR reunion, so too did Producers add more 101 Dates. Season 1 only featured three 101 Dates. The numbers rose steadily over the next few years to see peak 101 counts in Seasons 16 and 17, each of which incorporated twelve 101 Dates, before settling into the ten or eleven 101s we see almost every season in the current era.

Although Producers changed the number and presentation of the 101 Dates over time, they have forced someone to read the 101 Date Card in front of the entire player pool since the very first season—a tactic seemingly designed to induce jealousy and animosity wherever Producers see an opportunity. Whether you're the Date Card reader or one of the listeners, right after the anointed name is read the players realize that it's not just the first of many on a GD Card and they often gasp and bizarrely squeal. Feel free to join in if your name is not read. But if you are the special 101 Date recipient, try not to project too much overt happiness, as it can seem like you're rubbing the other players' faces in their misfortune. Burying your face in your hands is a valid way to hide uncontrollable glee at receiving this honor.

While all 101 Dates hold incredible value, not all 101s are created equal.

Some involve lavish pampering or exotic locales, while they design others specifically to force you into a Fool archetype or to make it easier for the Bachelor to dismiss you based on your reaction to the date type.

101 Types and Elements

Just as with Group Dates, the 101 Date combines two primary parts—a daytime activity followed by a nighttime activity that's almost always a seated dinner. And just like the Group Date, the 101 contains a basic type and a wide array of smaller thematic or activity-related elements that Producers add to enhance the moment. We've listed on the next page the various types and elements of all 101 Dates since the beginning of the game in 2002.

With such a wide possible array of potential 101 Date types, you cannot prepare for all of them. But because the 101 offers you a reprieve from the pulse-pounding competitive environment of the group scenario, focus your strategy by targeting the First Audience when you get this opportunity. Realize that you can never directly influence when or if you will get a 101. Producers always make this decision without exception. The Bachelor can certainly tell them which players pique his interest, but only the Producers select the recipients of every 101 in every season. Knowing this, appear amenable to the Producers while trying your best to capture the Bachelor's interest so that both the First and Third Audiences do everything in their collective power to generate a 101 for you. Help the Producers do their job by loading a strong PTC, either in an ITM or to other players, that you're ready to tell the Bachelor or load an early Love Level raise. Set up your own story arc and maximize the possibility of attaining this key reward.

If you hear your name on a 101 Date Card, lock in your strategy and prepare for an intense but incredibly beneficial twelve-to-sixteen-hour day of individual play in which you must give the Producers as much usable footage as possible to warrant the maximum amount of screen time.

And the first thing you need to think about is . . .

The Huju (Hug Jump)

The Hug Jump—wherein a player runs at the Bachelor, leaps into his arms, and wraps her legs around him—is a staple of every modern season. But this

101 TYPES/OCCURRENCES (196 101S)

50s Diner (1)
Adventure (19)
Animal Husbandry (10)
Art Gallery/Museum (2)
Artistic Activity (4)
Athletic Activity (4)
Bachelor's Element (1)
Beach/Lake/Ocean (13)
Boat/Yacht (30)
Brewery/Winery/ Champagnery (5)
Cabin (1)
Child's Play (3)
Classic Car (1)
Day Trip (2)
Driving (1)
Early MOTF/Hometown (Bachelor) (12)
Fishing (1)
Foreign Exchange (1)
Glory Days (1)
Gunplay (1)
Historical Monument (2)
Home Cooking (11)
Hot-Air Balloon (3)
Ice Skating (6)
Memory Lane (6)
Mi Casa (7)
Movie (Drive-In or otherwise) (1)
Natural Wonder/ Waterfall/Grand Canyon (2)
Overnight (1)
Package Deal Reunion (2)
Picnic (29)
Plane/Blimp (16)
Pool (1)
Prank (2)
Pretty Woman (19)
Private Amusement Park (7)
Private Island (1)
Private Musical Performance (924)
Private Sports Stadium (2)
Private Theater (2)
Public Performance (3)
Recreational Vehicle (2)
Roughing It (4)
Scavenger Hunt (2)
Sledding (1)
Sleigh Ride (1)
Spa (5)
Spirit Guide (3)
Spotlight Concert (5)
Tourism (5)
Wedding Crasher (92)
When In Rome (16)

ONE-ON-ONE ELEMENTS

C.O.T.A. (Ceremony of the Ancients)
Celebrity
Charity
Ferris Wheel
Fireworks
Forced Nudity
GTTC (Get To The Chopper)
Home Invasion
Hot Tub

hasn't always been the case. In fact, the Huju didn't debut in our beloved game until Season 6, when Ring Winner Mary Delgado invented it on a softball field during her Hometown Date in Tampa, Florida, when she vaulted into the arms of Byron Velvick. From that moment forward various players have indulged in this acrobatic subsport, adding to its rich legacy, like Melissa Rycroft in Season 13, who added incredible leg flourishes to her Hujus, a skill born from years of professional cheerleading before her playing days. Lauren Burnham in Season 22 introduced a koala-like high, seemingly perpetual cling around the torso of Arie Luyendyk Jr. And perhaps most notably, Kelsey Weier brought Olympic-level athleticism to her Hujus in Season 24 with frenetic sprinting and double leg leaps. Some players still view the Huju as superfluous or foolish. But as more and more players openly admit that Producers coaxed them into performing Hujus, it is, beyond doubt, an important part of any deep run. Although some brave players like Season 25's Katie Thurston and Kit Keenan have performed them on Group Dates, the 1O1 is most usually the first time you get an isolated attempt to pull off the game's most beautiful embrace.

How to Huju

A Huju consists of four separate parts, each requiring its own set of physical talents. Practice each of the following elements with a partner who is at least six feet tall to mimic the stature of whoever the Bachelor might be before you appear in the game. Only four Bachelors have stood below six feet tall and Jake Pavelka was the shortest at five-ten.

Part 1—the Approach

Producers will set the stage for a Huju to take place by positioning you and the Bachelor fifty to seventy-five meters apart. They will focus separate cameras on both of you and will quite literally tell you to "go." Once Producers give the signal, convey excitement to see the Bachelor both by smiling as wide as possible and by running toward him as fast as possible with arms outstretched in preparation to leap. A high-speed approach serves the double function of conveying excitement and building momentum for the next phase of the Huju. . . .

THE 4 PARTS OF THE HUJU

The Approach

The Mount

The Cling

The Dismount

Part 2—the Mount

This is perhaps the most difficult component of the Huju and where many players falter. A good mount requires you to leap and stick to the Bachelor in a single fluid motion that allows your arms to clear his shoulders and your legs to clear his hips. The kiss of death for most mounts is not gaining enough speed to jump high enough, which forces the Bachelor to do all the lifting. Ideally, the Bachelor does not even have to move his arms at all. He could stand there still as a tree with arms outstretched, as a good mount will land you with your legs around the lower part of his abdomen, just above his hips, and your arms around the back of his neck—a position that leads to the third segment of a Huju. . . .

Part 3—the Cling

Once mounted, find a way to maintain your aerial embrace for as long as possible. A perfect mount includes a double ankle lock around the small of the Bachelor's back and a double hand-to-elbow lock around the back of his neck. This allows you to support your entire body weight almost indefinitely, leaving your head and neck free to maneuver around the Bachelor's face, peppering him with kisses or possibly even engaging in deep chemistry game kissing, which concludes with . . .

Part 4—the Dismount

This is easily the most overlooked component of a Huju. Most players feel the job is done once they've leapt, clung, and kissed, but to seal the Huju, do not ignore the dismount. For a proper dismount, unlock your ankles, swing your legs back around, and plant your feet together just like an Olympic gymnast finishing a floor routine. Do not back bend or take unnecessary secondary steps to regain balance, and maintain eye contact with the Bachelor through this entire process. What's more, never break physical contact. Transition the double hand lock around the back of the Bachelor's neck into a double or single hand hold by sliding your hands down the length of his arms as you come to stand before him, gazing into his eyes and smiling.

Your Huju is vital to establish the appearance of enthusiasm for the Bachelor as well as the process. Critically, it also subtly gives the Bachelor some idea of what physical intimacy might be like with you, which helps to build your chemistry game.

Think of the Huju as the opening ceremony to a 1O1, a brief but brilliant flash of acrobatic artistry to set the tone of the entire date, no matter what Producers have planned for the activity. Date types and elements are much less relevant for designing your 1O1 strategy than they are for Group Dates. Your performance on a 1O1 isn't dependent on any other player's actions or on the Bachelor comparing players against one another. For that reason we recommend a basic pattern of linked actions to guarantee the highest likelihood of securing a 1O1 Rose, which we saw work with aplomb over and over during our Hyperbinge. Study and employ this formula, a tried-and-true series of cause-and-effect maneuvers that will help you make a strong case for passage into the next round of play. It's called . . .

The 1O1 Pattern

Players have perfected this technique through season after season of use. Tailor it to your specific archetype and brand, but the 1O1 Pattern always consists of using three tools (also used on Group Dates) in the following sequence:

1. The Wall

No matter what the day portion of the 1O1 might entail, play a wall during daylight hours for the first step of the 1O1 Pattern. Base your Wall on a past trauma, making it difficult for you to open up or, if the 1O1 occurs in an earlier round, you can even base it on nothing more than your cautious optimism about the possibility of the process actually working for you. Whatever the nature of the wall, make sure it serves as a noticeable obstacle for the Bachelor, a reserved demeanor that he feels needs to be shed in order to move on. For ideas, study the originators of wall strategy, Trista Rehn and Shannon Oliver (Season 1—Alex Michel). Your wall sets the stage for the next step, which you should play after dark.

2. The PTC

Once night falls, Producers will give you a few hours to sit alone with the Bachelor at a staged dinner. While they demand that you don't eat the actual food, you will pour drinks and engage in conversation. If you played a strong and overt wall during the day portion of the date, it's entirely possible that the Bachelor himself will actually bring up your walls that he sensed earlier. If this is the case, then you have a natural segue straight into the playing of a PTC. If he doesn't bring it up, simply acknowledge that although you had such a great time during the day, you found it hard to let your guard down and there's a reason . . . then play your PTC. The specific nature of the PTC doesn't matter, but playing it at this moment justifies your wall play earlier in the day and implicitly lowers it. And, of course, as all PTCs do, it will generate sympathy from the First Audience as well as the Fourth Audience, making it almost impossible for the Bachelor to withhold the 1O1 Rose that sits right next to you. But just to be safe, follow up the PTC by raising . . .

3. The Love Level

This will obviously depend on where you are in the season when Producers grant you a 1O1. If it's early, simply raise to Love Level 1 with something like, "Thank you for listening to me and for letting me share my story with you. You know it's been a long time since I've felt like this. I really like you." If it's later in the season, escalate to a Love Level 2 or possibly even 3 if it's called for. Determine the specific Love Level in the moment, but let it serve as the perfect icing on the 1O1 cake you have been baking all day and the Bachelor without question will award you the Rose.

During Season 25, Sarah Trott performed a textbook 1O1 Pattern on her first 1O1 Date with Matt James. She acted distant and aloof during the day when they flew in a 1930s biplane and then walked through the forest. In her ITM she described, "I am a little bit more private and it takes time for me to open up and take down those walls. I want to be vulnerable but don't want to bring up important family topics or uncomfortable things right off the bat."

James specifically asked about her father during the day and Trott vaguely described him as "the most sincere, loving dad ever." James described this initial portion in his confessional: "I had a great time but could tell Sarah was struggling with something. I need her to be open and vulnerable." Later that night, the pair went to dinner. Trott started it off saying, "You were asking questions earlier about my dad and my work. It's really hard for me to take down those walls; I am a private person. . . . It's so hard for me to open up. I want to share this with you." She then played her PTC, that her father had

ALS and that she quit her journalism job to act as his caretaker. It was heart-wrenching. She finished it off by raising an LL1, saying, "I feel so comfortable . . . I think there's something special." James immediately rewarded her with the 101 Rose. It took finesse to save that story for the dinner portion, but it created a story arc that both the Bachelor and the Producers recompensed.

Unlike the Group Dates, different types of 101s don't really require different strategies. Apply this standard pattern easily to every type of 101 you encounter. That said, some 101 Date types have special qualities, offering certain benefits and in some cases producing special reactions from other players.

Important 101 Date Types

Adventure

Producers have crafted nineteen Adventure Dates over the course of the history of our beloved game, and they are the only 101 Date type that requires you to overcome some element of fear. Players have skydived, bungee jumped, climbed mountains, rappelled down buildings, and even climbed to the top of the historic San Francisco–Oakland Bay Bridge. The Adventure Date offers you a built-in obstacle story if you're savvy. Whether you have a fear of the specific activity or not, pretend to have one—most commonly you'll use fear of heights. Once you establish the fear, coerce the Bachelor into helping you overcome the fear by engaging in the activity with you, protecting you from your fear in a sense, and snag a good-luck kiss. Then upon completing the activity, you win a heightened moment of bonding that non-Adventure Dates don't offer. Often, this includes a fear-conquering make-out session at climatic, cinematic moments, such as at the top of a giant rock you both have climbed or when you're both swinging at the bottom of a bungee jump's rip cord. Paired with the accompanying adrenaline rush, plus the swell of dramatic music, this moment produces one of the most memorable types of kisses.

Animal Husbandry

As the name implies, this type of date requires you to interact with animals. Those animals can be innocuous, like baby sea turtles who just need a little help getting to the ocean, as was the case in Season 20 when Lauren Bushnell and Bachelor Ben Higgins invoked the power of a Christian prayer to aid the tiny reptiles. But more often than not, you're sitting on the back of one of the most popular beasts of burden in the world—a horse. Many players make the mistake of entering the game without experience on one of these majestic creatures, which often results in comically terrible results and an unwelcome Fool Edit. To combat this possibility, and if you have the funds, find a stable near your hometown and spend a few weekends taking riding lessons. It's not a guarantee that you will have to saddle up, but as the American cowboy famously said, "Better safe than sorry."

Boat/Yacht

The most common 101 Date type, occurring thirty times (15.3 percent of all 101s), is the Boat/Yacht, a time-honored tradition in our beloved game. There is no magic formula to turning in a solid 101 performance on a yacht or boat. But one thing to avoid is getting seasick, which can destroy the mood immediately and possibly even ruin the rest of the date. If you've never been on a boat, much like taking riding lessons, take a few trips on a boat at the nearest lake or ocean. Get some sea legs before entering the game, because while some players indulge in wine and strawberries on smooth-sailing luxury yachts, others heave to and fro, wind-whipped on the choppy seas in a tiny catamaran. Bring Dramamine and use it as necessary. Indulge in one common boat play by taking the Bachelor to the very front or back tip of the boat to re-create the iconic spooning with outstretched arms of the *Titanic* pose. After laughing together at performing the overused trope, transition this moment into strong chemistry play.

Early MOTF

This coveted 101 Date offers you the chance to meet the Bachelor's family before Hometowns and, more important, before any of the other players. In some cases Producers structure this prestigious early MOTF around an important familial event like a parental vows renewal, as was the case for Madison Prewett (Season 24—Peter Weber). The early MOTF is immensely beneficial if you can get early approval from the family. It also comes with some cost in that the rest of the players will become jealous when they learn the date type. It immediately puts a front-runner target on your back. But there is absolutely no 101 that generates more jealousy and in some cases outright vindictiveness than the . . .

Pretty Woman

This is the holy grail of 101s. While Group Dates occasionally feature a *Pretty Woman* element, only on the 101 does the *Pretty Woman* element become the entire date activity. These 101s often start with Producers sending a dress, jewelry, or a private driver to the house for you. This serves only one purpose—to enrage the other players. Once you are on the date, Producers make you try on an endless array of designer dresses and more jewelry. The Bachelor will then whisk you away to a luxurious restaurant or concert hall. Often, you will have to enact a movie-montage-style dressing room performance of various outfits. The most valuable aspect of the *Pretty Woman* is that you almost always get to keep the clothes and sometimes even the jewelry, associating significant financial gain with this date type, more than any other 101. But, like most things in our beloved game, you incur no benefit without a cost, and the cost you'll pay in this case is a forced walk of embarrassment. If you receive the *Pretty Woman*, Producers will make you return to the house and parade yourself in front of the other players, arms comically heavy with designer bags and boxes for all to see. What's more, the Producers sometimes require you to sift through your spoils in a haul-style show-and-tell, specifically designed to negatively affect the other players. The *Pretty Woman* is certainly a 101 to covet and celebrate, but not too overtly, lest players paint a target on your back.

An experimental *Pretty Woman* strategy that has never been employed but would likely create an iconic and historic moment would involve you sharing your haul with the other players. When you return from the date, select one item that you want to keep and offer everything else to whoever wants it. For extra emphasis you might even add a speech that goes something like this: "Any one of us could have had this date and I just want to share it with you all. Don't get me wrong, I love these earrings. I'm keeping these earrings, but please, everybody go through this stuff and take whatever you want." This would elevate your Second Audience status to near untouchable and it would make a Third Audience Villain Edit virtually impossible. It would endear you to the Fourth Audience who would have never seen anything like this. And eventually this information would get back to the First Audience who would perceive it as proof that indeed you were there 4TRR.

Elements

Just as with Group Dates, 1O1s feature an array of elements added to the primary activity. Many are pleasant or inert enough that you need not prepare. Producers use celebrities, elderly couples imparting romantic wisdom, charity work, helicopter rides, and hot tubs commonly, but there is one element that stands above all others as a signifier of success. . . .

Fireworks

Once you complete a successful 1O1, with Rose in hand, the Bachelor will lead you to a balcony or a beach where he holds you tight as you both look up into the sky and witness a private fireworks show. Producers design this moment specifically to generate footage of a cinematic kiss, which is an incredible benefit for any player. It initiates a mandatory chemistry play in a perfect setting. What's more, in the current Professional Era, all players know what the fireworks mean and Producers make absolutely sure that the other players left back at the hotel or house see the fireworks exploding in the sky to signify that they are falling behind. During Season 25 Bri Springs went on a 1O1 Date that ended with a fireworks display. The other players not on the date openly discussed how that noisy symbol in the sky represented a successful date and implied a simultaneous make-out session. If you receive the fireworks date, accept the small victory, but always express false humility when you return to the house later that night.

101 by the Numbers

We've often debated the importance of 101 Date order over the course of a season, and after extensive examination we've determined that there are two 101s that have significant statistical importance. The first 101 and the last 101 each season. Although you cannot influence which 101 you get, use this knowledge to determine a strategy based on the likelihood of outcome.

First 101 Dates of the Season

The inaugural 101 has produced three Ring Winners:

Amanda Marsh—Season 1
Helene Eksterowicz—Season 2
Becca Kufrin—Season 22

But it has produced more Bachelorettes than any other 101 with seven:

Meredith Phillips—Season 4
Jillian Harris—Season 13
Ali Fedotowsky—Season 14
Ashley Hebert—Season 15
Clare Crawley—Season 18
Becca Kufrin—Season 22
Hannah Brown—Season 23

The average final placement for a player who gets the first 101 is 4.88th place. Bachelors have only eliminated two players on the first 101 Date of the season, giving it a 92 percent RSR (Round Survival Rate).

Last 101 Dates of the Season

The final 101 of each season has produced a staggering eight Ring Winners:

Helene Eksterowicz—Season 2
Sarah Brice—Season 7
Sarah Stone—Season 8
Jennifer Wilson—Season 9
Tessa Horst—Season 10

Courtney Robertson—Season 16
Nikki Ferrell—Season 18
Vanessa Grimaldi—Season 21

And it has produced only two Bachelorettes:

Ali Fedotowsky—Season 14
Hannah Brown—Season 23

The average final placement for a player who gets the final 1O1 is 3.58th place. Eight players have been eliminated on the last 1O1 Date of the season, giving it a 68 percent RSR (Round Survival Rate).

Since the start of the Paradise Era (Season 19) there have been an average of 10.6 1O1 Dates per season. Season 21 is the only modern season with fewer than 10.

There have been 196 total 1O1s. Thirty-four players have had two 1O1s in a single season and only one player has ever had three 1O1s in a single season—Season 15's runner up, Chantal O'Brien. Only three players have had both the first and last 1O1s in the same season:

Helene Eksterowicz—Ring Winner
Ali Fedotowsky—Bachelorette
Hannah Brown—Bachelorette

If you manage to avoid elimination through several Group Dates, navigate the cruel gauntlet of house life, and even properly utilize your tools on one or more 1O1 Dates, you will graduate from the regular season into another level of play where you will compete directly against the other three best players of the season in the Top 4.

Welcome to the play-offs.

Chapter 7

PLAY-OFFS ROUND 1:

HOMETOWNS

After meeting her parents, I could see where her big heart comes from. Her mom and dad were both so kind and loving and I could tell they genuinely wanted their daughter to be happy. It was easy to imagine myself being part of her family.

Sean Lowe, the seventeenth Bachelor

The long process of the Hyperbinge, collecting data, analyzing it, and relentlessly discussing it ad nauseum for the past year as we've put this book together has given rise to furious debates between us. We've spent countless hours trying to come to consensus on big topics like who is the greatest player in the history of the game, and we've probably spent even more time probing seemingly inconsequential subjects like does wearing sneakers with your cocktail dress truly qualify as a TOT Limo Exit? The answer to that question, by the way, is yes.

But one thing we've always agreed on is that the Hometown round of the play-offs is the most chaotic week of every season. Imagine what it would be like in any other sport if players' parents were brought in and made to play in a game. And not just any game, literally the first game of play-offs. This is at least part of the reason that *The Bachelor* is our favorite sport—baseball, football, basketball, and hockey don't have the guts to do something like Hometowns.

The Final Four players bring the Bachelor home to see where his prospective partners grew up and meet their respective families. For the first time you will have to rely on the skills of other people to help you through to the next round. You have to orchestrate an interaction with your family and possibly other denizens of your hometown to show the Bachelor that your family is normal enough to present no obvious problems in your possible future lives together. You have to make the most out of Hometowns to benefit you strategically, both in what you choose for the day portion of your date, as well as in crafting the perfect MOTF portion. The best Hometown Dates showcase you in a new, positive light that you could only really accomplish during this week due to the available new team of players and locations. During this important week of play-offs, most players up their Love Levels, drop their walls, and perform some strong future-casting moves. And throughout the history of the game, players have met this challenge with a wide array of successes and failures.

The History of the Hometown Date

The first round of play-offs every season has featured a trip to visit a player's Hometown since the beginning of our beloved game back in 2002. Every season has included four Hometown Dates except Season 6, when the Producers switched the Hometowns and Fantasy Suite weeks, which produced only three Hometown Dates, bringing the grand total to ninety-nine Hometown Dates. Almost all of them require travel by Production, except Season 25, which instead took place entirely in a bubble at the Nemacolin resort in Pennsylvania due to the COVID-19 pandemic. But the MOTF remained such an integral part of this first round of play-offs that Producers re-created this round by flying out key members of the Final Four players' families to meet Matt James.

While we are now used to the familiar pattern of modern Hometowns—a daytime activity and then the MOTF—we were amazed to experience the tumultuous and unstructured first Hometown Dates of Season 1. The day portions of the dates were short or nonexistent, offering almost no new information or opportunities for players to escalate their games. During the MOTF portions, Bachelor Alex Michel conducted an open discussion with each entire family. Producers didn't break up the time into smaller 1O1 segments of either Michel or the player with each of their key family members.

Kim Karels had the first Hometown Date of all time in Phoenix, Arizona. She featured a Weirdo MOTF portion, during which Karels's father, Pete, proudly showed Michel the family's entire taxidermy collection of animals that various members of their family had killed. Michel pointed at a deer head and Pete happily exclaimed, "Missy shot that one!" Michel floundered and told them that he loved swimming and books. He attempted to ingratiate himself to the family by playing with a child-age nephew, Drew, and picked him up off the ground by his still-forming arm. Drew immediately started bawling in pain. Despite Michel earlier describing Karel as "one of the most beautiful women in the world" and "my dream girl," he eliminated her at the next Rose Ceremony, a powerful omen of what awaits players who do not put their and their family's best foot forward.

The Hometown Date has evolved somewhat since that very first iteration into a much more streamlined two-step process of an activity day portion, followed by a structured MOTF meal portion. In Season 4, Mary Delgado brought Bob Guiney to visit her Cuban family in Tampa, Florida, where her brother played the role of translator for her father, who only spoke Spanish. It was the very first non-English Hometown Date and the first Hometown Date to feature a Latinx family.

Certain essential elements of Hometown Dates didn't develop until later on. One of the most important was the Glow—a verbal acknowledgment by a family member that the player looks happy or in love. Brooke Smith's aunt bestowed the first Familial Glow upon Smith during her Albertville, Alabama, Hometown Date with Aaron Buerge in Season 2. And a parent didn't grant the first Hometowns Familial Blessing until Season 14, when Ali Fedotowsky's mother granted it to Jake Pavelka. We break down the Glow and the Blessing more in depth later in this chapter.

Ring Winner Tessa Horst was the first Asian player to make it to Hometowns in Season 10, when she brought Andy Baldwin home to meet her family in Washington, D.C. She was also the first of two players to ever engage in a Hometowns Snowball Fight. The first Black player to get a Hometown Date was not until Season 21, when Rachel Lindsay took Nick Viall to her Dallas, Texas, megachurch and then to meet her family. Lindsay's family grilled Viall about how he would handle building an interracial relationship and family. Lindsay's White brother-in-law even pointed out to Viall, "I can't help but notice you are a White." Viall deftly deflected the familial attacks and said with conviction that he thought his and Lindsay's differences "would make [them] stronger."

As the show gained fame and notoriety, so too did the possibility for family members to earn fame and notoriety of their own as part of a Colorful Family Hometowns story line. Krisily Kennedy's grandmother, Nanna, arguably innovated the "Star Family Member" strategy during Season 7 at Kennedy's Hometown Date in Warwick, Rhode Island. Bachelor Charlie O'Connell danced with Nanna and gave her a Rose during the MOTF portion. Nanna then told Kennedy that she should "use her powers" to up her chemistry game during the Fantasy Suite round. For the dramatic Live Finale that season, Producers flew in both finalists' families and Chris Harrison checked in with Kennedy's family, during which Nanna reprised her little dance. Echoes of Nanna's signature dance would ripple throughout the ages.

JoJo Fletcher's mother, Soraya Fletcher, added a flourish to the "Star Parent" strategy during Season 20. When Ben Higgins came to meet their family, Soraya chugged straight from a champagne bottle to help get through the proceedings. However, this familial star player strategy rose to new, unprecedented heights with the introduction of an icon, Peter Weber's mother, Barbara Weber, during *The Bachelorette* Season 15.

She was over-the-top and passionate, earning Fourth Audience fans for herself after her very first appearance. She reprised and built upon her role when her son wore the twenty-fourth Crown. She starred in an early MOTF 101 Date during which Peter Weber took Madison Prewett as his plus one to the ceremony where Barbara and her husband renewed their wedding vows. Barbara even threw a bouquet. This was her show. She was such an emotional and beloved character that season that a scene of her crying "Bring her home to us" to Peter Weber became the key moment of that entire season. Producers played it over and over in promos during almost every single episode, representing the emotional climax of Season 24. Barbara Weber had no social media following before appearing on *The Bachelor* and today she has become an influencer herself, with a solid 114K IG followers. She does spon-con, gets paid to create Cameo videos for fans, and serves as an inspiration for all future family members of *Bachelor* players that they, too, can capitalize off of this beloved game.

Hometown Date Types and Elements

Modern Hometown Dates consist of two parts. For the Hometown Day portion Producers make you take the Bachelor to a location that was meaningful to you in the town where you grew up (or a suitable stand-in town), and for the second portion they require you to introduce your family to the Bachelor and to the entire production staff, where you must conscript mothers, fathers, siblings, aunts, uncles, and best friends into your strategy.

A solid Hometown Date hits multiple positive elements, highlighting the local flavor of your hometown as well as creating a high entertainment value. Hometowns also contain implicit future-casting should you win the Crown. What cast of characters might the Fourth Audience demand to see more of should Producers grant you your own season? Use Hometowns to showcase yourself in a new and beneficial light through the revelation of an interesting family business or your own job. Tailor these dates specifically to your brand and the Bachelor's interests if at all possible. Some types are definitely more beneficial for larger goals in this game. We've listed here the various types and elements of all Hometown Dates since the beginning of the game in 2002.

HOMETOWN TYPES/OCCURRENCES (99 HTS)

Adventure (5)
Ancestor's Blessing (4)
Animal Husbandry (6)
Aquatic Activity (6)
Artistic Endeavor (2)
Arts & Crafts (3)
Athletic Activity (9)
ATV (2)
Bar (10)
Beach (9)
Be A Man (4)
Boat (6)
Carriage Ride (2)
Celebrity (2)
Christian Invocation (14)
Cultural Indulgence (5)
Docks (2)
Dogs (17)
Familiar Home (74)
Family Business (6)
Family Dance (4)
Glory Days (3)
Gun (3)
High School (3)
Hotel (5)
Instant Family (3)
Kids (8)
Kite (2)
Local Tour Guide (20)
Local Tradition (3)
Mechanical Bull (2)
Meeting Of The Family (6)
Meeting Of The Friends (6)
Memory Lane (8)
Mi Casa (14)
Off-Road Vehicle (2)
Overbearing Siblings (5)

Park (18)
Picnic (17)
Prank (4)
Restaurant (9)
Roommate (3)
Scrapbook (4)
Shopping Spree/ Pretty Man (2)
Show-off (5)
Skeleton (3)
Skydiving (2)
Snowball Fight (2)
Spanish (2)
Split Home (12)
Take Your Bachelor to Work (8)
Taxidermy (2)
TOT (2)
Waterfall (2)
Wedding Role Play (2)
Weirdo (4)
What I Do for Fun (3)
Winery (2)

HOMETOWN ELEMENTS

A Different World
Animal Funeral
Apple Picking
Army Base
Billboard
Cat
Carriage Race
Country Club
Failure To Launch
Family Artistic Activity
Family Athletic Activity
Family TOT
Family Refusal
Horseshoes
Hot Tub
How Will You Support My Daughter
IFI
Lighthouse
Nanny
Pageant Room
Pool Party
Private Amusement Park
Private Arena
Private Concert
Racetrack
Religious Date
Sporting Event
Surprise Aunt

Most Common Hometown Date Types

The world is your oyster when choosing between the many different kinds of Hometown Dates, the world being the regional specifics of the locale where your parents currently reside. Producers make exceptions to this limitation only in extreme circumstances, such as during Chris Soules's Season 19, when they limited international travel and made Canadian player Kaitlyn Bristowe debut her Hometown in Phoenix, Arizona, where her family summered, instead. You have some influence in selecting the type of date, but Producers and their described production limitations will heavily influence those decisions. Whatever you and your Producers decide, here are the most common types and their outcomes.

Local Tour Guide (20)

The most common day portion of the Hometown Date is the Local Tour Guide. When you choose this date type, you show the Bachelor around your hometown, jumping between several different local sights. The LTG is a Hometowns version of a When In Rome 101 Date, but in this case you have an advantage over a WIR, as you can give facts as well as personal anecdotes about the various locales, putting your expertise on display. This gives the Bachelor both a feel for your background and some future-casting about what potential family reunions would look like. However, if your hometown is remote and desolate, this date type can backfire, as it did when Chris Soules brought his players to meet his own family in his tiny hometown of Arlington, Iowa. The players questioned if they could even accept a proposal if it meant spending the rest of their lives in a town with a population of 450 people. The best versions of the LTG day portion include fun, personal anecdotes (a Memory Lane) and trying local cuisine that allows you to perform a little food play and re-up your chemistry game.

Five Ring Winners and two Crowns have chosen the LTG route. Future Crown Ashley Hebert (Season 15—Brad Womack) utilized the LTG at its best during her Madawaska, Maine, Hometown by introducing Womack to a local flavor of poutine at the same restaurant where she had her first job in high school, combining many strong elements into one. It was novel for Womack, it portrayed a positive piece of Hebert's history, that she had always been hardworking, and perhaps most important it soothed Womack's mind with tasty, tasty French fries. She integrated these elements with a little French language lesson, an Aloha cherry on top of a powerful Memory Lane. This also benefited the later MOTF portion, as Womack could chat more in depth about Hebert's childhood with her family.

Ring Winner Catherine Giudici (Season 17—Sean Lowe) chose this same date type for her Seattle, Washington, Hometown. She guided Lowe through a tour of the fish market, where they ate lunch, took photo booth pictures together, and even took part in a Local Tradition: throwing and catching a fish with some local vendors. Giudici gifted Lowe a future-casting glimpse into what a typical day could look like when they would visit her family as a married couple. Lowe was also able to keep a photo memento of this day from the photo booth, to remind him of Giudici's excellent play, and this helped convince him to ultimately make her Catherine Lowe.

Picnic (17)

The second most common day portion of a Hometown Date is the tradition of a square cloth upon the ground, followed by drinks and treats: the Picnic. The advantages of a Picnic are as bountiful as the unlimited supply of wine and cheese on which you and the Bachelor dine. Picnics tend to take place in a beautiful, picturesque location. They often include food, alcohol, local creatures, as well as, most important, the ability for you and the Bachelor to focus on an important conversation. A Picnic is the perfect scenario for you to prep him for who he is about to meet in the MOTF portion, as well as to load any familial walls you wish for the Bachelor to overcome. The disadvantages of a Picnic are that it is static, not very memorable, and doesn't reveal a new facet of your identity. It also doesn't give you the chance to shine at any particular skill set, unless you have exceptional conversation skills or can open a bottle of wine with a unique part of your body.

Two Crowns and four Ring Winners have utilized the Picnic. The best Picnics contain strong emotional conversations in which you either load walls that you will eventually bring down or use them for strong future-casting. Season 16's Ring Winner, Courtney Robertson, performed one of the best Future-Casting Picnic plays of all time on her Hometown Date in Scottsdale, Arizona. Robertson's First Audience game was up there with the all-time greats. After an earlier MOTF portion, she brought Ben Flajnik to an innocent-appearing Picnic. The two discussed meeting her family, during which Robertson had upped her Love Level to LL3. Then Robertson introduced a twist to this Picnic—that this was a park where they conduct weddings. She pulled out a notebook for them to write their "fake" vows to each other as well as costumes for them to wear: two rings and a bow tie. Then they joined a wedding officiant at an altar nearby to perform a fake wedding ceremony, reading the vows they had just written to each other while wearing the rings and the bow tie. Robertson then upped her Love Level to LL4 at this very ceremony, which she had perfectly set up with their emotional work on their Picnic. It was future-casting at its best, showing Flajnik exactly what it would look and feel like to marry her. Robertson went on to ultimately win the Ring despite her incredibly strong Villain Edit. They did not ultimately, however, ever perform a real wedding ceremony.

Mi Casa (14)

Home is where the heart is, or at least that's what players who choose a Mi Casa date are hoping for. A Mi Casa sees you bringing the Bachelor to your own abode. It's a high-risk, high-reward type of date due to it revealing so much about yourself, positive or negative. You run the risk that the Bachelor doesn't like your neighborhood, your decor style, or even your pets. On the other hand, you can also show off a nice place to the Bachelor, which holds more power than the mystery spots of the other players. You're directly future-casting one of the two potential homes that you as a couple could ultimately choose to live in. Another benefit of the Mi Casa is that you're completely in charge of the production space and can tailor the rooms exactly to the needs of the Bachelor. You can even host the MOTF portion should the need arise due to a less-than-ideal home situation or wanting only specific relatives to attend. Players can't perform a Mi Casa date if they no longer live in the city where their family resides.

Five Ring Winners and three Crowns have chosen to bring the Bachelor into their homes on national television. Estella Gardinier (Season 4—Bob Guiney) won the Ring after her Mi Casa in Beverly Hills, California. She used her Mi Casa to station the MOTF portion of her Hometown, when her mother came over. Her mother instantly produced tears upon meeting Guiney, which came off very 4TRR, and eventually she bestowed Guiney with her Blessing. Gardinier made that moment all the more special because they were in her personal space.

Emily Maynard (Season 15—Brad Womack), one of the only players to achieve the Full Royale (win both the Ring and the Crown), also had her Hometown Date MOTF portion in her own home in Charlotte, North Carolina. While this date was primarily an Instant Family, as Maynard's young daughter joined throughout, Womack saw where the pair actually conducted their lives together, which made it more intimate. Womack played a game of Candyland in the living room and eventually helped tuck the child into bed. Maynard also performed a unique chemistry wall play due to this scenario, by making Womack too nervous to kiss her in the same house as her daughter. This built romantic tension, which Maynard ultimately released with a strong chemistry play when she kissed Womack on her doorstep. Emotionally structure a Mi Casa by erecting similar walls and bringing them down before the Bachelor leaves.

The Athletic Activity (9)

The Athletic Activity is a wonderful choice for a Hometown because it's fun, visual, and produces endorphins. Highlight either your own athletic ability or your charm in being a good sport at something you are terrible at. Bachelors are almost always incredibly athletic and we recommend letting the Bachelor show off his own skills and prowess, both to get screen time as a pair and to build chemistry between you and the Bachelor.

Madison Prewett (Season 24—Peter Weber) performed this date type in its highest form, and it's one of the best-executed and most important Hometown dates of all time. She previewed it early on, during her intro package, in which she and her father strategized about plays in both basketball and love. For Hometowns she then took Weber to the Auburn Arena at Auburn University, where her father was an assistant coach, combining a Private Arena, a Show-off Date, and a Family Business Date. Prewett put her basketball skills on display by doing some dribbling tricks and also showed off her connections by coaxing a celebrity NBA legend, Charles Barkley, to appear on the stadium's Jumbotron to wish the couple well. She shone in this environment and translated that Hometown Date activity into future parasocial play, by making basketball-related TikTok videos. She ultimately won an Under Armour sponsorship, with a TikTok collaboration that got 79.4M views, by far the most viewed TikTok of any *Bachelor* player. Prewett's day portion also prompted basketball stories at the MOTF later when Prewett's father described Madison developing grit from basketball IFIs growing up, including losing a tooth playing. While Prewett never won the Ring or the Crown, she did get the most TikTok followers in Bachelor Nation history (2M), as well as 1.7M IG followers—the most of any player from Season 24. In addition, two Ring Winners and two Crowns have chosen Athletic Activities.

Memory Lane (8)

Not to be confused with the LTG, although they often overlap, a Memory Lane requires you to take the Bachelor to specific locations in order to tell personal anecdotes about them. In many ways, the Memory Lane is a better version of the LTG, because it more explicitly reveals personal qualities about yourself and allows you to introduce characters via your backstory that the Bachelor is going to meet later that night. The Bachelor will then feel more connected to your family, as well as already have conversation starters in his pocket.

Make the MOTF more seamless for the Bachelor and have a structured story. If you plan it you can reap the benefits from this technique.

Three Crowns and one Ring Winner have used this date, meaning three out of eight Memory Lane Dates produced Crowns. That is some strong branding and excellent First, Third, and Fourth Audience play. Jillian Harris (Season 13—Jason Mesnick) utilized this date type to show Mesnick her hometown of Kelowna, British Columbia, Canada. She took him to a public square and the lake where her family spent most summers. Her tour guiding included a local myth about a Loch Ness Monster–style creature called Ogopogo that lived in the lake, adding her signature goofy flair to her descriptions. At a local winery she pivoted the conversation to be more serious and played a Hometown-specific PTC about her mother's depression and suicide attempts, punctuated with tears. This moment brought them closer together and better prepared Mesnick for meeting the family later. This was an ideal Memory Lane because it mixed lighthearted local stories with deeply personal anecdotes, rooted in locations around her hometown that connected her to Mesnick, and helped prepare and give him backstory for the MOTF. This date also deeply connected Harris to the Fourth Audience, who later demanded that she wear the Crown.

And Trista Rehn (Season 1—Alex Michel) performed the first-ever Memory Lane Date in St. Louis, Missouri. She took Michel to get some local fast food and then to her high school, a subgenre of Memory Lane called Glory Days, to show him where she was a cheerleader and continue playing her incredibly strong wall game. She lowered her walls briefly to give him their first kiss on the bleachers, using the backdrop of the high school to create a nostalgic make-out session. This date solidified Rehn in Michel's mind as the hard-to-get cheerleader up on a pedestal, whom he eventually rewarded with runner-up status and Producers rewarded with the first-ever Bachelorette Crown.

Take Your Bachelor To Work (TYBTW) (8)

The TYBTW is one of the strongest day portions you can choose because of the unique, positive glimpse into your life, highlighting you in your element. Display your skill set during Hometowns by picking this perfect opportunity to showcase one of your theoretically best skills, the one you get paid to do. It's 4TRR because it shows that you have a job outside of social media and your job also often displays an interesting background with colorful characters.

Three Ring Winners and one Crown have selected the TYBTW Date. Whitney Bischoff (Season 19—Chris Soules) played an effective TYBTW Date when she took Soules to her fertility clinic in Chicago, Illinois, where she was a nurse. She utilized TOT play by having them both wear scrubs, and then she showed him how to fertilize an egg. She also made it fun by pulling a lighthearted prank, asking Soules to give her a specimen and demanding that he "collect it" in the other room, before revealing that it was a joke and making out with him instead. She topped the date off with an LL4 raise, complete with tear play during the MOTF portion, which helped solidify her later Ring Winner position.

The only future Crown so far to use the TYBTW Date was Minnesotan schoolteacher Michelle Young (Season 25—Matt James). While Young's season filmed in a COVID-19 production bubble in Farmington, Pennsylvania, she made do by re-creating her classroom via a giant Zoom screen in an auditorium facing her and James. She conscripted an entire classroom of her students who had clearly been well trained to join them, complete with matching "Team Miss Young" T-shirts. It was a play for the Crown and it worked. It was very endearing and made her seem extremely 4TRR, like a true professional and not an influencer.

Young revolutionized the future-casting game. She was able to fully script this entire interaction, including asking James questions via the children about their relationship and their future. She was able to mute the children as well as have them convey things via hand gestures. Her date choice was also extremely topical, as parents across the country were trapped at home, trying to adjust to distanced learning during the pandemic. Young capitalized on the cultural moment, during which people arguably had never appreciated teachers more, and tapped into that sentiment flawlessly. She even had one student read a letter that Young had written to her for encouragement. It was future-casting at its best, implying to James that this was the type of conscientious, capable, and loving mother Young would eventually be, and at the same time she melted the hearts of Bachelor Nation, who demanded she get her own *Bachelorette* season when Producers gave her a Heartbreak Edit. She also paired this iconic Hometown Date with an iconic parasocial play by posting a perfectly parallel IG post the week this date aired: a photo collage of her students wearing the "Team Miss Young" T-shirts, with her in the center. This combination play utilized every element of a TYBTW Date to its fullest and garnered her a historical first: Producers added a second season of *The Bachelorette* that year onto the production schedule to accommodate this phenomenal player and the demands of the Nation.

Aquatic Activity (6)

Open waters are a dangerous place for players who seek the Crown, as no player has ever won it after choosing this Hometown Date type. However, three Ring Winners have brought their Bachelor into the deep blue sea (or midsized lake) for activities. Whether it's fishing, surfing, or even inner tubing, the benefits of a water activity date include combining fun with a picturesque and interesting location. Producers have choreographed many underwater kiss shots during such dates as well.

One of the most successful players to utilize the Aquatic Activity was Ring Winner Vienna Girardi (Season 14—Jake Pavelka). She brought Pavelka on a swamp tour in her hometown of Sanford, Florida, combining an Aquatic Activity with both a Local Tradition and Animal Husbandry (feeding gators). It was an interesting environment with a hint of danger and it assured pilot Pavelka that they shared a sense of adventure.

Animal Husbandry (6)

While pairs of lovers riding horses have dominated the covers of romance novels for many years, picking an interaction with creatures for your day portion date is risky. Horses may film beautifully on television, but the reality of riding horses is less romantic. You can't be that physically close to the Bachelor, so you cannot play a PTC or load walls as easily, and associated smells can kill the vibe. We do not recommend incorporating beasts of burden into your day portion, but if you must, choose activities with creatures that do not interfere much, like feeding ducks or alligators.

While only one Ring Winner and one Crown chose an Animal Husbandry Date, you can succeed if you have skill. Clare Crawley (Season 18—Juan Pablo Galavis) was one such skilled player. She took Galavis to a park in her hometown of Sacramento, California, and they fed ducks, which she combined with a powerful story about her late father. She told Galavis that she and her father used to come to this park and perform this same custom. She merged Animal

Husbandry with an Ancestor's Blessing type–date as they skipped rocks in honor of her father, a ritual to invoke a spiritual implied Blessing from a family member that had passed.

Prank (4)

Only four players have selected incorporating a prank into their Hometown Dates, but they were by far some of the most memorable. Many Bachelor Nation fans remember when future Crown Desiree Hartsock (Season 17—Sean Lowe) pranked Lowe with a fake Skeleton by hiring an actor to play a jealous ex-boyfriend who stormed into her Mi Casa trying to win her back. This worked on Lowe, who appreciated her paying him back for a prank he pulled on her earlier that season on an art gallery 1O1 Date.

However, few probably remember the pioneer of this Hometown Date strategy, Amanda Rantuccio (Season 12—Matt Grant), who brought Grant to her familial home in Tallahassee, Florida, and introduced him to her parents. She then left Grant to chat outside with her mother, who instantly started coming on to and fondling the British Bachelor. Rantuccio then revealed to Grant that she had hired actors to play her parents and quickly brought in the real parents, who did not make any subsequent passes at Grant. While you lose the opportunity for a genuine emotional moment with a prank and perhaps a little trust from the Bachelor, they do convey a lighthearted, adventurous spirit and make for excellent television, thrilling the Third and Fourth Audiences alike.

Common Hometown Date Elements

Just as with Group Dates and 1O1 Dates, Hometown Dates feature an assortment of elements added to the primary activity. Players and Producers commonly include date elements of dogs, parks, and religious invocations. However, one date element is the most utilized and most often hosts the MOTF portion: the familial home.

Familial Home (74)

By far the most common Hometown Date element is the familial home. Players have chosen to locate most MOTF portions here, although occasionally they pick a hotel, restaurant, or public park. Many times Producers portray a setting as the familial home, but they've actually rented and dressed a home to convey the feeling and vibe of the familial home, most likely due to size and production limitations. Familial home portions often begin with hugs, the Bachelor giving flowers to the player's female relatives, and introductions. Frequently a family dinner follows this, but families have incorporated all types of traditions into activities inside their home, including dances, prayers, and even silly hat TOTs.

Park (18)

The grass is green, the birds are chirping, and you're upping your Love Levels and loading familial walls! A park is one of the most common elements of a *Bachelor* Hometown Date. It's easy to film in, looks good on-camera, and hosts a variety of activities. A park's wide-open expanses also offer one of the best opportunities to perform a Hometown Huju. Five Crowns and four Ring Winners have chosen parks to host their Hometown Dates.

Dog (17)

Dogs may be man's best friend, but they are not the best friend of a potential Crown. Interestingly, we found that no player who has eventually worn the Crown ever had a dog on her Hometown Date. These loyal creatures don't necessarily spell doom, however, because seven Ring Winners have included a canine influence during their Hometowns.

Christian Invocation (14)

While *The Bachelor* is not an outwardly religious show, various players have uttered religious invocations on fourteen of the ninety-nine Hometown Dates, all of which were Christian. This includes three Ring Winners and four Crowns. Only one player chose a day portion where Christianity was the main event for their Hometown Date, however. This was Rachel Lindsay (Season 21—Nick Viall). She brought Viall to her predominantly Black megachurch in Dallas, Texas, where the two took part in a religious service, including performing some audience participation. Viall summarized the experience with the pithy quote "Amen is amen," to demonstrate that while it was not the religious practice he was used to, he could relate to the experience and enjoyed it. Although she was sent home after Fantasy Suites, Lindsay went on to become the first Black player in history to wear the Crown and one of the most successful players in the postgame whom the game has ever seen. Was this a part of God's plan? We will never know.

Split Home (12)

Does it matter if your family doesn't look like a traditional family portrait, as your parents are divorced? Not really. Two Ring Winners and two Crowns have brought Bachelors to meet a family with a Split Home out of twelve players total. Kaitlyn Bristowe (Season 19—Chris Soules) proved you don't need a conventional family by hosting both sets of parents at the same dinner table.

Kids (8)

At first glance, you might think that incorporating children on a Hometown Date would scare off the Bachelor, going a little too hard and on the nose with the future-casting. However, we've learned that you can never go too hard on future-casting! Four Ring Winners and one Crown have featured children present on their Hometown Date.

Kindergarten teacher Sarah Stone (Season 8—Travis Stork) choreographed a transcendent day portion Hometown date in Nashville, Tennessee. First she brought Stork to her apartment and then to the park, where she and Stork mused about where they would live and how they would raise their children. After setting those conversations up, she pulled off a surprise early MOTF when her sisters appeared at the park and brought some plus ones in tow, an army of children. Stone exhibited her incredible teaching chops by leading the kids through a series of games, in which they obeyed her every command. This demonstration of emotional and authoritative skill impressed Stork and he eventually rewarded her with the Ring.

Family Business (6)

Perhaps it is the implication of 4TWR for a player incorporating their family business into their Hometown Date, but no player who chose a family business type ever won the Ring or Crown. Focusing your date on how your family makes money and your possible future role in that endeavor can be entertaining, but is this free press worth the cost?

Overbearing Siblings (5)

Players whose siblings have blatantly overstepped boundaries have won two Rings and three Crowns! These stunning statistics show why you should heavily consider the Overbearing Siblings route. While you may think that incredibly abrasive familial walls would of course interfere with a good First Audience game, the perceived inability of your power to control this unfolding disaster actually garners a ton of sympathy from the Fourth Audience, who feel that you've been victimized and should therefore get more screen time, in the form of a Crown. Both Desiree Hartsock (Season 17—Sean Lowe) and JoJo Fletcher (Season 20—Ben Higgins) utilized Overbearing Siblings in the brotherly form to perfection. Hartsock's brother accused Born-Again Virgin Sean Lowe of being a "playboy" and Fletcher's brothers grilled Ben Higgins, charging him with being less emotionally invested than Fletcher, which caused Fletcher to erupt in 4TRR tear play. Both Hartsock and Fletcher went on to wear the Crown, have successful IG careers, and are still with their respective Ring Winners today. Whether real or contrived, that over-the-top familial tension seems worth it to us!

Family Strategies/the MOTF

The Bachelor takes the backseat to players in terms of strategy for most of the season, but in the Hometown round of the play-offs he has to dust off his playing shoes and take the field once again. The Bachelor attempts to secure two main prizes from the family during the MOTF, the Glow and the Blessing. Bachelors often encounter familial walls in the pursuit of these two goals, but you can help the Bachelor achieve both of these goals in an emotionally fulfilling process, bringing him closer to you as he achieves them. And neither of the goals should be too difficult for the Bachelor to overcome, as you should loosely script this entire interaction with your family beforehand.

The Glow

"You're glowing!" These magical words of joyous affirmation have fallen from many family members' lips during the MOTF portion of Hometown Dates. The Glow requires a family member to tell the player or the Bachelor that they are emitting some physical sign showing their love, e.g., "I can tell you're really in love!" or "You have a sparkle in your eye!" The Glow lets the player and Bachelor Nation know that this family member certifies that you're happy and probably in love. Your love reflects out of your body externally, producing a 4TRR physical transformation. A magical field of energy, a visible aura . . . a Glow. A family member issuing this play signifies that the emotional metamorphosis is rare for you and therefore shocking! You don't just Glow for anybody, so your connection with the Bachelor must be special. Any family member or friend can issue a Glow.

The aunt of Brooke Smith (Season 2—Aaron Buerge) issued the first Glow in history in Albertville, Alabama. She announced that Smith now had the "Glow" after developing a relationship with Buerge. Since then, family members have bestowed Glows upon twenty-eight players. A player who receives a Glow places on average 2.54th and Glows have produced three Rings and nine Crowns. The strong Heartbreak Victimization Edits that follow Glows that don't lead to Ring wins are part of this phenomenon.

While you should set up your family to Glow beforehand, one of the best ways to extract a Glow from a family member is by using touch play. You and the Bachelor touch each other over the course of the date to let your family know you have chemistry and are crazy about each other. Other Glow activators include excessive smiling, maintaining close physical proximity, effusive compliments, and sometimes even tear play.

The Blessing

A suitor asking a father for his daughter's hand in marriage is a hallmark of a somewhat bygone patriarchal era in which fathers sold their daughters, but it is shockingly still a mainstay in our beloved game. Colton Underwood (Season 23) even asked multiple fathers for "permission" to marry their daughters, an interesting choice of phrasing. And while generally the father gives the Bachelor the Blessing, another family member can dole it out if that is not an option. In this game, families traditionally reward the Blessing during this first round of Hometowns, although on occasion they have given it out during the Finale. In Season 20 Ben Higgins called Lauren Bushnell's father via Facetime right before proposing in the Finale. Higgins shouted into the phone, "I love your daughter! . . . I would like to ask for your daughter's hand in marriage." He received the remote Blessing instantaneously.

Surprisingly, this integral component of the Hometown round of the playoffs didn't occur for the first time until Season 9, when Lorenzo Borghese became the first Bachelor in history to secure dual blessings from Sadie Murray's and Jennifer Wilson's fathers in the Finale. Jake Pavelka landed the first Hometown Date Blessing during Season 14. He received Ali Fedotowsky's mother's Blessing during their MOTF after she effusively Glowed Fedotowsky and Pavelka told Fedotowsky's mother that family was one of his top priorities.

Since Season 14, Bachelors have attempted to get Blessings in every single season, except for Peter Weber (Season 24), who made no Blessing endeavors, at least none that Producers chose to include in the document. Chris Soules (Season 19) solicited a singular Blessing from Whitney Bischoff's sister and failed, joining Weber as the only two Bachelors to receive zero Blessings since Season 14.

While many family members have turned down this somewhat bizarre request, Bachelors have made twenty-four total successful attempts. Nick Viall (Season 21), Arie Luyendyk Jr. (Season 22), and Colton Underwood (Season 23) all tied for most secured Blessings—three apiece. Both Luyendyk and Underwood took their best shot at the elusive four-Blessing record but were denied, and no Bachelor has cracked it yet.

Use your own family to set up a Good Cop/Bad Cop situation during the mandatory dinner conversation that will ultimately strengthen your bond with the Bachelor. This helps your family maintain familial walls early on, without the whole experience feeling hostile for the Bachelor. Sure, Dad is glaring while cleaning his gun, but Mom has engaged the Bachelor in a traditional family dance while wearing a fun hat! By the end of the evening, instruct your selected Bad Cop family member to let down their walls, ideally shed some 4TRR tears, and ultimately deliver the Bachelor the Familial Blessing. Psychologically, this structure makes the Bachelor feel like he has overcome a giant obstacle in order to find love with you, which will make you seem like more of a prize. Producers also crave this sequence narratively.

Colorful Family

Navigating the MOTF can be especially tricky because during this round the three pertinent audiences all demand different things. The First Audience, the Bachelor, wants this portion to go as smoothly as possible so he can fit in with your family, collect his Glows and Blessings, and get through the whole thing in a frankly boring manner. The Third Audience covets a dramatic story arc, making the Bachelor conquer familial walls, and they want an explosive wild card to bring the drama for at least one of the four families. As the Fourth Audience we enjoy the drama, too, but we also demand a Colorful Family. We fall for families blurting out awkward remarks and performing weird traditions. We prefer to make players with the most interesting families the future Crowns so we get to see that family return to play again in a future season of *The Bachelorette*.

So your family should treat this as their time to shine for Producers to prove they can handle the spotlight. Coach them to convey added value to the Producers and that they would be entertaining on a subsequent season. While this is still your game, this is the one round that gives you the opportunity to launch the parasocial careers of other members of your life as well, such as an overly involved mother (Barbara Weber, Peter Weber's mother) or even an IG influencer sister (Michelle Randolph, Cassie Randolph's sister—Season 20). Both family members incurred massive IG gains as a result of their appearances on Hometowns.

Familial Walls (the Five Attacks)

For the family member you've chosen to play the Bad Cop role, teach them the Five Attacks. These are conversational tactics designed to knock the Bachelor off guard and set up familial walls that he will have to overcome. The Five Attacks are:

1. Time
2. Location
3. Other Women
4. Heartbreak
5. Values

Time: Your family demands to know how the Bachelor can possibly be ready to propose to their daughter, sibling, roommate, et cetera, given the short timeline of the shooting schedule.

Location: Your family expresses concern about the Bachelor possibly taking you away from them to another, faraway city. Shawntel Newton's family did this expertly in Season 15 by guilting Brad Womack about taking Newton away from the family funeral business in Chico, California, in order to help manage bars with him in Texas. Womack eliminated her after this round.

Other Women: Your family can attack the Bachelor by bringing up the remaining women. How can he propose when he is going to sleep with multiple other players? How emotionally involved is he with these other women? This is one of the most commonly used attacks.

Heartbreak: Your Bad Cop can also besiege the Bachelor by requesting that he not break your heart. They may even bring up or re-hit a Heartbreak PTC—that you were hurt before and they never want to see that happen to you again. If you can train your family in the arena of tear play, it will aid this 4TRR attack greatly.

Values: And lastly, your family can assail the Bachelor by questioning his values. Is he ready for marriage? Is he too young to settle down? Does he share or at least value your religious conviction? How will you handle being a mixed-race couple? All of these different lines of questioning are fantastic for the familial walls portion, as long as they ultimately come down by the end of the segment. The Bachelor will feel like he's run through a gauntlet by the time the Hometown is over, so when he finally receives the Blessing it will feel like a prize hard won. There is one situation, however, in which you will want to keep the familial walls left standing.

"The Addams Family," AKA Familial BOG (Blaze Of Glory)

If you decide you want to eject during this round for any reason, such as avoiding the Fantasy Suite, or maybe the timing feels right for the *Bachelorette* audition you've crafted, consider the "Addams Family" Blaze Of Glory strategy during the MOTF portion of Hometown Dates. The Addams Family takes its name from the classic TV show of the same title about a family of monsters who were too strange to exist in normal society. This bombastic game plan simultaneously saves you from having to contend with the rest of the play-offs, while also giving you high odds of becoming the next Bachelorette. The Overbearing Siblings date type falls under this category. You need to express to your family that you want to choose this route. However, because Production completely monitors communication, devise a plan with your family before going on the show, preparing them with a code word you'll utter to initiate this strategy on the fly even as cameras are rolling to seemingly "blow up" your own game.

After you utter your code word, your family should all start acting wildly when you bring the Bachelor to meet them. The Weirdo behavior can manifest in many different varieties—from the extremes of theo-political zealotry, to making the Bachelor endure a bizarre animal funeral (Naomi Crespo—Season 13), to the more subtle overly protective brother techniques and everything in between. The Bachelor is always, every second of every date, looking for his socially acceptable out. So if you present one he will take it every time.

When he walks outside and your father is nude in the pool, it will give the Bachelor pause when he thinks about attending summer barbecues. And Bachelor Nation can all accept that. The Bachelor will utter something along the lines of, "I'm so sorry, I think you're a really wonderful woman, and you have so much to offer, but family is very important to me and I just don't think I'd fit in with yours." Your family can play multiple roles to leave the Bachelor with no choice but to end his relationship with you and potentially give you a redemptive arc as Crown when it seems like your family caused you to lose the Ring and your one chance at true love.

Finish the Addams Family by feigning true emotional devastation in your Limo Exit. You saw the rest of your life with him. You're still very much in love with him. You're crushed by the family members responsible for turning the Bachelor away. This reaction generates sympathy in the viewer for the pain you've suffered and a sense that the Producers owe you another chance. Because, through no fault of your own, the Bachelor eliminated you from the game.

PreCog

An important element of future-casting is the PreCog, which takes its name from the three psychics in the film *Minority Report* who could predict future crimes. In our beloved game, a PreCog describes a play in which you tell the Bachelor that you will accept a theoretical proposal. Load a PreCog by telling other players or your family members that you would accept a proposal if the Bachelor were to offer one. It's very important to time the PreCog well. Too soon, and it comes off 4TWR. Too late, and the Bachelor won't want to risk being rejected at the RC altar. Traditionally, players begin PreCogging in the Hometown round and they escalate through the other rounds of playoffs.

The Fond Farewell (Autozone Love Levels)

By Hometowns you should have raised your Love Level to LL3 or maybe even LL4. While some players choose to save LL4 for Fantasy Suites, only do this if you're certain you will survive another week. In that case raise to LL3 or stay at LL3. But don't be shy about raising to LL4 during Hometowns. Bachelors sometimes use not LL4ing as an out, so you never want to leave your LL4 on the table. Your justification comes off naturally in this setting, after you saw how the Bachelor got along with your family. For maximum power and impact, perform this LL raise either sitting down on a bench outside the familial home or standing up in the "Autozone."

The Autozone is the space between your familial home and the car that will take you away from each other. It is where you make your last impression on the Bachelor this round. Do everything possible to make this moment the crescendo of the entire Hometown Date. Begin by summarizing the MOTF portion, concluding that it went well and your family loved the Bachelor. After all, he got their Blessing. Then up your Love Level. And finally seal the MOTF portion with a kiss. A few players have implemented experimental Autozone strategies, such as a weather-dependent snowball fight, to create a cherry-on-top "spur-of-the-moment" fun romantic occasion. Make sure the Bachelor drives away from this date thinking that he's driving away from his future mother- and father-in-law's, or that he's going to have to issue a crushing but justifiable breakup, leaving you with a solid Heartbreak Edit.

Your strategies in this round vary depending on your goals, from seemingly setting your game on fire in coordination with your "wild-card" family for the potential Crown or weaving a perfectly 4TRR game for the Ring. If you're able to construct a fantastic Hometown Day Date, a powerful MOTF portion, and ultimately survive the first Rose Ceremony of play-offs, you will graduate to the second and final round of play-offs, Fantasy Suites.

Chapter 8

PLAY-OFFS ROUND 2:

FANTASY SUITES

Wait, so Madison saying that Peter's actions with me and Victoria will determine if she can move forward with him or not . . . I was thrown off by that. We knew what we signed up for.

Hannah Ann Sluss, Ring Winner, Season 24,
during the Fantasy Suite round

Before the Hyperbinge, the Fantasy Suite episodes were our favorite round of the game, bar none. We loved the extravagant day activities, the exotic locations, the candlelit dinners, the reveal of the card, usually tucked under a plate of cold chicken, the golden key, and the eventual entry into the Fantasy Suite itself by hopeful players and hopeful Bachelors alike. But after the Hyperbinge, the Fantasy Suite round took on an entirely new meaning for us. To simply say that it was our favorite week in the game was a gross degradation of how much it had come to mean.

"Should you choose to forgo your individual rooms, please use this key to stay as a couple in the Fantasy Suite," repeating over and over again, seventy-five times on 2X speed, changed us. This invocation became a mantra that represented so much more than just an invitation to a night alone with the Bachelor away from Producers and cameras to ask the tough questions that aren't permitted on network television—what religion are you? Would you relocate to my city? Is there any photographic evidence online depicting you celebrating the Old South?

That twenty-three-word poem written into every Fantasy Suite Card since the dawn of the game held within it all of the hopes and dreams of every player who ever had the honor of reciting it. It represented a moment they had worked for all season, a moment they had planned for, a moment that allowed them a game-sanctioned chance to initiate the final glorious level of a chemistry strategy they had been building since Night One.

We took the quote that opened this chapter from a moment in Season 24 when Producers forced the greatest Night One player of all time, Hannah Ann Sluss, to recline on a bed with superstar Good Girl Madison Prewett to discuss Prewett's aversion to the very concept of the Fantasy Suite—that the game holds at least the very real possibility, if not an outright expectation, for each of three remaining players to engage in intimate congress with the Bachelor, one after the other. The underlying logic of Sluss's comment implied an expectation of all contemporary players having now seen enough seasons throughout childhood and adolescence to understand what each round expects of them. Furthermore, any attempt to avoid or denounce these expectations is unacceptable.

The shock generated by the very premise of the Fantasy Suite round might have been valid in bygone eras, but not now. After almost twenty years it is not only an accepted part of the game but also one that should not, *cannot*, be disrespected. Sluss would even go on to describe Prewett's inability to embrace this fact as "madness." This crucial moment gave birth to what we called the Slussian Protocol—the open acceptance of all the uncomfortable circumstances this process creates, including Fantasy Suites as a mandatory part of the game.

But this wasn't always the case.

The History of Fantasy

While attitudes about the Fantasy Suite round have certainly changed over the years from adamant skepticism to blind acceptance, this final round of play-offs has proven to be one of the most constant elements of the game, undergoing only slight practical modifications since its inception.

For example, Producers called the Fantasy Suites of Season 1 "Exotic Overnight Dates" and they did not set them all at the same international resort, as is the norm in modern seasons. Instead, Producers granted each player the privilege of a separate American city to serve as the setting for the best chemistry play she could muster. This hallmark of the Classic Era also forced Production to budget an extra day between the Bachelor's encounters for travel time. The "twenty-four-hour-sleep-and-shower" buffer that current Bachelors must contend with was actually closer to a forty-eight- or in some cases even a seventy-two-hour period of rest and reset.

The first player to ever experience the Fantasy Suite was Season 1 Ring Winner Amanda Marsh. Although the idea of engaging in intimate activity on national television was certainly shocking in 2002, Marsh's sex-positive outlook allowed her to march boldly into history by not only accepting the offer to forgo their separate rooms in favor of the Fantasy Suite but also ordering an item from the room service menu called "Sex in the Sheets." This in-room aphrodisiac included ice cream, chocolate sauce, rubber sheets, and the implication that they were all meant to be used together in a messy food-as-foreplay start to the evening's activities. Marsh and Michel set the Fantasy Suite tone for all time by covering each other in the sweet sauces and creams and taking Polaroids of the event, which Producers featured in the televised episode, adding an unexpected homemade-porn vibe that very clearly conveyed the idea that Fantasy Suites certainly included sex.

But the very next player to be offered the Fantasy Suite that season had, shall we say, a slightly different reaction. Shannon Oliver's Fantasy Suite Date started with a round of skiing at Lake Tahoe. The snowy ground served as a metaphor for Oliver's disposition where televised sexual congress was concerned. That afternoon when Michel leaned in for a kiss, Oliver recoiled from the Bachelor, saying, "Some of the things you want to do . . . just not gonna happen." Later at dinner when Michel produced the card, Oliver half joked that she expected him to have pulled out the wrong one, perhaps meant for one of the other two players. When finally she acquiesced to the idea, she did nothing more than walk into the Fantasy Suite for a few brief moments without any lights turning off or any doors closing. Her impeccable Good Girl strategy would echo through time to its most recent incarnation with Madison Prewett's Good Girl ultimatum in Season 24 that left Peter Weber reeling.

The third Fantasy Suite of Season 1 belonged to the eventual first Bachelorette, Trista Rehn, and Producers chose the island paradise of Hawaii. As the couple flew over the lush greenery of the islands on a romantic helicopter ride, Alex Michel began violently vomiting into an airsickness bag, destroying any chance to generate chemistry play for Rehn. But she powered through enough to care for him in his sickbed later that evening. Producers rewarded her with a dinner the next day at which she very openly divulged to Michel that she had never achieved orgasm through intercourse. This was a bold statement in 2002 and remains so to this day, having laid the foundation for several PVC (Personal Virginity Card) strategies through the years.

This format of the Bachelor propositioning three players to spend the night with him one after the other via greeting card during dinner would remain in place from this moment forward. The locations would continue to feature a variety of climates from topical to frigid, all over the globe, allowing for an equally wide variety of activities from snow skiing and ice skating to helicopter rides and tropical snorkeling.

It wouldn't be until Season 5 that the first anomaly to this pattern appeared in the form of a particularly fiendish machination Producers brought to life. As then-Bachelor Jesse Palmer enjoyed dinner with Mandy Jaye Jeffreys, a female silhouette appeared behind a glass door leading into their dining room. The door opened and revealed none other than Trish Schneider, Season 5's most notorious Villain, whom Palmer had eliminated in the Hometown round of the play-offs the prior week. Schneider was the first player to ever perform a Resurrection. Back from the dead, she marched in, interrupted the dinner, and performed a successful Steal to pull Palmer away into a nearby kitchen, where she slipped him her room key. Palmer was smart enough not to take the bait and Production filmed Schneider spending the night alone in her hotel room, waiting in vain, while Jeffreys accepted Palmer's Fantasy Suite offer. Schneider's interloper strategy failed, but more important, this was the first moment the Producers gave us an indication that this round of play-offs was not off-limits for their devious experimentation.

Two short seasons later the Producers again attempted to sabotage the Fantasy Suite round with a new twist on the format by selecting a single location for all three dates. They forced Sarah Brice, Sarah Welch, and Krisily Kennedy for the first time to stay at the same resort in Aruba and wait their turn with Bachelor Charlie O'Connell. What's more, they made Welch and Brice "accidentally" run into each other at the resort on one of their off days so they could engage in a "Girl Chat" about Krisily. This moment laid the groundwork for what we see in all recent seasons with regard to Producers forcing players to live together and interact with one another during this sensitive round of play.

This move to international resorts took players who made it to the Fantasy Suite round of subsequent seasons all over the world to places like Cabo San Lucas, Barbados, New Zealand, St. Lucia, South Africa, Switzerland, and Thailand just to name a few. And in Season 15 the Producers decided to move away from the functional hotel room key that came with the FS Card and replace it with a ceremonial golden key, more fitting for a Harry Potter movie than any hotel room door on planet Earth in the twenty-first century. This superficial change elevated the ritualistic reading of the FS Card to something more magical and less mired by the hard reality of the situation—that one man was having sex with three women he had spent a handful of hours with, one after the other, and advertisers were selling us toothpaste and trucks while we watched.

Season 18 marked the first Fantasy Suite disaster when Andi Dorfman revealed in her ITM the morning after that she could not wait to escape the Fantasy Suite after Juan Pablo Galavis had shown his true colors in the absence of the crew. She used her claims that he was a different person in the Fantasy Suite than she had seen so far to warrant a face-to-face reprimand and subsequent self-elimination before the Rose Ceremony that afternoon. Dorfman expertly wove her outrage into a victimization play that garnered her the Crown in the following season of *The Bachelorette*.

Season 23 brought the first-ever mid–Fantasy Suites breakup. The season before, Producers had tested the limits of how overtly they could attempt to destroy a relationship. They facilitated Becca Kufrin's ex-boyfriend flying to Peru to confront her the day after she consummated her relationship with Arie Luyendyk Jr. in a cramped tent in the middle of the Peruvian desert. In Season 23 they flew Cassie Randolph's father to Portugal to meet her in the middle of her Fantasy Suite Date with Colton Underwood. As she was changing to get ready to attend dinner with Underwood that night, Randolph's father entered her hotel room and sowed seeds of doubt in her mind that led her to break up with Underwood before he could even produce the FS Card. The resulting fallout included one of the most notorious moments in the history of the game when Underwood jumped a fence in an attempt to flee from his tormenters. The following day, Underwood broke up with Tayshia Adams, whom he'd already spent the night with, and Hannah Godwin, who did not get the opportunity for her FS Date that season. Underwood later convinced Randolph to give their relationship a shot and the Producers ultimately granted the couple a full Fantasy Suite–style date outside the context of the normal round of play.

Then in Season 24 Producers upped the ante yet again when they forced the three remaining players to live not only at the same resort but in the same suite and in some cases to have conversations with one another six inches apart, while lying on the same bed. With the shooting of Season 25 in a bubble entirely in the Nemacolin resort, it is difficult to know what structural changes might be in store for the Fantasy Suite round in seasons to come, but one thing is certain—that it will remain a favorite week of the Fourth Audience for all time.

Every Fantasy Suite round except two has had three players. Season 6 had four Fantasy Suite Dates and only Season 23 had two Fantasy Suite Dates. In Season 6 the tables were turned and it was the players who had to present Bachelor Byron Velvick with an FS Card at dinner. Cheresse (last name lost to time) declined to give Velvick the card, citing the fact that in the real world it would have only been their third or fourth date. Velvick sent her home that week. And Season 7 was the only one that saw the Bachelor, Charlie O'Connell, refuse to use the card-and-key technique in favor of simply inviting players back to his room.

Fantasy Suite Structure and Strategy

The Fantasy Suite Date is constructed from three distinct portions, each with its own setting, activities, and strategies. The first portion you will encounter is . . .

The Day Portion

This first leg of the date is extremely similar to any 1O1 that might take place during the regular season, because they choose the activities from the same pool. Helicopter rides, yacht excursions, spa days, zip-lining, and When In Rome–style strolls through local thoroughfares are all common daytime fantasy endeavors. The only mainstay 1O1 Date type they never use in this round of play-offs is the *Pretty Woman* Date. This late in the season, Producers have no more players left to make jealous with you returning from a *Pretty Woman* with arms full of expensive prizes. So they have no use for it.

No matter what the activity, they usually design the day portion to allow you the opportunity to showcase your sincerity and to build some necessary momentum for your chemistry game after not having seen the Bachelor for a week or more. But be wary, because on occasion the Producers will attempt to slip in an uncooperative horse or donkey on an Animal Husbandry–style date for the purposes of giving you a last-minute Fool Edit. If this is the case, play an IFI or outright refuse to partake in any sort of silly costume or interaction with an animal. Because above all, you must convey seriousness in the penultimate round of the season.

Whatever the type of date might be, when the sun is up there are two main goals:

1. Increasing chemistry play
2. Erecting a false emotional obstacle

At this point ideally you have escalated your chemistry game every time you're with the Bachelor in a situation by yourself. This includes all 101 Dates, 101 time at After Parties and Cocktail Parties, any IFI alone time, and even stolen moments in the middle of Group Dates. Constant touching and ending every encounter with a kiss are surefire ways to increase the effects of strong chemistry play during the regular season. But once it gets to the Fantasy Suite round, you have one last, all-or-nothing twenty-four-hour period to turn your chemistry game up to the highest level of the season. Whether at a Picnic or holding hands walking through a quaint Italian villa, remain engaged in virtually constant physical contact with the Bachelor in order to reassure him that all signs are pointing to the Fantasy Suite of his dreams with no drama at all. Just a fun time between two consenting adults.

Make this physical connection immediately with an aggressive and enthusiastic Huju at first encounter that culminates in a flurry of kisses during the cling, leading to a dismount that transitions flawlessly into a double hand hold, all while maintaining eye contact. A well-executed Huju lets the Bachelor know you're enthusiastic about not just seeing him again but the Fantasy Suite round and all it implies as well. You want the Bachelor to feel like you're both on the same page as far as how the day and evening that follows shall transpire.

Keep the day free of any emotional labor or concern. Laugh, demonstrate physical affection, and proclaim how incredible and unbelievable it is that you met someone like the Bachelor. Perform some future-casting about potential other adventures you could enjoy together. He will move through initial relief that you still have feelings for him to excitement for the night to come. Then when his guard is completely down, when he can't fathom the rest of the date not being equally perfect, just before the Producers separate you and the Bachelor for ITMs and to get ready for dinner, initiate your false emotional obstacle. Become increasingly visibly concerned about an unknown emotional discomfort, followed by quickly withdrawing physical touch to introduce the final magic ingredient to a strong day portion—the threat of loss.

With his mind spinning from the joy and certainty he felt during the entire date, he will be blindsided by the quick turning of the tables and the jeopardizing of all of his hopes and dreams of smooth sailing straight to the Fantasy Suite. He may even ask you, "What's wrong?" And you say something like, "It's just this situation. It's a lot and it's starting to get to me," and then punctuate it with well-timed tears just before the Producers whisk you away. In one move you will have planted the seed of doubt in the Bachelor's mind and you will have erected a wall, giving him an obstacle to overcome in . . .

The Night Portion

Candles flicker across the room. The camera crew lurks in the shadows. Food taunts you on the table, but you can't eat it. Although we always recommend giving the toast to guarantee screen time, the Fantasy Suite is one instance in which we recommend you let the Bachelor give the toast if you're following the strategy outlined in these pages. Even a slightly overly enthusiastic or celebratory toast can reduce the effectiveness of the emotional wall you erected in the day portion. It's much better to let the Bachelor use his own toast as a tentative litmus test to gauge your mood. After he gives his toast, join in graciously with a nod and pursed lips. Do not give him a smile. Do not give him any information about the tone or mood of what the rest of the night holds.

After some brief generalities about the beauty of the location just sit there, silent. This forces the Bachelor to initiate the conversation. He might say, "I can tell something's been bothering you since today. What is it?" Then you deliver the most important performance of the night, perhaps the entire season.

Sheepishly smile and take his hands in yours and recite the following speech with alterations to suit any archetype or dialect as you see fit:

I'm sorry about today. Everything just got very serious for me. I haven't really been jealous or even thought about the other women until today. When we were [insert activity] I looked over at you and I was having a great day and then I started thinking about you with someone else and it hurt so bad that I knew . . . It's so crazy to be saying this, but [Bachelor's first name], I'm falling in love with you.

This speech is designed to erase the Bachelor's insecurities and negative emotions while replacing them with not just happiness but also relief—a far more powerful emotional influencer than happiness alone. And of course finish it off with a final raising of a Love Level. If you've played correctly through the season and encountered no emergency circumstances that require a preemptive LL raise, you should be at LL3— "I'm falling in love with you."

The Bachelor will feel an overwhelming sense of accomplishment and progress in this moment. You'll have successfully avoided remaining static in your love story, a common error for players at this phase in the game. Even in the condensed timeline of dating within the game, complacency can be the death of an otherwise successful courtship.

End the moment with a kiss, which will prompt the Bachelor to remove the FS Card from his jacket pocket and hand it to you. Read the twenty-three sacred words with enthusiasm and accept the offer to share the Fantasy Suite. Make a joke about leaving dinner to get there as soon as possible, either verbally (e.g.: "Check please!"), by chugging your drink, or by excitedly pulling the Bachelor from his chair.

Behind Closed Doors

The final portion of the Fantasy Suite Date takes place in the suite itself. The camera crew will follow you in to get some traditional fast shots of you exploring the view, checking out the rose petal–covered bed, popping some champagne, and of course taking a dip in the hot tub. Then the Producers exit with the camera operators, the doors close behind you, and for the first time all season you're completely alone with the Bachelor and nothing but your First Audience game.

The power of privacy in this moment is absolute. Not only will Production not air footage of anything that happens in the Fantasy Suite (although you should assume they're still recording everything), but also an unspoken

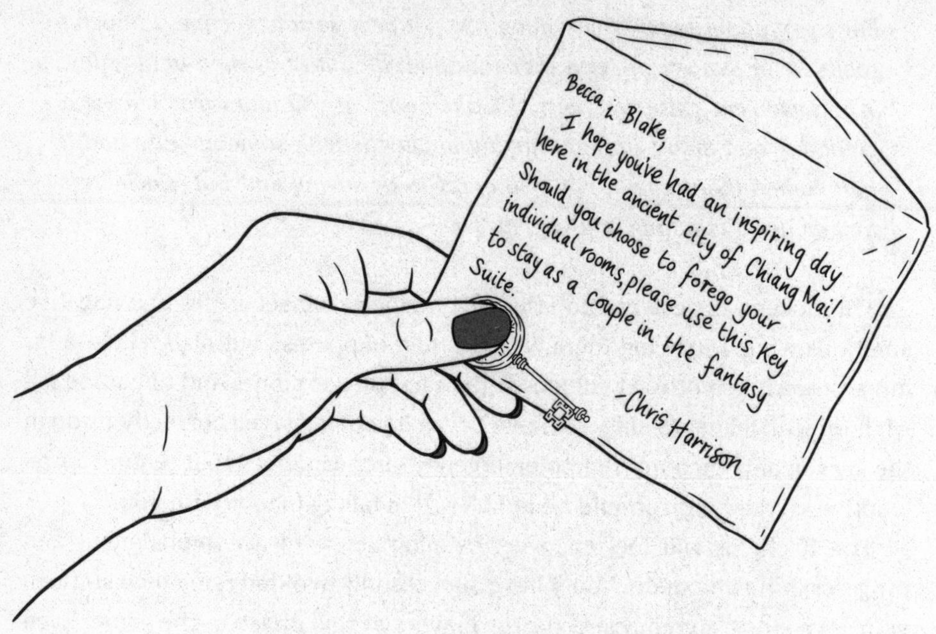

code of conduct guarantees the Bachelor will never reveal unflattering details about anything that transpires. So whatever your strategy might be, rest assured no one will ever know what happened in the Fantasy Suite outside the Bachelor, NDA-contracted production staff, and you.

The question every player must answer in the Fantasy Suite is whether to consummate the relationship or not. Successful players have traveled both paths. Catherine Giudici, the only Ring Winner to ever marry the Bachelor, chose not to consummate on her night with Bachelor Sean Lowe. And Hannah Brown, the IG champion for the entirety of Bachelor Nation, famously had sex four times with Peter Weber in a windmill, and Jesus, as she put it, "still loves [her.]"

A non-consummation strategy involves a full night of cuddling and prone embracing as well as hours upon hours of conversation about things that you might not have brought up in front of the cameras. Prepare for all lines of questioning, including religion, number of future children, and where you might live as a couple. Ironically, if you engage in a non-consummation strategy you'll have to utilize your chemistry game at the highest level. You have to convey that although you will not be having sex in the Fantasy Suite, you still want to very badly. And if you decide to fully indulge in all the Fantasy Suite has to offer, then you've got one more decision to make—Ring or Crown.

If you're after the Ring, this night should be as perfect as you can make it. You want the Bachelor to come away feeling confident and connected to you. Leave no doubt in his mind that you are the perfect woman for him.

But if you're looking for the higher prize, the Crown itself, use an experimental strategy that could secure it here in the Fantasy Suite round. Instead of giving the Bachelor a night to remember, give him one that he wants to forget. Whether you cool down your chemistry game or you decide to throw up a last-minute wall or maybe you just get overtaken by the anxiety of the moment, you have the option to derail this night and not be penalized for it by the Fourth Audience. We will never know what actually happens in the Fantasy Suite. To us it will just look like you got dumped less than a day after you raised your LL. This gives you an incredibly strong victimization identity, which the game often quickly repays with a Crown.

The Morning After

Eventually dawn breaks and whether the Producers will be getting shots of you in your chaste pajamas underneath a bathrobe or of telling disheveled piles of clothes strewn across the floor, you still have work to do. Morning snuggles followed by breakfast in bed are common staging areas for the final plays of the Fantasy Suite. In these moments, reiterate your LL raise, reminding the Bachelor exactly where you are on the chart. Kiss, hug, and perhaps even perform a standing Huju if the mood is right in these last moments with the Bachelor. And most of all convey that you don't want to see him go; you don't want to be without him. Never make this moment about the other players. This sorrow at seeing the Bachelor go is only ever about your personal desire to spend more time with him.

And then as the Bachelor walks away waving good-bye, wave back and blow a kiss, giving him reassurance that all is well in this relationship even as he is walking to his next Fantasy Suite Date.

Fantasy Home Life

Two of the three players in this round will have to return to their rooms or even a common suite while the remaining player takes her turn with the Bachelor. Only the final player will have the luxury of going straight to the Rose Ceremony after her Fantasy Suite performance, but she will have suffered through two full Fantasy Suite Dates taking place before her own.

Whatever order Producers dictate, one thing is certain—you will have to interact with the other players during the course of Fantasy Suite week. Not only will the Producers force you all together during this sensitive week, but they will also demand that you participate in "Girl Chat" segments designed to elevate your anxiety, stress, and jealousy.

This is a prime opportunity to praise the process. Every season of our beloved game sees one or more players fall prey to the green-eyed monster of jealousy, despite knowing full well the construction of the game dictates the Bachelor will be dating thirty women simultaneously and engaging in acts of physical intimacy with multiple players. If you start to feel the pangs of jealousy emerging, swallow them down and instead convey pure acceptance of the situation. The basic philosophy behind praising the process requires you to acknowledge the unorthodox nature of dating in the context of the game but ultimately accept that the Bachelor can't make the correct final decision unless he fully indulges in the process. You want him to thoroughly explore his options and choose you. By extension this conveys that you're in the game 4TRR as you also yield to the power of the process.

The Bachelor always maintains that he must adhere to the process, that it was the reason he agreed to participate in the game at all, so if you don't praise the process, you run the risk of giving him an acceptable reason to dismiss you. This can be devastating so late in the game, so close to the finish line.

The Penultimate Rose Ceremony

Just as with Hometowns, the Fantasy Suite round doesn't include a Cocktail Party before the Producers force you to stand shoulder to shoulder as the Bachelor renders his judgment, a decision that will determine the two finalists as well as the third-place finisher. The finalists will, of course, move on to one last riveting head-to-head performance in the final round of the season and the Bachelor will send the third-place finisher home. But a third-place finish is certainly not a loss. It is, in fact, statistically the best possible final position if you're interested in the Crown.

The average final placement of all players who went on to be the Bachelorette is 3.18th place. Of the nineteen players to be crowned Bachelorette, six of them finished in third place—roughly 31 percent. This is the most common finishing place, with five instances of second-place finishers becoming Bachelorettes as the next closest. Only two future Crowns have finished worse than fourth place—Hannah Brown, who came in seventh place in Season 23, and Katie Thurston, who concluded her run in eleventh place in Season 25.

A third-place finisher's time in the *Bachelor* universe is far from over. Because before the two finalists give their all in a heart-stopping head-to-head face-off, each season gives all players of note one last chance to make a case for their invitation to Paradise. *The Bachelor*'s version of an All-Star game occurs in the week just before the final showdown. It is the WTA.

Bachelorettes and Their Finishing Placements

BACHELORETTE SEASON	BACHELORETTE
1	Trista Rhen
2	Meredith Phillips
3	Jennifer Schefft
4	DeAnna Pappas
5	Jillian Harris
6	Ali Fedotowsky
7	Ashley Hebert
8	Emily Maynard
9	Desiree Hartsock

FINISHING PLACEMENT	PLAYER SEASON
2nd	*Bachelor* Season 1
4th	*Bachelor* Season 4
Ring Winner	*Bachelor* Season 3
1 of 2 Finalists (No Ring Winner)	*Bachelor* Season 11
3rd	*Bachelor* Season 13
4th	*Bachelor* Season 14
3rd	*Bachelor* Season 15
Ring Winner	*Bachelor* Season 15
4th	*Bachelor* Season 17

BACHELORETTE SEASON	BACHELORETTE
10	Andi Dorfman
11	Kaitlyn Bristowe
12	Joelle "JoJo" Fletcher
13	Rachel Lindsay
14	Becca Kufrin
15	Hannah Brown
16	Clare Crawley
16	Tayshia Adams
17	Katie Thurston
18	Michelle Young

FINISHING PLACEMENT	PLAYER SEASON
3rd	*Bachelor* Season 18
3rd	*Bachelor* Season 19
2nd	*Bachelor* Season 20
3rd	*Bachelor* Season 21
Ring Winner	*Bachelor* Season 22
7th	*Bachelor* Season 23
2nd	*Bachelor* Season 18
3rd	*Bachelor* Season 23
11th	*Bachelor* Season 25
2nd	*Bachelor* Season 25

Chapter 9

WOMEN TELL ALL

Welcome to my nightmare.

Bachelor Ben Flajnik at the
Women Tell All of his own Season 16

In our more innocent days before the Hyperbinge, we discounted this reunion episode as boring, lacking the emotional and dramatic weight of the rest of the season. We sometimes even skipped watching this episode, as it didn't seem important. But throughout our journey, we realized that the WTA is actually a crucial part of the season for players. The WTA is the first of two *Bachelor* reunion shows each season and it is your first chance to play again after your season has started airing. It's therefore the first time you can study and internalize all of the information from the episodes already televised so far in order to help you achieve a few different goals, like getting one last IG bump, possibly securing an invitation to *BIP*, or even issuing a last-minute Hail Mary play in an effort to become the next Bachelorette. Whatever your objectives, we recommend a few tried-and-true strategies to keep in your tool kit for this performance. And in order to use those tools to the best of your ability, it certainly helps to know how the modern WTA has evolved.

The History of the WTA

The WTA didn't always feature only the top players going head-to-head one last time, in a carefully constructed series of Hot Seats. The first WTA aired on April 25, 2002, right before the Season 1 Finale later that night, and watching it felt like a fever dream. Alex Michel returned to confront every single player who had been dismissed from his season in a giant studio. Chris Harrison sat in front of a fireplace on a stage. Producers placed all the players on their own individual couches, spaced bizarrely far apart in a stadium-seating manner. The N.OG.'s sat so far back from the main stage that they probably couldn't hear anything. Selected members of the audience asked questions and many of the queries reflected Bachelor Nation at its infancy, still wrapping their heads around the very premise of the show. While this first iteration included many of the video reel types featured in the modern WTA, such as Heartbreak, Villain, and bloopers, the overall presentation had a much more haphazard quality, as opposed to the formalized structure it has today.

Producers gifted the very first Hot Seat to twenty-two-year-old graduate student Cathy Grimes, a fan favorite they bestowed with a Fool Edit for her bombastic, party-driven behavior. Chris Harrison teased her Hot Seat in a bumper in which he said cheerfully, "When we come back, find out which Bachelorette passed out from drinking too many margaritas!" Harrison then played the first reel for a player, a Fool Reel video package of Grimes passing out in the bathroom after overindulging at the open bar and then finding a burst of drunken energy that fueled an impromptu dance presentation for the other players. Grimes then utilized her Hot Seat moment to make history. When Chris Harrison questioned her intentions for going on the show, Grimes uttered the phrase "for the right reasons" for the first time ever in our beloved game. These words would bake into the fabric of everything to come from this moment forward.

Grimes also told Harrison she'd made a few "enhancements" since the show and he reflected a boob-obsessed era of American culture by continuing to press her into discussing her breast augmentation by repeatedly asking, "In what way?" and by saying he'd noticed she'd made a few "changes." He also later joked about Grimes by asking the other players, "The old Cathy or the new Cathy?" We will get into what we perceive to be some of the unfortunate misogynistic, homophobic, and racist elements of our beloved game in more detail in a later chapter, but the show focused so much on women's bodies, and particularly fake breasts, both in discussions and in slow-motion zoom montages, that it could have been considered a staple of the early game. We came up with a term to describe the rampant misogyny, ableism, and focus on thin bodies, particularly during the older seasons, which we loosely deemed the "Boob Zone." Despite Grimes's treatment by the show, we owe so much to this pioneer.

The first WTA also included the very first "*Bachelor* Watch Parties" Reel, which ultimately became a mainstay of the Fourth Audience. In this case, however, the package of *Bachelor* Watch Parties depicted players from the season themselves, watching the game with their friends and family at home and at a bar, as opposed to members of Bachelor Nation at large.

Starting in Season 6, Producers placed players in chairs as opposed to on couches, but they still asked all twenty-five back. They played a reel of the season's Villain, twenty-eight-year-old financial analyst Krysta (last name lost to time), talking shit about the other players, pointing out which ones had fake boobs, and issuing cutting one-liners, including, "There's so much silicone around here if I were allergic I'd be dead." Right after that, Producers for the first time included the image of a magazine article, an *In Touch* spread of Krysta dressed in a dominatrix outfit and riding a motorcycle. This was the first time Producers featured newfound fame from the show prominently, juxtaposing it against her Villain Reel depicting the viciousness that was required to earn herself that moniker. Back in those early seasons, Harrison introduced the "drama reel" by speaking about the players in a manner that no longer holds up today, saying things like, "Up next, the catfight begins!" and "The claws came out!"

The first major change to the reunion's structure occurred in Season 7, when Producers no longer invited all of the players back and reduced the cast to only twelve. The group was made up of mostly front-runners with Heartbreak Edits but also included a few characters who had Villain Edits or memorable moments. Megan (last name lost to time) referenced her story line of changing her hair color to suit Bachelor Charlie O'Connell's physical preferences by donning the first-ever WTA TOT, a T-shirt saying: "Brunette is the new Blonde." Players started to see this as an opportunity to re-hit their brands and make one last impact. From then on, all WTAs only featured the top-placing and most memorable players, except for Season 10, when there was no WTA. Season 11 debuted the first Live WTA as well as the modern studio that they record in today. Season 14 featured a few different WTA firsts. It presented the first "Cast Reunion" Reel, a video package of previous players from many seasons meeting up in Vegas, getting drunk, and hooking up, a precursor to *BIP*. Season 14 also contained the first player to openly attack the show on a reunion, Rozlyn Papa, when she struck down the accusation by Harrison that she had engaged in inappropriate relations with a Producer from her season. Coincidentally, this was also the first season to insert a "Bachelor Gives Back" Reel, showing players painting murals and Chris Harrison handing checks for various charities to Ellen DeGeneres.

Season 16 highlighted the first finalist to return to the WTA. Generally, the top two or three players sit this round out, so as not to give any hint of a spoiler at the final ending. However, in only this one season, Ring Winner Courtney Robertson came back to confront the women and Bachelor Nation about her own heavy Villain Edit. She used strong tear play to try to counteract the multitude of the 4TWR attacks against her.

In Season 17 Chris Harrison and Bachelor Sean Lowe crashed Bachelor Nation viewing parties for the first time, and the WTA displayed a reel of this raucous adventure, including a group of screaming young women demanding that Lowe take his shirt off. He obliged in a very *Hunger Games*–esque moment. The game owns you even after it's over.

It wasn't until Season 19 that Chris Harrison issued the first on-camera invitation to *BIP*, to Weirdo Edit recipient Ashley Salter, a reward for her entertaining game spent talking to inanimate objects and performing strong face play.

The Hierarchy of the WTA

While at first glance the WTA appears to be a reunion show for all of the players of *The Bachelor* to come back and hash it out as one big Bachelor Nation family, this is a fallacy. Producers bake a definitive hierarchy of importance of players into the physical and temporal structure of this round. It is possible for deft players to engineer a transition up through the ranks of the WTA caste system, but the Producers often handcuff you by your own body of work in the main game in terms of possible screen time and story lines. The two main types of positions they assign you are Hot Seats and Chairs. All players asked to participate receive Chairs, but Producers give only a select few a Hot Seat, during which the host interviews the player one-on-one onstage. The average placement of a player who receives a Chair is approximately 11.72, while the average placement of a player who receives a Hot Seat is around 6.51.

The Cheap Seats/the Chair People

Chairs are the most common and the lowest rung of the WTA power structure ladder. While in the first few seasons Producers invited every dismissed player back, the title of Chair itself became more exclusive during Season 7 when they only brought back players in the top twelve, with a few exceptions. In the Modern Era, Chairs consist of roughly the top twenty players. They maintain a hierarchy even within the Cheap Seats, though. Producers place key players closer in physical proximity to the main stage. In the Modern Era, they seat Lead Villains and more important players who generally finish with a higher placement in the first of two rows, while they relegate the lesser-known characters to the back row. This positioning makes it easier for featured players to chime in on each of the various story lines discussed throughout the episode and more awkward and difficult for the second-row Chairs.

Hot Seats/Reels

Most skilled players covet the Hot Seat because it gives you potential screen time and the possibility of a continuation of your story. The top players whom Producers give Heartbreak Victimization and Villain Edits generally dominate Hot Seats.

Occasionally, huge characters and Colorful Narrator or Fool fan favorites get Hot Seats as well. Producers do not always air all Hot Seats that they film, so it is critically important for you to make the most of yours should you receive one. And while Producers predetermine most Hot Seats, it is possible for highly skilled players who find themselves relegated to the Cheap Seats to elevate their own story lines and even join these illustrious ranks. Cheap Seats players can incorporate strong victimization tear play and prompt the host or a benevolent Bachelor himself to ask them to join him for an impromptu Hot Seat.

If you get a Hot Seat, Producers will cut a package together for you, outlining your story through the season. This is your reel. If you had a Heartbreak Edit, the reel will outline your romance, but if you had a Villain Edit, it will highlight all of your main fights with other players and they will expect you to answer for all of your 4TWR behavior.

The Next Crown

This is a rare Hot Seat and the most ideal position for a player at the WTA. The Next Crown announcement depends on both the casting and production schedules, but sometimes they will announce the next Bachelorette at the end of the WTA episode. Producers will frequently tease this throughout the episode and use it as part of their strategy to retain their audience from season to season. If the production does not announce the Next Crown at WTA, they will generally do it at the second reunion special of the season, the ATFR.

The Types of Hot Seats

When you learn that you will get a Hot Seat, you can usually pretty easily determine what type it will be, depending on your edit. Were you one of the last people to leave and did you leave crying? You'll probably get a Heartbreak Hot Seat. Were you one of the lowest-placed players who was asked back but had some conflict? You'll probably be getting a Villain Hot Seat. Depending on the type of Hot Seat, you can determine the line of questioning and therefore pivot the Hot Seat into what you want it to be, a platform for you to achieve your future goals, the first of which is making your Hot Seat interesting enough to make the WTA final edit.

Heartbreak/Victimization Hot Seat

The Heartbreak/Victimization Hot Seat is by far the most common type of Hot Seat. Producers award them to players who generally finish from third to sixth place and have developed pretty strong relationships with the Bachelor, which ultimately ended in their dismissal and victimization. This is the coveted spot for a player who ultimately wishes to wear the Crown, although it is an excellent audition space for good sand placement as well. Eleven Heartbreak Hot Seats became future Crowns, so it truly is the audition stage for you to get that ultimate prize.

Before the Hot Seat examination begins for players who receive Heartbreak Edits, you will have to watch your Heartbreak Reel first. This package showcases your entire love story from start to finish, from your Limo Exit, through your Love Level raises, through your PTC plays, a glimpse at your chemistry game, and ultimately your Victimization Elimination scene, ideally with a tear play finish in an ITM or during your final Exit. In the Modern Era, Producers will film your face while you watch this sequence and show it in a small box in the lower corner of the screen. Keep in mind the Fourth Audience is scrutinizing you the entire time. Good face play is a must, from a 4TRR wistful look during your emotional moments to cringing and laughing at yourself during a blooper. It's a bonus if you can pull tear play just from watching the tapes back so that when you come out of your reel you're already crying, already suited up in your 4TRR armor.

The host then begins the interrogation of you, the victimized player. The mainstays of these conversations include asking you to relive your relationship, your breakup, as well as indicate where you are at emotionally today. The host will often ask if you are still at LL4 (if you played it in-game) and whether or not you need closure. Sometimes players will even play a postmortem, previously unplayed LL4, i.e., "I actually did love him, before he broke my heart into a thousand pieces." This heightens the victimization level even more. The best players convey that their emotions were real—that they were in love and will always "have love" for the Crown, though they're not currently "in love."

Praise the process for being effective and offer up some future-casting in terms of possible other romantic avenues. An easy way to display this is by saying, "I loved the Bachelor. He didn't choose me. I know I deserve a man who will choose me just as much as I choose him and [insert branding metaphor here—"be my teammate," "be my copilot," "be a world changer with me," "be my sexy equal," et cetera]. I know he's out there." Let Bachelor Nation fill in the blanks and desire to start matchmaking for you from the previous player pool or generate ideas of what new rookie players would be good for your own season.

Heartbreak Reunion Hot Seat

The Heartbreak Reunion Hot Seat is a specialty Hot Seat that generally follows a Heartbreak Hot Seat, although most Heartbreak Hot Seats don't receive Heartbreak Reunions. A Heartbreak Reunion occurs when the host of the WTA brings out the Bachelor to have an emotional discussion with the victimized player. Producers usually reserve it for the most important heartbreak story lines of the season and for the breakup that Bachelor Nation itself most demands closure from. A Heartbreak Reunion Hot Seat earns you the chance to get double the screen time, as well as a chance for a public closure conversation that can pivot your story line in a new direction, often toward sand and even sometimes toward a Crown.

Prepare a couple light grilling questions for the Bachelor, to show you took the relationship and heartbreak seriously, as well as some lighthearted material to wrap it up with a feel-good ending. Bonus points if you can coax the Bachelor into teeing up your own Crown run by asking him positive branding things like, "What do you think it's important for my future husband to know about me?" or "What would you say are my best qualities?" or "What was your favorite moment we spent together?" And if you don't get a Heartbreak Reunion Hot Seat, it doesn't hurt to publicly ask for one once they bring the Bachelor himself out, i.e., "Bachelor, I have one last question for you. Do you mind if I come up there with you?" Benevolent Bachelors are compelled to oblige.

Villain Hot Seat

The Villain Hot Seat is the second most common Hot Seat type after the Heartbreak Victimization Hot Seat. As much as the Producers demonize 4TWR players, Bachelor Nation wants to hear from them and there is almost always at least one Villain Hot Seat, as there have been roughly twenty Villain Hot Seats across twenty-four WTAs.

The strongest Villain Hot Seats show another side of the Villain. Corinne

Olympios did this during Season 21's WTA by actually playing a previously unaired PTC at the WTA. She told the audience that while Bachelor Nation made fun of her for having a nanny, "Raquel is a very, very special person because she's someone who has been there with me through the hardest times in my life. My mom had ovarian cancer. I was told that she was going to pass away. I was told that my dad needed to get her funeral in order. And Raquel was there, and she was my rock." This revealed a new, softer part of Olympios's backstory, which she paired well with a few of her signature comedic elements, like serving everyone in the audience Raquel's signature cheese pasta dish during the reunion show to absolutely dominate the entire round.

Fool Hot Seat

The Fool Hot Seat is an exotic Hot Seat. While it was the first-ever Hot Seat, they are pretty rare. Generally, Producers utilize them to relive the wildest moments of the season, often accompanied by a blooper reel, and to also build up the particular player for going on to *BIP*. If you should find yourself sitting in the Fool's Hot Seat, indulge in self-deprecating laughter and do your best to reprise your role as the Fool for your best chance at a Paradise invitation right there on stage.

The Bachelor

The host always conducts a solo interview with the Bachelor when they first bring him out, another mainstay of the WTA. The Bachelor will generally discuss his journey and sometimes hint at whether or not he has found his happily ever after. He will sometimes join the Hot Seats of Heartbreak and/or Villain Hot Seats for closure conversations as well. If you've played a decent season, you'll be given the opportunity to ask the Bachelor a question or engage in some small conversation with him at the very least. But if you're not afforded this opportunity, you must create it. Do not leave the stage without having at least some minor interaction with the Bachelor to reinforce your relevance in the Nation.

The Next Bachelorette

Sometimes Production announces the next Crown at the end of the WTA as a way to get everyone excited about the next season as this one wraps up. The host generally asks the new Crown a couple softball questions about what she is looking forward to in her season. This is the ideal place for the next Crown to re-hit your brand and even launch your catchphrase for your season, e.g., Becca Kufrin: "Let's do the damn thing!" This is also your first opportunity to get a real social media boost, so rehearse these lines as much as possible and make the most of the moment if you should be crowned.

And if the Crown has been placed atop another player's head, be supportive and happy for her. If you've done well in selecting your team and making friends, there is a distinct possibility that you might be called onstage to share in the moment with the new Bachelorette like Becca Kufrin's team was at the Season 22 WTA.

Prop Work/Audience Participation

Perhaps the most infamous example of audience participation was during Ben Higgins's Season 20 WTA. A fan jumped out of the audience, seemingly impromptu, got onstage, and lifted his shirt to reveal a rib cage tattoo of Villain Edit recipient Lace Morris. While she only placed seventeenth, this moment helped solidify her brand and her invitation to *BIP*, where she made a strong run with then-partner Grant Kemp. But don't count on anomalies like this to help you in your efforts. It's entirely up to you to make sure that you get everything you can out of what might be your last chance to convince Producers that you still have some playing days ahead of you.

And after you make your best case for additional followers, screen time with an invite to sand, or even potentially a possible Crown contention at WTA, the game resumes with the Super Bowl of the Bachelor—a head-to-head final showdown of the last two players standing: the finals.

Chapter 10

THE FINALE/ATFR

I miss you every time we have to say good-bye. I don't want to say good-bye anymore. Catherine, I want to spend the rest of my life telling you "I love you" and making you feel like the most special, beautiful woman in the world.

Sean Lowe's proposal speech to
Catherine Giudici (Season 17 Finale)

For us this is the NBA Finals, Stanley Cup, Olympics, Wimbledon, World Cup, World Series, and Super Bowl all rolled into one. It's not just the end of a season, not just the culmination of a TV show, not even just the final moments between the top two players. Every year the *Bachelor* Finale hosts the pinnacle of competitive display across the whole of the sporting world, where superstars are made and future *Bachelor* royalty is crowned. It is the event around which our calendar year begins and ends. It is, simply put, what we live for.

When Sean Lowe uttered the words that opened this chapter, he might not have known he was making franchise history, but that's exactly what we witnessed. After seventeen seasons, over the course of eleven years, Lowe ended up being the first and only Bachelor Crown to ever marry his Ring Winner. It was also the only relationship from the Bachelor and his Ring Winner that resulted in children, and the franchise would bring this pair back again and again on subsequent seasons as the prototypical romantic coupling, aka Hero Couple, for all future generations to emulate.

It all began with Catherine Giudici playing this Finale round of the game flawlessly.

While you may have left it all on the field up until now, this final round of play-offs is where you clinch the entire season. In it, you must navigate meeting the Bachelor's family, one Last Date, and the many components of the FRC, wherein you will find out if you'll become the Ring Winner or perhaps get a strong enough Heartbreak Victimization Runner-Up Edit to win the Crown. And players have contended with these same elements since the very first season.

The History of the Finale/ATFR

The modern televised structure of this Finale episode consists of the last round of the game, featured within the larger construct of a live viewing party navigated by a host. The first Live Finale wasn't until Season 17, however. As soon as the Bachelor makes his final decision, the modern Finale transitions to the ATFR, where the final players and Bachelor give a postseason debrief to us and discuss their plans for the future.

While the Finale/ATFR three-hour special has been a tradition of the game for a long time, the last round of play was not always what it is today. The first Finale aired April 25, 2002, and it was one hour and there was no ATFR. The final two players, Amanda Marsh and Trista Rehn, met with Alex Michel's family at their home in Dallas, Texas. Michel's mother urged him not to propose. Michel then went on a Last Date with each of the players back in LA, during which Marsh played the first LL3 in history. Michel then went to a ring store where he picked out a Harry Winston ring. The diamond king of the Bachelor Franchise, Neil Lane, was nowhere to be found back then. Michel then broke up with Rehn at the first FRC altar. Moments later at the same altar, he told twenty-three-year-old Marsh that while he wasn't proposing, he wished to continue a relationship with her, which they ended ten months later.

This last round has gone through many iterations since that point. The structure and order of the Last Date and MOTF have varied. Sometimes the Finale and ATFR have aired as different episodes and sometimes as the same.

Bachelor Charlie O'Connell (Season 7) turned his Finale episode upside down when he went rogue and decided he didn't want to make his final decision until the ATFR. He then continued his polyamorous relationships and dated both of his top two players, Sarah Brice and Krisily Kennedy, for two months, with some filming of phone calls and dates throughout. At the end of the two months, Producers shot the ATFR, which served as the de facto Finale, when O'Connell made his Final Rose choice on live television. This was the first time a Bachelor was able to make his final decision having seen the airing of the show. O'Connell then dumped Krisily Kennedy backstage and gave Sarah Brice his Final Rose in front of a live audience, on a stage decked out to look like a traditional FRC. Chris Harrison toasted them at the altar with champagne and gifted the happy couple a trip to Aruba. The pair dated on and off for five years before calling it quits.

Many surprise guests have appeared in the Finale and often Producers incorporate the families of the top two players. In Season 8 (Travis Stork), Producers flew the mothers of the final two players out to Paris to help pick out dresses and rings with their daughters for the FRC. During Season 20, they flew out Ben Higgins's and his Ring Winner Lauren Bushnell's entire families as well as Higgins's pastor in order to try to force a live, onstage wedding between the pair. The couple politely declined the offer.

The Finale has also included breakups between the Bachelor and his Ring Winner and then romantic reunions between the Bachelor and his second choice for wife, the runner-up . . . three times! This bizarre phenomenon's pioneer was Jason Mesnick in Season 13, who ended things with his initial Ring Winner, Melissa Rycroft, live on the ATFR studio stage in favor of pursuing a relationship with Molly Malaney, whom he informed of this intention live onstage as well. The couple married, had a child, and are still together to this day.

The second switcheroo was during Arie Luyendyk Jr.'s twenty-second season when Producers filmed one of the couple's clandestine postseason visits. Luyendyk took the opportunity to break up with Becca Kufrin on-camera, giving her one of the most intense Heartbreak Edits of all time, and then Luyendyk later reunited with Lauren Burnham in front of the cameras at her home. He even later performed a second in-season proposal, this time to Burnham, live on the ATFR stage.

Season 24's Peter Weber also ended his engagement with Ring Winner Hannah Ann Sluss on-camera, but his pursuit of his runner-up, Madison Prewett, took a bizarre turn when host Chris Harrison flew in his stead to Alabama to try to convince Prewett to reconsider Weber. Producers then flew Prewett out to LA for a surprise on-camera reunion with Weber, which fizzled right after the ATFR.

The Producers regularly find themselves in a quandary at this point in the season. They've spent twelve weeks setting up elaborate situations designed to undermine every relationship on the show in order to generate nervous breakdowns on-camera, but then they realize they need to at least present the illusion that this process worked, that it did indeed succeed in its stated goal of helping two people find love. So more often than not, they'll force the Bachelor and either his Ring Winner or another top player to pretend they're still trying to make it work.

The Bachelor's MOTF

Before the ATFR portion, the Finale round traditionally begins with the Bachelor's MOTF. This often takes place during the daytime, in the days leading up to the Last Date and the FRC. Producers fly the Bachelor's family out to whatever exotic location they've selected for the Finale, where the family meets with both finalists in quick succession (on the same day in some cases) in hopes of providing further clarity on the important decision. The Bachelor will generally meet with the family before and after each MOTF to consult. You want to leave the family feeling like you are the best choice for their son, that you are . . .

The Ultimate Daughter-in-Law

Generally, the Producers will give you a gift of some kind (usually flowers) to present to the Bachelor's mother or mother figure during this round, which combined with hugs will start a very similar but reverse Hometown MOTF date. Occasionally they've set this Bachelor's MOTF at the Bachelor's parents' abode and not an exotic location.

This is one of your greatest opportunities for a final push for the Ring or for a strong Heartbreak Edit, which involve related strategies. Convey strong 4TRR to whoever represents the Bachelor's family, repeat all of the Love Levels you've already raised for their son to the family, and even produce tears for them. Similar to your own Hometown, tears, Blessings, and/or Glows from the family signify a round well played.

Only convey positive ultimate daughter-in-law sentiments during this date.

Research his family in the preseason and come up with some future-casting ideas for activities you could do with various family members. For instance, if you share a passion for or even a mild interest in golf with the Bachelor's family, suggest a future family golf tournament and joke about giving the father a handicap. Fathers almost universally like a player who can give them a little spirited competitive attitude.

Common traps to avoid during this round include speaking negatively about the other remaining player or expressing any doubts about the process or the Bachelor. The family might also utilize some of the same five attacks that families on Hometown Dates use (see chapter 8 Hometowns for defensive strategies). Ideally, convey to the Bachelor's parents, especially his mother, that you will be a fitting replacement for her maternal caregiving, that you will be able to take care of him and the family you will eventually have together.

The Last Date

This is it. Everything you've been working for. The final round of play before the Bachelor proposes to or dumps you on national television. Producers split these dates almost always into a day and night portion, with a day of adventure or beautiful scenery in the exotic location and the nighttime portion an intimate conversation back in your hotel room.

Daytime Fun

Kick off the daytime portion with a conversation about how great it was to meet the Bachelor's family. Include new things you learned about the Bachelor, new inside jokes with his family, as well as some future-casting about what reunions with them later on might look like. Utilize the rest of the day portion by playing a strong chemistry game. You're fun and attractive—just think about how fun and attractive your future life of traveling and selling spon-con together could be!

The Last Last Date

Execute any remaining emotional play during the night portion. If you somehow still have an LL4 on the table, raise it here. Again, never leave the game with Love Levels on the table! And absolutely avoid revealing any unplayed PTCs. At this point they will only hurt your game and will translate as last-minute red flags or desperation. Focus on sincerity—being as genuine as possible and building the foundation of a strong heartbreak story line should you be dismissed, which can include conveying strong future-casting and PreCogs, as well as tearful fears of heartbreak. Leave no walls erected. You're as vulnerable as can be. Players have discussed future Costco trips and even names of their children during this last round of play. The Bachelor is often going through a high level of emotional turmoil at this point. Ask him about his feelings in a well-timed How You Doin'? (HYD) to convey to him that you sincerely care about his well-being. Ideally, even if you suspect you are the runner-up, do not question the Bachelor's final decision here or demand an answer. Taking this course of action can prompt an early dismissal. And if you're going to go out in second place, locate your heartbreak at the FRC Sacrificial Altar in full makeup with your hair done, wearing the perfect dress, as the star of the entire moment.

One Last Kringle

Give the Bachelor a gift at this point, one last grand gesture or emotional token of your affection. Players often put together pictures or scrapbooks chronicling their love story or some other meaningful 4TRR item. During Season 22's Finale, Becca Kufrin Kringled Arie Luyendyk Jr. a scrapbook with photos from their *Bachelor* journey together.

During her Last Date on Season 25, Michelle Young told Matt James she "came into this looking for a teammate" and "can't imagine another teammate—it's you that I want and it's hard to picture leaving here without you." She then pulled out a couples Kringle of matching jerseys that read "Mr. James" and "Mrs. James." She called back to them playing basketball with her family on her Hometown Date, she future-cast their potential sports family, and she hit Matt James's love for sports. This play fit well into Young's branding of looking for a "teammate" and set up an essential, powerful Heartbreak Edit with this thoughtful, visually interesting gesture. It was so emotionally powerful, in fact, that it demanded Matt James make a decision and eliminate her on the spot, as opposed to putting her through the gauntlet of getting dumped at the FRC. She was almost instantaneously rewarded with the Crown.

Neil Lane, Master of Sparklers

Once the dates are done and you've left it all on the field, Producers make the Bachelor go ring shopping. This process has ranged from him entering a physical store in Beverly Hills, to Bachelor Ring Broker Neil Lane flying in to St. Lucia to let the Bachelor stare at his open suitcase of sparklers as he ponders his final two.

While Neil Lane is as much a staple of the game as FIMP Roses, he actually did not enter the game until 2009. Producers presented the game's first official Neil Lane Sparkler during Season 13 (Jason Mesnick). Neil Lane himself didn't appear in person until Season 14, when he met with Bachelor Jake Pavelka to display his wares and treat us to his spritely, ring-focused presence. When *InStyle* asked Lane about his important role and his sparklers, he answered, "I make each and every ring . . . with the couple's lasting love in mind. . . . It's my hope that the spark between them lasts forever. And if it doesn't, I like to think that the ring goes to heaven."

If the couple breaks up before a year, the contract you each sign supposedly states that you have to return the ring, but if you can make it past that threshold, you get to keep the expensive ring. Ben Higgins's ring for Lauren Bushnell from the Season 20 Finale was allegedly valued at $100,000. So if you do win the Ring but don't want anything to do with the Bachelor, you'll have to factor in the monetary gain associated with maintaining at least the image of a happy couple for a calendar year.

The FRC

The morning of this grand event, Producers and makeup, hair, and wardrobe teams will wake you up and you will start getting ready for your final performance. Despite the fact that you'll have professional hair and makeup, the Producers will force you to pretend that you're doing it all yourself so they can get shots to build your getting-ready montage. They always want shots of you putting on makeup, looking into the mirror, gazing off your balcony, writing in a journal, laying your dress out on a bed, and ultimately riding in a limo to the final destination. You'll also have to participate in final ITM interviews to talk about the journey and your hopes for the outcome. Producers will cut the audio of this ITM apart and use it as voice-over for your final montage. And if you haven't already written it, you should absolutely focus on generating both an acceptance speech for a proposal and an exit speech in the event of a dismissal that sets you up as the next Bachelorette, to the best of your ability.

Their Big Finale

The Finale is certainly going to be a big deal for you and an equally big deal for the Bachelor. With casting included, the past four months of your life have focused only on this moment. And for the Bachelor it's been even longer. He's most likely had to go through an entire season of play in *The Bachelorette* before this and possibly even a season of *BIP* to get to this final moment.

But never forget whose show this is. It belongs to the Producers. Some of them have spent over a decade in service of the game and building up to these moments at the ends of seasons. They have boiled it down to a science of trauma and pain designed to deliver uncontrollable crying from as many players as possible. So remember, no matter what the Producers tell you, their primary goal in this final round is to destroy you on national television. And if they need to pick up the pieces to salvage the semblance of a love story, that is an afterthought.

Former *Bachelor* producer Sarah Gertrude Shapiro revealed her strategy for approaching the runner-up in a *New Yorker* article, saying, "The night they were going to get dumped, I would go to the hotel room where they were staying and say, 'I'm going to lose my job for telling you this, but he's going to pick you—he's going to propose.'" This would make the player think she was the Ring Winner, which would cause a more devastating heartbreak at the FRC. Unless you communicate directly with the Bachelor, do not trust the intel. During Season 24's Finale, Producers told Peter Weber that his only remaining player, Hannah Ann Sluss, might not be showing up, despite no indication by Sluss that that was her intention. They presumably even delayed her car coming to the FRC. This completely fabricated moment of uncertainty sent Weber into a tailspin, even though Sluss turned up and accepted his proposal.

It's incredibly unlikely that you'll know if you're the first player to arrive at the FRC, but if you should come into the possession of that intel, be aware that the first player is always dumped, with the single exception of Season 5. Jesse Palmer LL4ed the first player to arrive, Jessica Bowlin, then gave her a plane ticket before she was whisked away by Producers to hide inside a building. Palmer then dumped the second player to arrive, Tara Huckeby, and reunited with Bowlin once Huckeby was packed into the back of an SUV, face covered in tears.

The Path of Pain

Producers will take you from your hotel room and put you in a car or, in some cases a helicopter, which will transport you to the location of the Final Altar, where the Bachelor waits to deliver his final judgment. The host will greet you as your vehicle comes to a stop and they'll make you have a brief conversation with them. There is just time enough to make a joke about nervousness that gives way to resolve and readiness to face whatever is about to happen and then . . . you must then walk the Path of Pain.

Sometimes straight, sometimes curved, sometimes cobbled, sometimes paved, the Path of Pain is the thoroughfare from the host to the elaborate Final Altar where the Bachelor waits to begin the last Rose Ceremony. Producers will force you to walk this path alone so they can get the all-important shot of you nervous and taking deep breaths as you approach the Bachelor with blind uncertainty about what they are presenting as the most important moment of your life.

And if the Bachelor eliminates you at the altar, they will make you walk the Path of Pain alone again all the way back to the car that will take you to the airport.

Sacrificial Altar

As you finish the Path of Pain, you will come upon the Sacrificial Altar, where the FRC takes place. Production elaborately decorates the altar and sets it against a magnificent landscape backdrop, and the Bachelor will be waiting for you there. The Final Rose lies beckoning on a pedestal.

The Bachelor will be smiling, but don't be fooled. This is mandatory—a tactic the Producers force him to employ to mask his intentions, good or bad. Sometimes engaging in some kind of physical contact can give you an indication of what he's decided. Some Bachelors have kissed their runners-up on the lips at the altar, though, so be warned.

FRC Speech

You must deliver your FRC speech to the Bachelor before he reveals his decision. Excellent FRC speeches include a summary of the love journey, hopes for the future, and some brand/couple-specific jokes. If he's going to eliminate you, the FRC speech is the most important setup to your heartbreak story line in the entire season. You want your heartbreak to be the furthest fall, so convey being the most in love, ready for the happiest day of your life. Reiterate your LL4, and ideally conjure tears in this passionate display of 4TRR. It should come off like you are baring your entire soul and that you have never been more certain of anything in your life—the Bachelor is *your person* beyond any doubt.

The Dumping

Under 50 percent of players who have gone to the FRC receive this outcome due to early eliminations. Prepare for it, no matter how well you think your Ring Winner strategies have gone. If you're going to be eliminated, prepare your reaction. Should you wear the Crown, this is the scene Producers will use over and over in your promo videos for the upcoming season, so try to use a few tricks of the dumping trade to generate the most possible sympathy from the Fourth Audience.

You can play the victim and for that you'll need tears, tears, tears. And we're not talking just a few trickles. Use everything you've got. Put your whole body into it. Unleash guttural noises. Make us feel like the rug has been pulled out from under you and your world is ending. JoJo Fletcher employed this technique perfectly in Season 20 when Ben Higgins eliminated her at the altar.

Alternatively, you can also forgo the emotionally injured strategy in favor of the outraged anger position. One of the most famous reactions to an FRC elimination was Clare Crawley during Season 18. After Juan Pablo told her she wasn't the Ring Winner, he tried to hug her and she refused. She said, "I lost respect for you because I thought I knew what kind of man you are, but what you made me just go through . . . I would never want my children having a father like you." She would later re-create this iconic moment as part of her take-no-shit branding in another takedown of a 4TWR player on her own Crown season.

Lindsay Yenter, the runner-up on Sean Lowe's seventeenth Season, played a version of this strategy as well. She took off her shoes mid-FRC and walked back down the Path of Pain barefoot in a bold rebuke of both Lowe's decision and the formality of the event itself. Yenter said of the moment during *The Bachelor: The Greatest Seasons Ever*, "Truth be told, my feet had swelled, and it was hurting so bad that in the middle of the breakup I was like, 'Listen, if you're not gonna get down on one knee, I'm taking these bad boys off, because you're not gonna break my heart and my feet at the same time.'" While Yenter never wore the Crown, these kinds of moments *create* Crowns and should be well thought out. We recommend an experimental modernized version of taking off your shoes, like taking the chicken cutlets or bra out of your dress, removing your false eyelashes, or taking off your Spanx. Bachelor Nation will relate to this reaction, you will be memed, there will be articles about it, and you will be remembered.

Proposal

If you wanted the Ring, congratulations! You've won one of the most difficult prizes in this game. If you were going for the Crown, do not be too distraught, as it's not impossible to win the Crown after the Ring. Jen Schefft, Emily Maynard, and Becca Kufrin can all claim the Full Royale among their accomplishments. After you give your FRC speech, then it is time for the Bachelor to give his proposal speech, which almost always ends in either a Proposal of Marriage or an indication of wanting to keep dating or a promise ring, et cetera. Positive indicators of being the Ring Winner include FRC kissing, the use of LL4, and jovial body language, although these are not perfect barometers. Generally, this is the first time the Bachelor will LL4 all season, with a few exceptions.

As he kneels before you and pulls out that Neil Lane Sparkler, your job as Ring Winner is to seem surprised and overwhelmed by blinding happiness. Cry tears of joy. Catherine Giudici's hand famously started shaking uncontrollably during the Season 17 Finale, appearing extremely 4TRR. The Bachelor will then place the Ring on your finger, possibly spin you around a few times, and then turn his attention to the Final Rose of the season. He'll offer it to you and you will accept it knowing that you are the only player to have received the full array of ten Roses (if your season concludes in a standard fashion).

You will do final interviews as a couple, holding the rose, and then often do some gesture of riding off into the sunset, be it a carriage ride or an elephant ride together. In the most recent seasons, players film some selfie video updates of their life together as a pair after the show. Producers shoot these videos during the secret rendezvous that they grant all couples after the Finale, but before the outcome of the season has been made public.

ATFR

"All I've ever asked for is for someone to give me their whole heart like I'm giving mine to them. You took away from me my first engagement. You took that away from me."

Hannah Ann Sluss said this to Peter Weber when he ended their engagement during the ATFR of Season 24. While this was a powerful moment, Sluss was a studied player and, knowingly or not, she used the same language that Hannah Brown had used only one season prior on her season of *The Bachelorette* when she found out her Ring Winner, Jed Wyatt, had allegedly had a girlfriend during her entire season. Brown told Wyatt in their Finale breakup, "I feel like this experience has been taken away from me." Both Brown and Sluss subconsciously chose words that would set up their Heartbreak Victimization Edits. Setting up the next leg of your journey in-game is your goal during the ATFR.

The structure of the modern ATFR changes depending on the ending of a season. The last three seasons have ended nontraditionally in that both final players were not at the FRC because the Bachelors dismissed the runners-up beforehand. This resulted in some part of the romantic journey being documented postseason and aired during this time. But usually both finalists are present, as are some family members. Peter Weber's mother, Barbara Weber, was interviewed repeatedly in the Season 24 ATFR, even earning her face a spot in the small reaction box at the bottom of the screen while watching some of that season's footage.

Every so often, the Producers bring back key players from recent seasons to comment on the current season's drama and deliver sports analyst–style predictions about who they think will be the Ring Winner. This can include the show's Hero Couples—the couples brought together by the franchise in one way or another. These couples return to update Bachelor Nation on their romantic journeys and display how the game is 4TRR, that it is not meant to cause emotional upheaval and breakdowns but actually meant to help people find love. They've brought back Sean and Catherine Lowe to display their success more times than these two stats gurus could count. Jade Roper Tolbert and Tanner Tolbert have also cemented themselves as a go-to success story for the Producers.

These couples who are still married, who have had children, reinforce the idea that the game is about anything other than IG followers and spon-con money at this point, despite the fact that couples like Arie and Lauren Luyendyk from Season 22 have a company called IG Husband through which they generate constant spon-con revenue as professional influencers.

The Next Crown

Sometimes Producers announce the next Bachelorette in a Hot Seat, as a way to seamlessly transition into the next season. For Nick Viall's twenty-first season, they announced Rachel Lindsay as Crown and then the host surprised her. He revealed that her season was starting right now, which included Producers setting up a makeshift mansion on the stage for them to do the first four Limo Exits ahead of the actual production of her season. While this only happened once more, for Becca Kufrin during Arie Luyendyk Jr.'s season, all future Crowns should be prepared for this to happen again. And indeed if Producers select you as the Crown, they will obviously tell you ahead of time that they'll unveil you at the ATFR.

The Ring Winners' Circle/Couples Reunion Hot Seat

If you're returning to ATFR as the Ring Winner, your job is fairly straightforward. You want to convey love and happiness and reveal some surprise for your future as a couple that Bachelor Nation will want to continue to follow on social media. This includes plans for you both to move in together, or maybe you're getting a dog, et cetera. Sometimes the host will Kringle you a gift as a couple, to help you continue dating in the hopes that you'll become a Hero Couple, maybe even get married, and that they can then bring you back again and again to project the mirage that *The Bachelor* is a big happy family who continues to provide for past players.

These gifts often take the form of plane tickets and/or vacations back to somewhere the couple traveled on the show and are almost always provided to the show for free by the brand sponsoring them. When Jason Mesnick got back together with runner-up Molly Malaney in the Season 13 ATFR, Harrison presented them with a gift of a tent, a callback to their infamous overnight 101 tent date under the stars. In more recent years, the Couples Reunion Hot Seat has also involved the host asking the couple how they've dealt with the hate and bullying that comes along with being successful in this game. The best and most common way players have handled this is generically saying that "it's brought us both closer together."

Second Place Is Second Best/Heartbreak Hot Seat

If you're the runner-up, you're in the second-best place for potential Crown, only after the ideal position for Crown, third place. If you're playing this round as the runner-up, lean heavily into the heartbreak story line, similar to players with Heartbreak Edits on WTA. However, in this case, you have the gravitas and victimization of a runner-up, who possibly (and ideally) endured a humiliating FRC Elimination. Convey the hurt and disappointment, but transition into a lighthearted optimism and branding for the future. Let Bachelor Nation fill in the redemption story line they will want for you, be it via high sand placement or even as Crown!

F*** It, We'll Do It Live!

Whatever your path is at this point, feel free to experiment given the live show format. Kringle the Bachelor. Kringle the host. Kringle the mother of the runner-up! Reveal a hidden tattoo! As long as it is 4TRR, feel free to go for it, as they only have a seven-second delay in broadcasting and it's your last on-camera appearance . . . for now.

And once the cameras are off and the lights on the stage fade out, the game is over . . . or has it only just begun? After the ATFR you return back to the world of social media with what is hopefully a massive amount of new followers. This is the postseason and it is the part of the year in which you can finally start to exploit all of your social media gains from your time in-game.

Chapter 11

THE POSTSEASON

I'm not going to let people shame me into not going to a music festival. I'll be a little more careful, but I'm really looking forward to it. #imstillgoingtostagecoach

Blake Horstmann, *Bachelorette* Season 14 runner-up,
BIP Season 6

When we started our descent into madness we followed a few of the leads and top players from recent seasons on Instagram. But we soon began to realize it was necessary to follow every player on every platform, because after the season ends they make some of their most important plays in the world of social media. We became so obsessed with who got spon-con deals, who posted pics of their baby bumps, who appeared in photo shoots with other players, and generally who had the highest follower numbers that we devoted a weekly segment of our podcast to examining everything players were doing after their season ended.

We started to see that no matter when you were eliminated from the season, the postseason is when you really begin your career as an influencer if you've played a strong enough season to get yourself over 100K followers on a major platform. And we also saw that beyond making a living off spon-con, strong parasocial plays help you maintain relevance in the eyes of the Producers, so you're more likely to get an invitation to Paradise if you didn't walk away with the Ring or the Crown.

A proper postseason strategy is broken into three very distinct periods of time, each with its own rules and best practices. The first period is . . .

The Dead Zone

The Bachelor shoots from the end of September through the middle of November, but it doesn't air until the first week of January. The month-ish-long period of time that starts at whatever point you're eliminated from the game and ends the night the first episode of your season airs is called the Dead Zone. In prior years, when Producers gave players back their personal belongings as they left the game they had free rein to immediately post away on whatever social media accounts they wanted. But this made it obvious for Bachelor Nation to figure out who was still in the game as other players were returning home and the Fourth Audience was spoiling virtually every season by deductive reasoning months ahead of its airing. To combat this loss of control over the narrative, Producers recently started forcing every player to agree to remain silent on social media until a predetermined date that coincides with the end of that season's shooting. So unless you make it to the finals, you won't be allowed to post anything or comment or like for a few weeks to avoid unintentionally giving Bachelor Nation spoiler-level information. But you will be able to see the beginning of your social media gains.

Because they make the list of players public, you should see an uptick in followers (or requests if you've chosen to make your Instagram private), which will represent a taste of what's to come as your season begins airing. If you're not used to getting tons of DMs every day, you can start interacting with your growing audience and try to imagine it scaling up by many times as your numbers go up. Develop a plan for how you specifically want to handle your inbox. It will very soon be overflowing, and that can be an overwhelming experience. A good rule of thumb is to treat every response you send as though someone will absolutely post it to Reddit for everyone to see, because that's a definite possibility. Anything that can be screenshotted probably will be, so proceed with caution.

Then once shooting concludes and all players have returned home, the Producers give the OK for everyone to start posting again. But they control these posts. Producers monitor you and won't allow you to post much more than selfies with no context given in the image or the caption. These "Return to IG" posts serve the singular purpose of starting your social media engine revving once again. If you entered the game with 10K or more followers this post might do as well as any of your average posts. But if you're coming into the game with a smaller following it's very possible your "Return to IG" post will be your most successful post of all time. And as the season goes on, so will each successive post do better than the last.

Then finally, after languishing in the Producer-enforced social media cone of silence, Night One airs and the next period of the postseason begins. . . .

The Watch-Back

Once the first episode airs, things will change significantly. This will very likely be the first time you get to see yourself on television. It will also probably be the first time you have the strange experience of a team of Producers editing footage of you to create lines of dialogue you might have never said in an effort to make you seem like a type of person you never actually were. And it may well be the first time you start to see drastic increases in your follower count across the major social media platforms. In some cases players have seen increases of well over 100K IG followers in the twenty-four-hour period after an episode airs that featured them prominently.

The Producers will relax their control over your posts at this point, but they won't relinquish it entirely. You will be able to post selfies as before and they will also supply you with approved images and videos from the show itself to help promote various Group Dates or other events that might be airing on a specific night. Posting every Monday afternoon to generate excitement for your upcoming appearance that night is mandatory, as is a Tuesday morning post in reaction to the prior night's events. Any other posts are highly encouraged, but you should figure out your own comfort level with frequency of posting. Too many can burn you out unless you've got the parasocial stamina for it, but develop a consistent pattern so your followers know what to expect.

If a given episode isn't about you, make sure you comment on the posts of whoever it is about and on the *Bachelor* Instagram. Always insert yourself into whatever the main conversation is from week to week, especially if it's not about you. If you happen to have been eliminated early, find the line between entertainingly commenting on players' posts who made deep runs and coming off as thirsty. If Bachelor Nation smells desperation their parasocial interest may wither and it can mean the end of your chances at Paradise or any subsequent followers.

It's during the watch-back that talent managers and agents might reach out to you. If you have high enough numbers, plenty of people know how to turn that into money for a fee of their own. Do your research and ask who else they represent before agreeing to any contracts or terms. Get advice from previous players. Brands, too, might start reaching out directly during this period. This can be exciting, but you have to be careful and make sure any spon-con agreement doesn't violate any clause in a potential Paradise contract unless, of course, you don't plan on returning to the game at all.

If you had a great season and made a deep run, you're obviously going to have big numbers by the end of your season airing. The screen time to follower count ratio isn't exactly 1:1, but Top 4 finishers overall have many more followers than those who went home earlier. So if you did well enough to make it to the play-offs, you can bide your time during the watch-back. You can post with less frequency and comment with less enthusiasm on other players' posts. Your quality of play will be enough to generate massive gains as the season unfolds. And once the season's Finale airs and the ATFR has concluded you will enter the most important period of time in the postseason. . . .

The Engagement Party

We're not talking about celebrating a decision to get married to the love of your life. We're talking about a five-month traveling marathon of music festivals, birthday parties, road trips, and IG posts designed to maximize your social media engagement. And in fact, marriage should be the furthest thing from your mind during the Engagement Party. Once the Finale airs, Producers will release you from their controlling demands and you can post whatever you want across all platforms. And now you can start telling your story—the story of a happy, capable single woman ready for a year of incredible new opportunities on the horizon—and maybe, just maybe, you'll find your person.

But before you post anything there is something much more important you have to take care of. Get your Stagecoach situation settled. Who are you going with? Where are you staying? And who is getting the tickets? Stagecoach is the mecca of Bachelor Nation. It's a smaller, more intimate version of Coachella that features only country music, which is the de facto soundtrack of *The Bachelor*. More players attend it than any other music festival and it takes place in April, a few months before *BIP* starts shooting. So, as we all saw in *BIP* Season 6 with the Blake Horstmann, Kristina Schulman, Caelynn Miller-Keyes

tayshia
Los Angeles, California
guccibeauty
allanface
nataliesaidi
raulromo
rubyvo_
ryanrichman
hairbykristingrip
306,130 likes
tayshia Can I get an amen for this @guccibeauty lip I think I may have found my new color

beach-spinning love triangle, Producers use events that occur at Stagecoach to lay the framework for strategies in Paradise. And you can use Stagecoach to set up relationships that the Producers will want to exploit, giving you a better shot at getting the invitation.

Stagecoach is also a good place to look for a partner for Paradise, a male player who will agree to give you his Rose every time if you don't have another one in exchange for the same. Play this strategy well and most important, subtly, and enjoy a deep run in a game that's much easier to navigate than *The Bachelor.*

And of course, chronicle the events of Stagecoach via social media as frequently as you can in an effort to generate questions in Bachelor Nation's mind about what other players you might possibly be dating. If a rumor like that gets big enough, *People*, *Us Weekly*, and *Cosmo* will cover it and it has the chance of becoming *the* story from Stagecoach.

But aside from Stagecoach, there are plenty of other activities that generate fantastic social media opportunities. Collaborating weekly with all of the members from the team you chose during the regular season is essential. The more collabs you can do with anyone from your season the better. These help drive your audience to your friend's account and theirs to yours. Many players from Season 25 all moved to New York City to jump-start their parasocial collabs last year.

Plan trips with players from your season, attend their birthday parties, and do IG lives and TikToks with them to maintain relevance. And for the bold among you, move in with one or more of your fellow players to turn a shared living situation into a twenty-four-hour-a-day content factory. It could turn out to be the best move you ever made. *The Bachelor*'s last episode airs in March and then the following season of *Bachelorette* is filmed from February to April and traditionally airs May to July. So you have to fill five months with highly engaging content to maintain relevance and have the best shot at an invitation to Paradise.

Two Suggestions:

Re-create iconic looks from prior era superstars like Kaitlyn Bristowe and Hannah Brown and then tag them in your post with a funny caption paying them homage to get them to comment on your post and drive engagement.

Flirting in the comments of players from other recent seasons to spin the rumor mill and get free coverage from *Us Weekly*, *People*, and *Cosmo* is a great strategy because it also serves the double purpose of hinting to the Producers that perhaps there is a preexisting relationship they could exploit in Paradise.

And then once the subsequent season of *The Bachelorette* starts airing, your strategy shifts. Stay in the current conversation by watching and live posting about every episode on Monday nights to give support to the Bachelorette, who will very likely have been a player on your season. But you also scout the field of *Bachelorette* players to see who you might work well with in Paradise. And definitely do not be afraid to start DMing them. Other players will certainly be doing this, and in some cases finding a good partner with whom you can confidently head into Paradise is just a matter of who sends the first DM. But be careful not to expose your plans or you could wind up on the wrong end of an angry Fourth Audience like Brendan Morais and Pieper James did on *BIP* Season 7.

And when you get your call to come to the burning sands of Paradise, hold your head high. You were prepared. You had a strategy. You executed it flawlessly. You earned your ticket to Paradise and now you have a whole new game to play.

Who Have We Become?

We are not the same people we were when we started this. And by "this" we mean a years-long journey into the deepest analysis of *The Bachelor* that we believe exists anywhere on planet Earth. Starting with our podcast, then the Hyperbinge, and ultimately reinforcing everything we learned by tabulating these statistics and writing this book has turned us into experts on a subject that some certainly think is frivolous or even pathetic (Mom and Dad). But what we've learned in all of this is that there are more people than we could have imagined who take this game just as seriously as we do. And as the show continues to forge ahead year after year, the audience who treats this sport the same way other fans treat football, baseball, and basketball continues to grow. We think it's only a matter of time before statistical analysis and earnest game commentary become incredibly commonplace in most mainstream *Bachelor* podcasts and coverage.

And in some ways we've seen firsthand how much more influential social media and reality TV are than traditional sports. We've never had a pro football player in the White House, but we have had a reality TV star who used Twitter to win an election.

Even as network TV ratings dwindle year after year and the show itself undergoes massive change with the ousting of longtime host Chris Harrison, *The Bachelor* continues to win its Monday night time slot every season, so it doesn't seem like it's going anywhere anytime soon. It is a part of American culture, referenced constantly across all other forms of media. We felt like it was deserving of an intense examination so we decided to do it ourselves and, as strange as it may sound, this process has taught us that there is still more to discuss about *The Bachelor* and we are masochistically looking forward to our next Hyperbinge . . . *The Bachelorette*.

Chapter 12

BEING COMPLICIT

My first reaction to when someone said, "You should be on **The Bachelor,"** ***[was] Black people don't go far on that show.***

Rachel Lindsay, the thirteenth Bachelorette

We've always had a complicated relationship with *The Bachelor* and we wanted to take one final chapter to address that before the end of the book because we have talked to plenty of other fans who feel the same way. On one hand, we are diehard addicts, scheduling our lives around the cycle of the game's seasons, the announcements of rookies, the pomp and circumstance of Night One Limo Exits, and the subsequent season of play that eventually culminates in a new Ring Winner and the crowning of a new Bachelorette. On the other hand, what we perceive to be the racism, homophobia, ableism, and misogyny inherent in the foundation of the game are present in every frame of every season, and continuing to watch it means, at least on some level, we are supporting the continued promotion of these discriminatory practices and their presentation as entertainment. So we're constantly asking ourselves—should we keep watching?

We could stop, and so could everyone else who recognizes these problematic elements of the show, and maybe that would actually make enough of an impact to see *The Bachelor* finally canceled after twenty years of dominating

the ratings. But *The Bachelor* has won the Monday night network ratings battle almost every year, even in its lowest-rated seasons. Instead of the network canceling the show, it's more likely they would cut budgets to maintain the bottom line and the show would remain equally profitable as it continued to cater to an audience who would have no remaining voice of dissent to point out the things that need to change.

So to silence that voice, especially now when it's growing louder every season, we feel would be a mistake because we have seen what it can do. An increasing number of ex- and current players, as well as bloggers, podcasters, and social media movements, have largely been responsible for holding the franchise accountable and fueling all of the changes toward progress that have emerged in recent seasons.

So instead of completely disengaging from the sport we love, we continue watching knowing that we are complicit, but we are also aware. And that awareness gives us an opportunity to do as much as we can on any platform we have, including this book, to point out what needs to change to push the game forward. We believe the show must become more progressive or be discarded as an antiquated relic of a past generation.

To a casual viewer the racism-related scandal that erupted in Season 25, which has since led to the removal of Chris Harrison as host, might have seemed like an anomalous event. Even more seasoned fans of the show who can remember back to 2017 when the Producers used racism as a plot point in Rachel Lindsay's season of *The Bachelorette* still might not recall how race has played a role in shaping the game since the very beginning. We certainly didn't until we completed the Hyperbinge.

Although we only cataloged seasons from *The Bachelor* in this book, we've included some incidents in this chapter from both *The Bachelorette* and *BIP*, as they help to illustrate the full context that led to the events of 2021 and just how much the racially discriminatory practices of the show have influenced outcomes for players of color. The most drastic effect being twenty full seasons without a single Black player reaching the play-offs. The uninitiated might see this as a fault of the first twenty Bachelors, but you have to remember that it's the Producers deciding who all but one of the Final Four will be in virtually every case. They purposely created a statistical ceiling that existed until 2016 by casting almost entirely White player pools and literally not allowing a Black player to participate in the most crucial rounds of the game.

And it all started in Season 1. We have attempted to highlight the incidents we felt were most important, but it is by *no* means a comprehensive list.

The History of Race in *The Bachelor*

Season 1 featured twenty-five players. Twenty-three of them were White, as was the Bachelor, Alex Michel. In 2002 most of the formal coverage of the show that we could unearth centered around the audacious premise of one man dating twenty-five women and the overwhelming success the show experienced in the ratings. We found no coverage of a major network game show selectively choosing a 92 percent White cast. This type of critique wouldn't come for many years.

In a rare moment of progress in Season 1, a Black player named LaNease Adams performed the first kiss in *Bachelor* history on a Group Date in Las Vegas, but Bachelor Alex Michel dismissed her in the round just before Hometowns. This hard-line barrier for players of color cemented itself in the game—an informal and unspoken rule defined by statistics that all but guaranteed that Producers only allowed White players berths into the play-offs. This unacknowledged pattern of seemingly racist casting and producing practices continued for almost two decades in plain view on network television, pumped into millions of homes every Monday night.

We were extremely surprised to see a moment in Season 3 that could have changed the trajectory of representation in the franchise early on. The first episode of that season included short video packages of multiple potential Bachelors, all leading up to a final reveal of the man Producers ultimately selected. One of the prospective Bachelors that season was an Olympic volleyball gold medalist named Dain Blanton. Blanton could have been the first Black Bachelor way back in 2003. Instead, the Producers selected Andrew Firestone, the White heir to the Firestone family fortune. For a glimmer of a moment the show revealed how different the entire franchise could have been.

Instead, Seasons 2–7 featured a player pool that was 87.5 percent White and Producers regularly eliminated players of color wholesale in the first few weeks or, in the case of Firestone's Season 3, entirely on Night One. Season 4 did represent a rare moment of progress for diversity in the game when Mary Delgado became the first Latinx player to make it to the play-offs. She was eliminated in third place by Bachelor Bob Guiney but returned for a second tour in Season 6, where she became the first Latinx player to win the Ring and secure her place in the pantheon of the greatest players of all time.

But as groundbreaking as Delgado's contributions were, they were short-lived, and in 2011 both Season 15 of *The Bachelor* and Season 7 of *The Bachelorette* were 100 percent White—all players and the leads. They cast this show subjectively. A room of Producers and network executives decide who gets to play each season. In 2011 everyone responsible decided to exclude anyone who was not White. We believe it was the most egregious display of inherently racist casting practices employed by the show, at least up to that point.

This completely White year didn't go unnoticed. The very next year in 2012 two Black men named Christopher Johnson and Nathaniel Claybrooks sued *The Bachelor* and ABC. After the franchise rejected them they claimed the show discriminated against people of color. ABC rebutted with a claim that no such practices were in place but added that even if they were, nothing would be wrong with that. It is their First Amendment right to cast whoever they want. A judge ultimately threw the suit out. But awareness was building in mainstream pop culture about just how seemingly racist the casting practices of the show actually were.

And beyond the overarching casting practices, even the in-game awards like the FIMP Rose seemed to be reserved only for White players. It wasn't until Season 18 that Sharleen Joynt became the first player of color to receive a FIMP Rose. This was, coincidentally, also the first season with a Latinx Bachelor, Juan Pablo Galavis.

Producers would crown a player from Galavis's season, Andi Dorfman, the next Bachelorette for Season 10 in 2014, and this was the first time that they overtly used racism to build a story line. In the fifth episode's Group Date a player named Andrew Poole was accused of using a racial slur to describe the two Black players who made it through the most recent Rose Ceremony, one of whom was still in the game—Marquel Martin. Martin was then forced by Producers to confront Poole in an awkward scene that they used as the dramatic through line of that entire episode. The burgeoning world of *Bachelor* blogging wrote about this scene and it became one of the most memorable moments from that season. Producers discovered that they could use racism to build dramatic plots and this would certainly not be the last time they employed it.

In Episode 3 of Season 20 a White player named Lauren Himle told a fellow White player that a Black player named Jubilee Sharpe "wouldn't get along with the other soccer moms." While Himle was certainly responsible for this arguably racist statement, it was still the Producers who chose to air the footage, as is the case with literally anything and everything in any episode. Once again they saw value in exploiting racism to drive plot.

At the same time Season 20 was airing, the Academy Awards announced their nominees and all twenty acting nominations went to White actors, prompting the hashtag #oscarssowhite to trend immediately. It didn't take long before the hashtag #bachelorsowhite was trending right along with it, and this was the first time we saw social media pressure actually have an effect on the game.

In 2016, as tension mounted over the upcoming presidential election, Producers selected the cast of Season 21, and it was the most diverse in the history of the game up to that point. Almost a full third of the player pool was non-White, a trend that would continue through all future seasons. But Season 21 was far more important than simply raising the level of diversity. Many people believe that Producers engineered that season to produce the first Black Bachelorette in Rachel Lindsay. She was the first Black player to ever receive a FIMP Rose and she was the first Black player to make it to the play-offs (both Hometowns and Fantasy Suites). And in a landmark article for *Vulture* penned by Lindsay herself, she corroborated that indeed Producers had her in mind to wear the Crown from very early on.

Rachel Lindsay's announcement as the first Black Bachelorette was historic. We had a real sense of hope that maybe, just maybe, the show was actually turning a corner, sincerely attempting to change what we believe to be the racist foundation on which the entire franchise was built. The first time we saw Lindsay as the Bachelorette was in the last few moments of Season 21's ATFR. Lindsay was brought out onstage and allowed to meet four players who would be on her season. One of them was Dean Unglert, who upon meeting Lindsay said full-throated, "I'm ready to go Black and never go back." This produced audible groans from both of us, as we had the sinking feeling that Lindsay's season might not be what we hoped for.

Although it was certainly incredible to finally see a Black lead and even the most diverse player pool up to that point by a large margin, with almost half of the players in Season 13 being non-White, the season was marred by the addition of one player specifically, who seemed to completely overshadow any attempt at greater inclusion. A White player named Lee Garrett was quickly embroiled in a racism-based rivalry with a Black player named Kenny King.

The Producers did all they could to stoke the conflict, which ultimately featured Garrett using the racially charged term "aggressive" to describe King several times as he tried to present himself as a victim to Lindsay. A few weeks into that season airing, tweets surfaced from Garrett that people felt were overtly racist. The show and network claimed to be oblivious to these openly and easily viewable tweets, denying any culpability in fostering a racism plot, but virtually no one believes that. Rachel Lindsay herself has claimed to believe that the Producers purposely cast him on her season in order to generate a racism plot for the first Black lead in the show's history.

At that season's Men Tell All, the show got to double-dip into their racism pot by putting Garrett's tweets on a screen behind Chris Harrison and making Garrett answer for them in front of a live studio audience. It was the first time social media played a part in uncovering past actions by players, but it would certainly not be the last, especially where racial insensitivity was concerned.

Season 13 of *The Bachelorette* was difficult to watch. The guilt was starting to outweigh the pleasure. But we tried to focus on the good things—the first Black lead, the most diverse cast in history. We hoped that despite the turbulence of the season and the mistakes that were clearly made, the door would open a little wider for future players of color, and we settled in for what we were sure was going to be the mindless fun of *BIP*. The only problem was *BIP* Season 4 was rocked by another race-related scandal that involved a Black player from Lindsay's season named DeMario Jackson.

Jackson had already suffered a severe Villain Edit in Lindsay's season and Paradise was to be his chance for redemption. Instead, in Week 1 Jackson and a White player named Corinne Olympios engaged in what they both defined as a consensual sexual act, but a Producer who did not see the tape or the event itself filed a misconduct allegation that forced production to shut down. And when they resumed shooting, neither Jackson nor Olympios returned. In subsequent interviews Jackson openly expressed his concern that the allegation was racially motivated, and the only Black player left in Paradise at that point, Diggy Moreland, echoed the same feeling on the show itself. In interviews Jackson explained that the allegation ruined his life for a year because the first thing that came up when anyone Googled his name was "sexual assault." It didn't matter if it was true. And so the question has to be asked, what was the Producer's motivation to file the misconduct allegation if not to start a racially motivated dramatic plot, just as had been done on the most recent season of *The Bachelorette*? In response to the event, Warner Brothers issued the following statement: "We have become aware of allegations of misconduct on the set of *Bachelor in Paradise* in Mexico. We have suspended production and we are conducting a thorough investigation of these allegations. Once the investigation is complete, we will take appropriate responsive action."

It seems that this incident might have given the Producers some pause, because Season 22 of *The Bachelor* had a cast as diverse as Season 21, but it avoided using race as an overt plot point. And in Season 23 not only did they maintain the increased cast diversity; Tayshia Adams became the second Black player to make it to the play-offs (both rounds, just as Lindsay had). Once again it felt like the show might have been on the right track.

But then *Bachelor* Season 24 happened and, just like with Lee Garrett back in *Bachelorette* Season 13, the Fourth Audience uncovered social media that revealed racial insensitivity from one of the players. Victoria Fuller, who would later make it all the way to third place, was tagged in some IG photos as a model for a company called WLM, which claimed to stand for "We Love Marlins" but made apparel featuring the phrase "White Lives Matter" and used a version of the Confederate flag as a logo in some of their designs. Fuller issued a response to her involvement with the company via Instagram story in which she said, "My intention was only to support an endangered species . . . I want to say that I unequivocally reject the beliefs of the white lives matter movement or any propaganda that supports racism of any kind. I would like to specifically apologize to people of color that are affected by racism daily. It was never my intention to add fuel to the racial fire in this country. This has truly been an educational moment for me, and I hope to be a voice against racism moving forward. I hope I can be shown grace as I navigate through this process." *Cosmo* revoked a reward they gave to Fuller on a Group Date that would have allowed her to model for the cover of one of their issues. This was the first time there were real-world consequences outside the game for a player based on past transgressions, so it seemed like there would be some level of accountability. But at the WTA that season, instead of making Fuller face the social media evidence of her racial insensitivity like the Producers did with Lee Garrett, they completely ignored it.

Instead, they brought out Rachel Lindsay, the first Black Bachelorette, to deliver an anti-bullying monologue written by the Producers that featured verbatim readings of derogatory messages certain players received on social media. The segment was presented as a plea from Lindsay but crafted by Producers for Bachelor Nation to stop online harassment of players. At no point did they include the word "racism" in this monologue, but the message was delivered by a Black player. This seemed as close as the show was willing to get to addressing apparent racism within the franchise.

Then they announced the next Bachelorette—Clare Crawley. And then a few short weeks later, COVID-19 changed every element of life around the globe, and that included the production schedule of *The Bachelorette*. It halted everything, and just like everyone else, we went into quarantine. We had Zoom meetings by day, *Bachelor* Instagram and TikTok by night, and occasionally we wore pants just to feel important. And then a police officer murdered George Floyd on-camera and a world that had already changed so drastically just kept changing as BLM protests mobilized in every major city across the United States and even globally. Systemic racism in America was laid bare and people were doing everything they could to fight against it wherever they saw it. And that included Bachelor Nation.

Fans across social media started flooding the official ABC *Bachelor* IG account with demands for greater diversity in the show. Rachel Lindsay herself said she was done with the franchise if they didn't cast a Black Bachelor and the Bachelor Diversity Campaign gained enough momentum that, during the height of the BLM protests, ABC announced that the next Bachelor immediately after Crawley's season would be Matt James . . . the first Black Bachelor.

We already knew who Matt James was. So did anyone who followed the two biggest IG players of all time—Hannah Brown and Tyler Cameron. James was Cameron's best friend. At the time he was the third most important member of the Quarantine Crew, a group of Floridians led by Cameron who quarantined together for a month or so in order to produce social media content and merch. We also knew that James had been previously cast as a player on Crawley's postponed season of *Bachelorette*, but the pressure from Bachelor Nation for more diversity in the show propelled him to the Crown without ever playing a single day of the main game, as well as ABC making the earliest ever announcement of the following Bachelor. He would be the first Bachelor since Season 12's Matt Grant who had never stepped out of the limo as a player (except for Brad Womack's second *Bachelor* run in Season 15).

But before James could shoot his season, Crawley had to shoot hers. News started filtering in through social media that the show had figured out a way they could shoot while the world was still in quarantine. They were going to sequester an entire resort in Palm Springs and force everyone into a bubble similar to the one the NBA forced players into to finish the 2020 season. And it was also going to be literally 120 degrees the entire time, so everyone would be covered in sweat. It was already going to be a weird season, but then it got even weirder when we found out Crawley knew who her players were going to be and because of the postponed season she became the first lead in history to be able to look at her players on social media.

For five months she was sitting in her living room checking out Dale Moss's abs every day, essentially falling in love with him through Instagram. Meeting him was just a formality. Moss had already won the game before he even started playing. Crawley famously ended the season early because she was so smitten, and Moss became the first Black player of all time to win a Ring in either of the two main games (*The Bachelor* has still not produced a Black Ring Winner).

And with Clare and Dale gone after only four rounds of the game, the Producers were forced to bring in a second Bachelorette to finish out Season 16. They selected Tayshia Adams, who would be the second Black Bachelorette. And once again we found ourselves excited that maybe the show was actually changing. James's season would start shooting after *Bachelorette* Season 16, and by their slotting in Tayshia Adams just before his season, it truly seemed like they were making a big effort to start correcting what in our minds was eighteen years of openly racist casting and producing.

And then as Tayshia settled into her role as Bachelorette and started going on dates with her players, a 1O1 transpired between Adams and a player named Ivan Hall that was quite possibly the most historically important moment of all time where representation is concerned. As they sat at a table looking at food they weren't allowed to eat, they had an open conversation about being Black in America. Ivan Hall talked about his brother being incarcerated and abused by correctional officers. He invoked George Floyd's name. Adams herself recounted what it was like for her growing up in a predominantly White area of Orange County, California. Astonishingly, Producers left this conversation in the edit and sent it to air. We have imagined that throughout the long history of the game, conversations like this have to have taken place, but the Producers always tossed them in the cutting room trash can to uphold the illusion that race isn't an issue in the show or in the country at large. But in this moment, they let Bachelor Nation see a real conversation about it. It was remarkable.

Then later in the season, when Ivan Hall made it to the Hometown round of the play-offs, the show brought his brother to join the Hall family. They made him a part of the conversation and portrayed him as a human being. This season contained no forced racism plots like we saw with Rachel Lindsay. Instead, it had the exact opposite—people of color talking about their experiences. For at least some of Bachelor Nation, this was the first time they had seen anything like this in their living rooms and that felt like a massive step forward.

In prior seasons Chris Harrison had defended what we believe were the racist casting practices of the show by claiming that either they weren't getting high enough quality applicants of color or the *Bachelor* audience just wasn't ready for a Black lead. When *E! News* asked him in 2018 if there would ever be a Black Bachelor, he said, "Sure, yeah, absolutely, I mean no reason not to . . . My thing has always been, for Rachel; I'm glad that Rachel wasn't the first Black Bachelorette; I'm glad that she was the right woman . . . she's an amazing woman. That's what I want. Same thing for a man. When we do have, and we will, I just want it to be a great man. And a good man. And if he happens to be Black, great!" Tayshia Adams proved that Bachelor Nation was more than ready to see diverse stories being told in the game. She made history on November 6, 2020, by becoming the first Black player to break through the 1 million IG follower mark, a feat that Rachel Lindsay had flirted with but never achieved.

We were feeling great heading into Season 25. The seasons were ready to change. The show was ready to change. The audience was ready for it to change. The first Black Bachelor was ready to take the stage and he was pre-approved by the two biggest stars in the game in Hannah Brown and Tyler Cameron. What could go wrong?

It turned out . . . literally everything.

Everyone knew it wasn't going to be like Season 16 of *The Bachelorette* almost immediately. As soon as Chris Harrison met James in front of the castle-like main hotel at the Nemacolin resort in Pennsylvania, things seemed . . . off. Before James was allowed to meet the players of his season, the Producers forced him to have an on-camera conversation with Chris Harrison about the pressure of being the first Black Bachelor.

Before the first player even stepped out of the limo, all of the sincerity and humility we saw in Tayshia's season was replaced by Harrison's gleaming white teeth smiling under hollow eyes. As James was forced to talk about the pressure of picking a Ring Winner of a certain race, Harrison, who is now, in our minds, the exposed face of racism within the franchise, nodded knowingly, playing the role of caring confidant. But the reality was that this conversation was scripted and produced to eliminate any culpability the show might face for racist casting or producing practices they meant to employ that season. It was a purposeful preemptive strike meant to inoculate the show against any possible responsibility for the outcome of the product they were creating.

It wasn't a promising opening tone for a season that should have been a watershed moment in the franchise—the first Black Bachelor in eighteen years. But still we kept watching and there were promising moments. Right off the bat Season 25 was the most diverse player pool of all time with over 50 percent players of color. For only the third time in *Bachelor* history, the Bachelor gave the FIMP Rose to a player of color, Abigail Heringer. And they even featured an on-camera conversation between Matt James and a player named Chelsea Vaughn about the unique experiences she had with her hair as a Black woman. It was later revealed that Producers cut footage of James adding his own hair-related experiences from the show, but nonetheless, having this conversation pumped into millions of homes across America on a Monday night still felt like progress.

Then, early in the season a TikTok video emerged from a woman named Maddy Bierster that shot through online Bachelor Nation like wildfire. Bierster claimed that an early front-runner named Rachael Kirkconnell had harassed her in high school for dating a Black man. These allegations were unproven, but the accusation raised concerns about Kirkconnell's actual attitudes in regard to race and interracial dating and gave rise to the idea that perhaps she was not in the game 4TRR.

As the season wore on, Kirkconnell remained a front-runner, which always carries the weight of more intense online scrutiny. In the last half of the regular season, Bierster's initial claims were corroborated, at least in part, when a series of IG posts surfaced, all liked by Kirkconnell, depicting high school students engaged in culturally appropriative activity, and one post even featured the Confederate flag. The show ignored this completely, but the Fourth Audience, Bachelor Nation, certainly didn't. Even more damning images were unearthed from 2018, this time actually featuring Kirkconnell herself at an Old South party dressed in an antebellum gown.

We had seen something like this in Season 24 with Victoria Fuller. The show never dealt with her posing for a company wearing "White Lives Matter" T-shirts and hats. They completely ignored it and went about their business as usual, and it worked for them. Granted, this was before the events of the summer of 2020 and, perhaps even more important, Fuller wasn't the Ring Winner. She went home in third place that season. And quite possibly most important, the Season 24 Bachelor, Peter Weber, was White.

Kirkconnell, on the other hand, was the Ring Winner of Season 25. Bachelor Nation didn't know she won her season yet because the Finale hadn't aired, but the Producers obviously knew how the season ended. Reporting emerged that alleged the show itself had forbidden Kirkconnell from commenting on any social media platform until they could figure out what the official plan of action would be. It was quickly becoming a PR nightmare. So, Chris Harrison was called upon to appear on *Extra*. We believe this was in order to defend Kirkconnell, take some of the heat off the situation, and hopefully salvage what was left of a season that was quickly sinking in controversy that threatened to overshadow everything.

So on February 9, 2021, Chris Harrison appeared via video teleconference to talk with none other than Rachel Lindsay, who had become on-air talent for *Extra*, to discuss the Kirkconnell scandal. This was quite possibly the worst moment for progress in the history of the franchise and one of the most harrowing conversations to witness as two superfans. Harrison proceeded to not only defend Kirkconnell's past behavior by claiming that "fifty million people" a year attended Old South balls but also justify racist behavior because in his mind 2018 was a vastly different time than 2021 where public tolerance of racism was concerned. And he ultimately pointed a finger at Lindsay herself and the "woke police" as being a part of the problem. Harrison's marching orders had clearly been to defuse the situation, to smooth it over as best he could so the Producers might be able to salvage the illusion of a love story from the dumpster fire of the season they designed. Instead, Harrison inadvertently threw gasoline on it and watched it burn.

The outrage from his appearance was instantaneous, giving birth to a petition on Change.org titled "Fire Chris Harrison" that accrued almost fifty thousand signatures within a week. And conversely, members of the Nation also launched a petition to keep Harrison as host, which saw a similar number of signatures, if slightly less. Harrison issued a quick apology via Instagram, but it wasn't enough and he was forced to issue another apology in which he announced he would be stepping away from the show for some amount of time, which would include forfeiting his hosting duties for Season 25's ATFR, an episode he had hosted since the first one aired during Season 3.

Harrison had been the face of the entire franchise since its first days, but after he revealed his true feelings about race and the recent social justice movements, Producers were forced to edit him out of as many remaining scenes as they could and they replaced him at ATFR with Emmanuel Acho, a former NFL player turned YouTube host, activist, and *New York Times* best-selling author of *Uncomfortable Conversations with a Black Man*.

The season had been entirely overshadowed by the exposing of what many believed to be Harrison's true views and the scandal that resulted. And some wondered if, like with Producers purposely casting Lee Garrett on Rachel Lindsay's season to stir up a racism plot, Kirkconnell was a purposeful plant. It's true Producers might not have dug deep enough to find her Confederate flag and antebellum appreciation posts, but they did know she came from an infamous sundown county in Georgia. At the very least that seemed a suspicious choice. And if indeed Kirkconnell was cast in the hopes of giving rise to a racism plot, it had obviously gone far beyond the Producers' control and caused the entire season, which should have been a celebration of diversity, to collapse under the worst racism scandal the show has ever seen.

After the season's conclusion on ATFR, James admitted that the scandal and Kirkconnell's past actions led him to break up with her. He cited thinking about what their prospective children might think when they would eventually see these things online about their mother. Kirkconnell apologized through tears. The pair split for a while and later got back together. And in an effort to quickly divert Bachelor Nation's attention from the disaster the Producers had created, they reserved the final moments of Season 25's ATFR for the announcement of the next Bachelorette!

A White player who was eliminated in eleventh place named Katie Thurston emerged from backstage and Acho announced her as the lead of *Bachelorette* Season 17, which would begin shooting very quickly. But that wasn't all. In a surprise twist, and a first in the history of the show, a second Bachelorette was announced simultaneously—a Black player named Michelle Young whose season would shoot after Thurston's and air after the subsequent season of *BIP*. The move was seen as a clear attempt by the Producers to pacify the divided audience in Bachelor Nation. But as the ashes of Season 25 were still smoldering we collectively turned our attention to the next big question mark . . . who was going to host what would now be three seasons of content almost back to back to back?

The Producers forced Harrison back on-camera a week later to deliver what appeared to be a scripted apology he was reading off-camera to Michael Strahan on *Good Morning America*. If this appearance was meant to be a litmus test for Bachelor Nation's readiness to see Harrison back on their TV screens, it failed miserably. It was too soon to be believable and it was delivered too robotically to be sincere. Despite this, ABC and the Producers still planned to have Harrison host the upcoming Season 17 of *The Bachelorette* and force him back into the franchise.

But as the off-season wore on, a series of incredible events transpired that started with most of the players from Season 25 banding together in an unprecedented act of solidarity. They all released an identical post to their main IG grids denouncing racism, supporting Rachel Lindsay, and in effect denouncing Chris Harrison himself as host of the show. It was a form of unionization by a group of players that had never been attempted before and it worked. The men of *Bachelorette* Season 16 issued a similar statement in solidarity and we even saw third-place player Ivan Hall publicly say that he would not participate in any future season of *BIP* if Harrison was host. It was a claiming of power by the Second Audience, the players themselves, that will very likely be remembered for all time.

And the final stroke of this power grab came from Thurston herself. Just before she made her way into the bubble to shoot her season she issued a tweet:

> *I stand with other alumni who have expressed that learning & growth require time. I hope that Chris Harrison continues to take more time to step away while sincerely educating himself & dedicating himself to the work . . .*

This was a historic moment, marking the first time an incoming Bachelorette wielded the full power of her position to dictate who the host of her season would or, more important, would not be. This all but handcuffed the Producers and they almost immediately announced that Harrison would not be hosting Thurston's season, but instead former Bachelorettes Kaitlyn Bristowe and Tayshia Adams would co-host it. And just like the choice to shoot two seasons of *The Bachelorette* almost back to back with leads of different races, the choice to cast two hosts of different races seemed to be an effort to appease a divided Bachelor Nation.

A few weeks into the airing of Thurston's historic Season 17 of *The Bachelorette*, news emerged that the embattled former host of the franchise had retained the same high-powered entertainment attorney who helped Gabrielle Union reach a lucrative settlement with NBC over her claims of racism and sexism in the workplace. NBC's reply to the Gabrielle Union lawsuit was, "NBC Entertainment appreciates the important concerns raised by Gabrielle Union and remains committed to ensuring an inclusive and supportive working environment where people of all backgrounds can be treated with respect." Could Harrison have leveraged the threat of exposing nineteen years' worth of dirty laundry about the behind-the-scenes practices of the show? Is that ultimately why he walked away from *The Bachelor* forever in exchange for a reported $9 million payout?

We had mixed feelings about this. On the one hand, Chris Harrison had come to symbolize the worst parts of the show and seeing him leave felt like progress. But on the other hand, he was only a figurehead for the entire system of network and studio executives, Producers, and casting directors who are all still in place and now protected from the possible threat of Harrison exposing whatever secrets he had used as threats.

The future of the show is unclear. We can only hope that these recent seasons and events have forced the show and those responsible for its production on a more direct course to make lasting and meaningful changes.

Impact of Race for Players

Although the game is changing with more diverse casting practices, it is crucial to understand the diminished odds of success that still exist for players of color in *The Bachelor*, especially if you are a player of color about to enter the game.

Odds of winning a Ring for a Black player in *The Bachelor*, for example, are still 0 percent. And Michelle Young was the first and only Black player to make it to the finals.

There has been one Latinx Ring Winner in Mary Delgado (Season 6). There has been one Filipino-American Ring Winner in Catherine Giudici (Season 17). And there has been one Chinese-American Ring Winner in Tessa Horst (Season 10). All others have been White.

Until Season 25 only two Black players had ever made it into the play-offs. As of Season 25 there have been four:

Michelle Young (Season 25)
Bri Springs (Season 25)
Tayshia Adams (Season 23)
Rachel Lindsay (Season 21)

So at this point in the game's history, Black players have a 4 percent chance of making it to the Hometown and/or Fantasy Suite round of the game. And again, we're hopeful that Season 25 is more indicative of things to come, which saw three of the Final Four players as players of color, but the numbers are the numbers and currently the numbers are very bad.

FIMP Roses are another indicator of unfair bias against players of color, with only three of twenty-five recipients being players of color (we are discounting Season 17, in which Bachelor Sean Lowe was allowed to hand out twelve FIMP Roses):

Sharleen Joynt (Season 18)
Rachel Lindsay (Season 21)
Abigail Heringer (Season 25)

And it's not just the main games that disproportionately favor White players. Social media preferences skew White as well, which is perhaps to be expected given the underrepresented screen time for players of color. Even in Season 25 with their record-breaking diverse cast, a popular *Bachelor* statistician, @bachelordata (on Instagram), found that the players of color had a disproportionately low amount of screen time compared to the White players. Only two Black players have ever broken into the 1 million IG Club—a group of thirty-four elite players that is 91 percent White. And all four sitting members of the 2 million club are White.

The current state of Bachelor Nation is in turmoil where diversity and representation is concerned. That is clear. But ABC and the official *Bachelor* IG account have issued statements claiming to hire more people of color behind the camera and at Executive Producer levels in an effort to be more inclusive. And indeed in April 2021 they named Jodi Baskerville their first Black Executive Producer in the franchise's history. As society changes, all professional sports must reflect those changes or run the risk of becoming irrelevant and antiquated. *The Bachelor* is no different. At this point the corporate entities behind the show are very obviously aware there is a problem and they have vowed to fix it. We remain hopeful that they will. And we wish all incoming players luck in the game, but especially players of color, who face a more difficult road than their White counterparts.

Appendix

THE HISTORY OF OUR BELOVED GAME

Congratulations. You've made it through everything we learned from the Hyperbinge and the countless hours of discussion and examination of our beloved game. Well, almost everything. There's still one last piece of knowledge, one grouping of information that we didn't really understand ourselves until the whole thing was over. The last lesson we learned was just how important the history of the game actually was.

Watching four to six episodes per day on 2x speed was like seeing time-lapse photography of the evolution of the game itself as it climbed out of the primordial ooze of early-century guilty-pleasure reality TV to become as integral to the American pop culture landscape as the NFL. If you started watching *The Bachelor* any time after 2010 you might think that things like FIMP Roses and riding up to the Mansion on a horse have been in the game forever. That's certainly what we thought. But we learned that huge, intrinsic pieces of the game weren't always there. In fact, they were invented by Producers season after season in the early years in what we believe was an effort to heighten drama at the cost of building relationships.

We encourage everyone to embark on their own Hyperbinge. It will absolutely enhance your understanding of every element of the game in a profound way. But if, perhaps like most people, you find yourself with a job, a family, or any kind of social life at all, you might not have three months to spend ten hours a day watching *The Bachelor*. So this final appendix is our best attempt to deliver the historical lessons we learned as we watched. On these final pages you will find an easy reference guide for all twenty-five seasons—every Bachelor in order, the basic facts about their seasons, and the most important things that happened during each one.

The Classic Era (Seasons 1–3)

2002–2003

There is no question when you watch the first three seasons that they were from a different time. They were simple, elegant, and even innocent. As of March 25, 2022, *The Bachelor* will have been on the air for twenty years. So much has changed in America just over the last year, let alone the last two decades, and the Classic Era reflects that change in every frame.

SEASON 1

Air dates: March 25–April 25, 2002

7 Episodes, 1 Hour Each

Players: 25

Bachelor: Alex Michel, a thirty-one-year-old Harvard and Stanford Business School graduate living in San Francisco

---

After twenty-five seasons, the premise of the show, that one man would simultaneously date twenty-five women, is something we take completely for granted. But when *The Bachelor* premiered it was beyond shocking. It was a social experiment in the same way *Big Brother* and *Survivor* were; the only difference was those other shows were open competitions with a monetary prize. *The Bachelor* billed itself as a dating show, nothing more. Certainly not a game with any obvious prizes. However, some of the most important game elements were there from the beginning even if they were a little different from what we now watch.

There were, for example, Limo Exits, but each of the twenty-five players delivered nothing more than a handshake and brief introduction before entering the Mansion—not even so much as a peck on the cheek. The pageantry and spectacle of the parade of costumes and classic cars that we've become used to on Night One was nowhere to be seen. There were Group Dates and 1O1s, but there were no Roses awarded on any of them. There was no jockeying for time because the Group Dates were evenly allocated in order to allow each player an equal amount of time. In some ways it was a more fair and civilized game in that it guaranteed every player a date in each round.

Notable players included Cathy Grimes, who used the phrase "right reasons" for the first time at the WTA. Rhonda Rittenhouse was the first player to ever say she was "not here to make friends," earning her the first Villain Edit. LaNease Adams entered the record books by securing the first-ever kiss and of course Trista Rehn (who would be crowned the first Bachelorette) was the first player to be rejected at the Final Altar as the runner-up. The very first Ring Winner was Amanda Marsh, although Michel did not propose to her but instead pledged to begin a dating relationship, which ended after several months.

SEASON 2

Air dates: September 25–November 20, 2002

9 Episodes, 1 Hour Each

Players: 25

Bachelor: Aaron Buerge, a twenty-eight-year-old banker/pilot/restauranteur living in Butler, Missouri

---

Nothing was done to change the format of the game, but because the first season was such a massive hit, ABC ordered two more episodes, one of which was a behind-the-scenes casting special that aired before Night One. Multiple potential Bachelors were highlighted in this first episode and we were granted a rare look at the process of creating a season. Producers, including the creator of *The Bachelor*, Mike Fleiss, were featured on-screen for the first time as they interviewed not only the prospective Bachelors but the players for that season as well. Season 2 included the first utterance of the phrase "Rose Ceremony" by host Chris Harrison in reference to the elimination portion of the game, which was called Invitation Night in the first season. In a moment that has only happened once in the history of *The Bachelor*, Buerge insisted on writing a check from his own bank account to purchase the ring that he would give to psychologist Helene Eksterowicz. This was a form of public-facing financial proof that he was there 4TRR and Buerge followed it up by issuing the first on-camera proposal in history. Eksterowicz accepted, but the couple broke up shortly after the final episode.

SEASON 3

Air dates: March 24–May 21, 2003

10 Episodes, 1 Hour Each

Players: 25

Bachelor: Andrew Firestone, a twenty-eight-year-old heir to the Firestone family fortune and businessman at the Firestone family vineyard north of Napa Valley, California

---

By the third season of *The Bachelor*'s dominance on ABC, rival network Fox set out to throw their hat into the reality dating arena with a similarly structured show called *Joe Millionaire*. The twist was their lead, Evan Marriott, was presented to the players as a millionaire even though he was far from it, a fact that would be revealed eventually to test the validity of the relationships he developed. In reaction to the blatant attempt to steal their audience, ABC and the production company behind *The Bachelor* not only cast Andrew Firestone, an heir to one of the largest fortunes in America, but also coined the slogan "We've got the real millionaire," which Chris Harrison delivered multiple times per episode. This marked the first overt inclusion of financial gain as part of the prize package for players.

The first nontraditional Limo Exit occurred this season—a Stand-Up performed by a player named Tina (whose last name is lost to time), who greeted Firestone with the prepared line "You have to pick me tonight because I have a lot of clothing I can't return." This season included the first two-hour episode. And the most important element of the final season of the Classic Era was without a doubt a player named Tina Panas. Panas was a different Tina than the one who performed the first Stand-Up, and the first player in the history of the game to utilize an aggressive, comedic, character-based play style, aimed at the viewing audience more than the Bachelor, which garnered her the first nickname of all time, Tina Fabulous. Contemporary comedic character players like Alexis Waters, Corinne Olympios, and Demi Burnett are all part of the legacy started by Tina Fabulous.

Firestone ultimately proposed to Jen Schefft, who accepted, but the couple broke up shortly after the Finale.

The Experimental Era (Seasons 4–12)

2003–2008

To put it simply, the Experimental Era is when things got crazy. Over the course of these nine seasons Producers made a series of radical alterations to the game, testing the limits of how far it could be manipulated and mutated from the original concept. There are things that happened in these seasons that are still in today's game, but there are many, *many* more that are not, and for that we should all be thankful.

SEASON 4

Air dates: September 24–November 20, 2003

10 Episodes, 2-Hour Pilot, 1-Hour Regular Season

Players: 25

Bachelor: Bob Guiney, a thirty-two-year-old owner of a mortgage company from Detroit, Michigan, and fifth-place finisher on the first season of *The Bachelorette*

Eliminated in the round just before Hometowns by Trista Rehn on her season of *The Bachelorette*, Guiney made a name for himself on the inaugural season of *The Bachelorette* as the "funny guy" who didn't fit the physical norm of a stereotypical player. The audience loved his high-pitched laugh and happy-go-lucky attitude so much that for the first time in *Bachelor* history the Producers gave the Crown to an ex-player. So this was also the first time the players already knew the identity of the Bachelor and had also watched him for a full season before meeting him. Because the players all felt like they knew him already, Guiney's season had the first-ever Night One kiss and several Night One tears being shed. But the experimentation didn't stop with Guiney's casting.

The Producers brought Guiney's mother to the Night One Cocktail Party in the first Night One Curveball. The Producers started augmenting Group Dates with an early version of the GDR and there were two new additions to Limo Exits. The Ring Winner of that season, Estella Gardinier, performed the first It Takes Two by coaxing Guiney into putting his hand on her heart when she exited the limo, a move that has been repeated multiple times since. And the first-ever Aloha was performed by Mary Delgado when she greeted Guiney by saying, "Hola, hola, señor." Delgado herself was a player who revolutionized the game on many levels, but in this season she became the first Latinx player to make it to Hometowns and the Fantasy Suite round. She was also the oldest player in the burgeoning history of the game at that point at thirty-five. Estella Gardinier was this season's Ring Winner, but the Ring was only a promise ring, as Guiney refused to propose. The couple dissolved a few weeks after the Finale.

SEASON 5

Air dates: April 7–May 19, 2004

9 Episodes, 1 Hour Each

Players: 25

Bachelor: Jesse Palmer, a twenty-five-year-old NFL quarterback for the New York Giants from New York

---

The love story between *The Bachelor* and the NFL truly began in this season with the casting of an active NFL quarterback as the Bachelor. In another first, Producers tested an element that was never seen before or since by including a Spy within the player pool. Jenny De Schiralli was a personal friend of Palmer and a willing infiltrator whose sole function was to secretly report conversations and behavior of the other players back to Palmer.

The fifth season also saw the rise of a player named Trish Schneider, who would be the game's most influential Villain up to that point. Schneider received the first blur box in history to cover a thong bikini she wore in response to the other players slut shaming her. Schneider's Villain story culminated in the first-ever 2O1 Date as she faced off against Pageant Queen Mandy Jaye Jeffreys. Though there was no Rose on this date, Schneider was ultimately eliminated from the game after Hometowns. However, Schneider displayed so much value in her strong Villain play style that the Producers granted her the first Resurrection of all time, when she was brought back to interrupt Jeffreys's Fantasy Suite dinner the following week. Even though the effort fell short, it was a turning point in the structure of the game that meant Producers were willing to openly act against the Bachelor's best interests in service of drama.

And the most important addition of Season 5 to the overall game was undoubtedly the first FIMP Rose. It was presented to Jesse Palmer by a young Chris Harrison just before he entered the Mansion after Limo Exits, without a silver platter or ceremony of any kind. After a brief explanation by Harrison of this SR's purpose, Palmer simply tucked it inside his jacket and later presented it to the first-ever FIMP Rose recipient, the true star of this season—Trish Schneider.

Jessica Bowlin was this season's Ring Winner, but the couple ended things only a few weeks later. An interesting bit of trivia about Season 5—it remains the only season of all twenty-five in which the first player to arrive at the FRC has won the Ring. In all twenty-four others, the first player was eliminated and the second was the Ring Winner.

SEASON 6

Air dates: September 22–November 24, 2004

9 Episodes, Pilot and Finale 2 Hours Each, All Others 1 Hour

Players: 27

Bachelors: Jay Overbye, a forty-year-old real estate agent from New Jersey, and Byron Velvick, a forty-year-old professional bass fisherman from Downey, California

---

The sixth season of *The Bachelor* was a blitzkrieg of experimentation. The Producers weren't just adding a few Roses here and there: they pushed the boundaries of what the game even was starting with the addition of a second Bachelor. Jay Overbye and Byron Velvick were presented to the player pool (who it is worth noting were not afforded the usual pageantry of Limo Exits this season) and it was the players themselves who voted on which man would be the Bachelor.

Not only were Velvick and Overbye both forty years old (still the oldest Bachelors in history), but once Velvick won the player vote, he moved into a house on the same property as the Mansion, where the players were staying, allowing what was basically unfettered access to him for the entire season. The Producers gave Velvick four Fantasy Suite Dates instead of the usual three and this season saw the first-ever return of players from a prior season. A Season 2 player named Heather Cranford and Season 4's superstar, Mary Delgado, returned for a second tour in Week 3 of this season, marking the first time the overall player pool exceeded twenty-five players. While Cranford was dismissed in the same round she entered, Delgado went on to revolutionize the game in more ways than one. She created the Huju during her Hometown this season and she also made history as both the oldest (thirty-six) and first Latinx player to win the Ring.

Delgado and Velvick engaged in a tumultuous relationship once the show ended that included a domestic assault incident on Delgado's part, but they didn't finally end their relationship until five years after this fateful season.

SEASON 7

Air dates: March 28–May 16, 2005

8 Episodes, 2-Hour Pilot, 3-Hour Finale, All Others 1 Hour

Players: 25

Bachelor: Charlie O'Connell, a thirty-year-old actor from New York, New York, and brother of actor Jerry O'Connell

---

Charlie O'Connell was the closest the Producers ever got to casting a real celebrity as the Bachelor. But that's no slight to him. He was, without a doubt, our favorite Bachelor primarily because he controlled the entire season in a way no one ever really has. In a first, he got the show to shoot in his hometown of New York instead of LA, where the players had to trade in the expansive Mansion for a cramped loft. O'Connell did away with the fake spectacle of Date Cards in favor of informal phone calls to the loft to ask the players out on dates. And for the first time ever 1O1s had Roses up for grabs, which required players to pack their bags in case they were eliminated.

Late in the season the Producers tested the boundaries of how far they could manipulate the game by waiting until Kimberly Choma was on a Hometown Date with O'Connell in Edmonton, Alberta, Canada. They brought in her ex-boyfriend as the first Skeleton to crash a date in an effort to derail her relationship, which worked as planned. Season 7 was also the first time all three Fantasy Suite Dates occurred in the same location (Aruba), which allowed the Producers the ability to have the players run into one another at awkward moments.

And perhaps the biggest flex of O'Connell's control of the game came in the Finale. O'Connell admitted he wasn't ready to select either of the finalists and he asked to continue dating them both for the next two months. The request was granted, and in another groundbreaking first O'Connell made his final selection live on the ATFR episode with both of the finalists' families present to bear witness. This was the first time the Bachelor was able to make a decision after watching his entire season as it aired. O'Connell selected Sarah Brice as the winner but did not propose. The couple had an on-again, off-again dating relationship until 2010, when it was off again for all time.

SEASON 8

Air dates: January 9–February 27, 2006

8 Episodes, 2-Hour Hometown, Fantasy Suite, and Finale, All Others 1 Hour

Players: 25

Bachelor: Travis Stork, a thirty-four-year-old doctor from Nashville, Tennessee

---

Season 7 took the game out of California, but Season 8 took it out of America and landed it in a six-hundred-year-old château in Paris, France. The FIMP Rose was brought in on a silver platter by a French bartender and placed on a communal table for all of the players to see, stoking their anxiety and competitive instincts in a way that had not yet been seen on Night One. Further experimentation with visible roses occurred on this season's 2O1 Date, which included the phrase "Two Women, One Rose, One Stays, One Goes" on the Date Card for the first time.

And in an attempt to mimic other popular reality franchises of the day like *Survivor*, in Week 3 the producers brought back two players who had been eliminated in earlier rounds and let them choose who would go on the dates that week. In the Finale, they also experimented with having the two finalists' mothers visit the players and help them pick out rings and dresses for their proposal or elimination. Instead of proposing, Stork gifted his season's Ring Winner, Sarah Stone, a ring on a necklace. Although Stork's relationship with Stone did not last, he went on to achieve relatively mainstream media success as the host of *The Doctors*, a reality show featuring doctors talking about medical issues.

SEASON 9

Air dates: October 3–November 27, 2006

8 Episodes, 2-Hour Hometown, Fantasy Suite, and Finale, All Others 1 Hour

Players: 25

Bachelor: Lorenzo Borghese, a thirty-four-year-old Italian-American cosmetics entrepreneur, heir to the Borghese fortune, and prince

---

Seasons 8 and 9 were twin seasons in the Experimental Era, matching each other structurally almost identically, including each of them taking place almost entirely outside the United States—the only two seasons to do so. Season 9 saw the game move to Rome, Italy, where the players got to stay in a building that was presented as the Borghese Castle. In keeping with a game mechanic the Producers unveiled in Season 8, an eliminated player was brought back in Week 3 to decide who would be granted dates. The "eliminated player choosing dates" mechanic was never attempted again, as it exposed a truth about one of the most fundamental deceits of the game—that the Producers are not actually trying to help people find love but are instead trying to sabotage relationships to produce as much "drama" as possible.

Season 9 also saw the introduction of two local Italian players who could speak almost no English. They put their mark on the history of the game when they invented the Italian Steal, a move that involves immediately stealing the Bachelor back from the player who initially stole him. The FIMP Rose this season came with a pair of diamond earrings that the recipient was benevolently allowed to keep, the first prize of monetary value associated with the FIMP. Jennifer Wilson was the winner of this season, but Borghese didn't propose and the couple ended their attempt to maintain any kind of relationship shortly after the airing of the final episode.

SEASON 10

Air dates: April 2–May 22, 2007

9 Episodes, 2-Hour Pilot, 1.5-Hour Regular-Season Episodes, 1-Hour ATFR

Players: 25

Bachelor: Andy Baldwin, a thirty-year-old US Navy officer, physician, and sportsman from Lancaster, Pennsylvania

---

Andy Baldwin was the first active-duty military officer to be cast as the Bachelor, and the theme of support for the US military bordered on propagandistic this season, including a 2O1 Date between Tessa Horst and Peyton Wright that took place on the deck of the USS *Midway*, an aircraft carrier docked in San Diego. By this point the FIMP Rose had been solidified as the featured appetizer to the main course of every Night One, but the Producers still saw cause to sprinkle some seasoning on it.

As Baldwin stood in front of the Mansion, the FIMP Rose sat right next to him on a small white pedestal so the players could see it before they even stepped out of their limos. Baldwin was then forced to award the FIMP Rose to a player during her Limo Exit before the players were allotted any time to make an impression at the Cocktail Party. And Baldwin himself pushed the game forward by being the first Bachelor in the rich history of our beloved game to tell two women he loved them. Tessa Horst was this season's Ring Winner, but she and Baldwin broke off their engagement later that year.

SEASON 11

Air dates: September 24–November 20, 2007

10 Episodes, 1.5-Hour Pilot, All Others 1 Hour

Players: 25

Bachelor: Brad Womack, a thirty-four-year-old bar owner from Austin, Texas

---

Nearing the end of the Experimental Era, Season 11 saw some of the last pieces fall into place that would give us the final version of the game. We had mansions in Malibu, châteaus in France, and lofts in New York, but it wasn't until Season 11 that the game finally came home to Villa de la Vina, the now-familiar ten-thousand-square-foot, seven-bedroom, eight-bathroom mansion in Agoura Hills, California, where every subsequent season has been shot (except Season 25 due to COVID limitations).

This season's lead, Brad Womack, was the first Bachelor to have an identical twin, a situation the Producers did not let go to waste. In Week 2 Brad's twin brother, Chad, was made to stand in at a Cocktail Party in an attempt to manipulate the players into believing he was the Bachelor. It was a basic identification test that most players passed, but not all.

A player named Solisa Shoop contributed the first voluntary nudity play in history when she took off her bikini top and ran into the ocean on a Group Date. And the most remarkable event of the eleventh season was beyond doubt a decision made by the Bachelor himself, who was promoted as "sexiest Bachelor of all time." At the FRC Womack opted to dismiss both of the finalists. He told DeAnna Pappas and Jenni Croft that he couldn't see a future with either of them and preferred instead to remain single in what was the most blatant rebuke of "the process" in the game's history. This is the only season ever to not produce a final Ring Winner. But Womack would be given a chance to amend this affront to our beloved game in the very near future.

SEASON 12

Air dates: March 17–May 12, 2008

9 Episodes, 1.5-Hour Pilot, All Others 1 Hour

Players: 25

Bachelor: Matt Grant, a twenty-eight-year-old financier from London, England

---

After eleven seasons' worth of tinkering with the presentation, number, and timing of the FIMP Rose, it was here that the Producers finally crystalized everything. For the first time Chris Harrison himself interrupted the Night One Cocktail Party to bring the FIMP Rose in on a silver platter and set it on the table for all the players to see. It added the necessary jolt of anxiety to the players' systems to elevate the back half of Night One with an extra layer of drama.

But quite possibly the most important development to come from this season was the addition of blatant commercialization in the form of product placement on a date. In Week 2, Grant selected Holly Durst for a 1O1 Date that included a private screening of the movie *Made of Honor*. The date featured scenes from the movie as well as a brief conversation about it by Grant and Durst. This in-your-face style of product placement would weave its thick tendrils through every season afterward to manufacture paid dates by McDonald's, Halo Top ice cream, several other movies, and the tourism boards of cities like Cleveland, Ohio.

Season 12 notably featured an incredibly experimental Hometown strategy by a player named Amanda Rantuccio, who hired a pair of actors to play her mom and dad, which culminated in her fake mother making a pass at Grant in order to see his reaction. Grant ultimately proposed to this season's Ring Winner, Shayne Lamas (whom he affectionately called his "little monkey"), but the two parted ways a few months after the final episode.

The Modern Era (Seasons 13–18)

Colloquially known as: The Mesnian Era
2009–2014

By this point in the Hyperbinge we were a well-oiled machine, able to generate a hundred pages of notes per day without blinking, speaking the language we created to describe the game fluently, and beginning to see the massive bigger picture of the entire scope of show's structure and influence.

By the thirteenth season the frenetic chaos of the Experimental Era had calmed into a stabilized structure built on the cornerstones of the game we know today: Roses on every date, all seasons taking place at Villa de la Vina, two-hour episodes, and perhaps the most important—starting with Season 13 all leads would come from within the franchise from this point forward. But this is not to say the six seasons that comprise the Modern Era didn't contribute lasting effects of their own to the overall game. Limo Exits specifically were adjusted and fine-tuned by players and Producers alike to ultimately yield all eight types by the end of the Modern Era in Season 18. And perhaps most notably, this period of our beloved game saw the first actual marriages and offspring to come from *The Bachelor*, lending it a new legitimacy where its stated goal was concerned.

SEASON 13

January 5–March 3, 2009

9 2-Hour Episodes, 2 1-Hour Episodes (ATFR1 and ATFR2)

Players: 25

Bachelor: Jason Mesnick, a thirty-three-year-old financial consultant from Cleveland, Ohio, who was the runner-up on Season 4 of *The Bachelorette* (DeAnna Pappas) and the first single-father Bachelor

---

Up until this point, all previous Bachelors save Season 4's Bob Guiney had come from outside the franchise. Mesnick was the genesis of the player-to-Crown precedent that guaranteed all future Bachelors would be selected from previous *Bachelorette* player pools (with the sole exception of Brad Womack's second season), and that would hold true all the way until Season 25 with Matt James (although he was technically cast as a player in Season 16 of *The Bachelorette* but was named Bachelor before that season began filming).

Mesnick brought with him a few other historic firsts as the only single-father Bachelor and the only Jewish Bachelor the game had produced at that point. The players' contributions to the game's development this season included Shannon Bair breaking new ground with the invention of the TOT Limo Exit by emerging from the limo wearing monster teeth. Jillian Harris performed an It Takes Two by questioning Mesnick about his hot dog condiment preference, which she followed up with a pre-planned hot dog cooking mini-date in the Mansion. This was a feat she could not have accomplished alone, demonstrating the first blatant Producer involvement in Limo Exits.

Season 13 also marks the first glimpse of what would become *Bachelor Pad* and later *BIP* when, at the WTA, Chris Harrison introduced a video package of some players from prior seasons getting together for a franchise-sponsored meet-up. Neil Lane rings were used for the first time this season, setting the stage for a decade of his glittering sparklers to adorn the delicate fingers of all future Ring Winners.

And Season 13 is certainly known for what was possibly the most dramatic ATFR to date. Mesnick eliminated his Ring Winner, Melissa Rycroft, and instead awarded the Ring to his runner-up, Molly Malaney—the first time a win had been reversed. And the most important structural change lengthened episodes to two hours apiece, which allowed for more time to be spent on various elements of the show, prompting for the first time ever B-roll intro packages of seven players before Limo Exits. Despite the emotional turmoil caused by Mesnick's switching of the Ring Winner, he and Molly Mesnick are now married and have a child together. Technically, this was the first marriage and child to come from any *Bachelor* season.

SEASON 14

January 4–March 1, 2010

10 2-Hour Episodes

Players: 25

Bachelor: Jake Pavelka, a thirty-one-year-old pilot from Dallas, Texas, who was eliminated in Episode 6 of *The Bachelorette* Season 5 (Jillian Harris)

Season 14 marks the beginning of a disturbing trend in the game with the least diverse cast up to that point. Twenty-four of twenty-five players were White and Channy Choch, the only player of color, was dismissed on Night One. But despite what was a clear backslide in diversity in a game that was already problematic in this area, the rules, format, and length of episodes were doctrine at this point.

Pavelka made history when he dismissed both players on a 2O1 Date, Ella Nolan and Kathryn Sherlock. And then again in the first round of play-offs (Hometowns), Pavelka continued to break new ground by securing the first Parental Blessing of all time from Ali Fedotowsky's mother and another from Tenley Molzahn's father.

One player in this season would find out the hard way that some rules were unbreakable. In Episode 2, a shock wave ripped through the game as Rozlyn Papa was accused of engaging in an "inappropriate relationship" with a Producer. Papa herself denied this claim, but the GDR she was awarded that very night was revoked in a stunning first for the game and she was dismissed immediately. And one of the most enduring figures in the game was granted his first on-camera appearance during the Finale. Neil Lane himself consulted Pavelka with his now-familiar briefcase of diamonds in tow, helping the Bachelor select his Finale sparkler.

Vienna Girardi was this season's Ring Winner, who herself was a trailblazer as the first-ever Ring Winner to have overcome a Villain Edit. While Pavelka proposed in the Finale, the couple broke up a few months after it aired but returned for a dramatic special interview with Chris Harrison in which they discussed their breakup and Pavelka engaged in what we saw as verbal abuse, causing Girardi to storm off the set in tears.

SEASON 15

January 3–March 14, 2011

11 2-Hour Episodes, 1 1-Hour ATFR

Players: 30

Bachelor: Brad Womack, a thirty-eight-year-old bar owner from Austin, Texas, and the first repeat Bachelor

---

Continuing the downward spiral of what we consider racist casting practices, this season featured the first completely White player pool. Statistically this is even worse than it might initially appear because this was also the first season to have thirty players, five more than the norm. Brad Womack made history as the first Bachelor to wear the Crown twice after he rejected both final players during his first season (Season 11). Second chances became the theme of the season, and for the first and only time the Bachelor's therapist was featured to discuss his emotional issues and his in-game decision-making.

The Night One Curveball hammered home the image of Womack as an apologetic, changed man when the two finalists from his first season, DeAnna Papas and Jenni Croft, returned to discuss whether he learned from his mistakes and was indeed finally ready for commitment. The Producers continued to test minor contextual alterations with the 2O1 Date by pitting two friends against each other for the first time—Ashley Hebert and Ashley Spivey. Emily Maynard also made history this season as the first single parent to win the Ring. Womack proposed to her, but they broke up later that year.

SEASON 16

January 2–March 12, 2012

11 2-Hour Episodes, 1 1-Hour ATFR

Players: 25

Bachelor: Ben Flajnik, the twenty-eight-year-old owner of Envolve Winery and the runner-up on *The Bachelorette* Season 7 (Ashley Hebert)

This season also had an almost entirely White player base (96 percent). The most important addition to the game to come from Flajnik's season was the final two types of Limo Exits. The fifteenth player to emerge on Night One, Brittney Schreiner, brought her seventy-two-year-old grandmother, Sheryl, with her for the first Sidecar in history. And the last Limo Exit of the night saw Lindzi Cox forgoing the luxury of the back of a limo in favor of riding in on horseback, the first Grand Entrance ever. With the Sidecar and the Grandy firmly in place the game finally had all eight types of Limo Exits.

The main story of Season 16 was undoubtedly the Villain, Courtney Robertson. She was the second player with a Villain Edit to win the Ring, but she revolutionized game play in order to do it. She openly discussed strategy and game theory in almost every episode and, simply put, played with a degree of deftness and skill that we wouldn't see again until many years in the future. Ahead of her time, Robertson engaged in voluntary nudity play, purposeful and overt sabotage of other players, Machiavellian laughter in celebration of successful deceits, and she was the only finalist to ever attend the WTA in order to defend herself. While Flajnik proposed to Courtney in the Finale, the couple ended their engagement the following year.

SEASON 17

January 7–March 11, 2013

11 2-Hour Episodes, 1 1-Hour Sean Tells All, 1 3-Hour Finale/ATFR

Players: 26

Bachelor: Sean Lowe, a twenty-eight-year old Born-Again Virgin and former Kansas State University football player from Dallas, Texas, who placed third on *The Bachelorette* Season 8 (Emily Maynard)

Season 17 is considered by the Producers to be the most successful season of all time due to the fact that Sean Lowe is the only Bachelor in history to marry his Ring Winner and the couple is still married, with three children. This is the only time the revered "process" has been proven to work for the Bachelor, though two other Bachelors married their runners-up and three Bachelorettes have also married their Ring Winners.

Lowe set a new standard for purity as the game's first "virgin*" Bachelor (*Born-Again). For the first time, he was allowed to give out twelve SRs on Night One, eliminating the FIMP Rose and instead allowing a dozen women to revel in early Night One safety before the daunting Rose Ceremony. Villainy evolved this season with a performance turned in by Tierra LiCausi, the likes of which the game had never seen. In a seemingly never-ending barrage of IFIs, she fell down the stairs, interrupting the start of another player's 1O1, and later claimed hypothermia on a polar bear plunge Group Date. She was ultimately eliminated in sixth place, but her theatrics are forever etched into the highlight reels of this season.

Selma Alameri made history as the first Muslim player and she made it all the way to Week 5. Social media made its first on-screen appearance during a bonus episode called "Sean Tells All," as they superimposed tweets about the season from Bachelor Nation on the bottom of the screen. This season's WTA featured Chris Harrison and the Bachelor crashing *Bachelor* viewing parties for the first time. Due to the massive ratings success of this season, ABC granted an extra hour to the Finale, producing the first-ever three-hour event in which the Finale was intercut with ATFR. Sean and his Ring Winner, Catherine Giudici, are routinely brought back to appear on-camera in later seasons as examples of success within the game.

SEASON 18

January 6–March 10, 2014

11 2-Hour Episodes, 1 1-Hour ATFR

Players: 27

Bachelor: Juan Pablo Galavis, a thirty-two-year-old single father and former Venezuelan professional soccer player from Miami Beach, Florida, who was eliminated in the sixth Rose Ceremony of *The Bachelorette* Season 9 (Desiree Hartsock)

In what seemed like a deliberate move by Producers to shift the game toward diversity, they cast the first Latinx Bachelor since the show's inception in 2002. Although Galavis seemed to be a move in the right direction, Bachelor Nation and the game soon learned this might not be the case, as he became the first Bachelor to earn a Villain Edit through a series of what we perceived to be misogynistic reactions to plays made by Clare Crawley and Andi Dorfman as well as homophobic remarks about the possibility of a bisexual or gay Bachelor, which he later apologized for. Despite the dark shadow of Galavis's regressive demeanor, there were bright spots in Season 18, like Sharleen Joynt, who made history as the first player of color to receive a FIMP Rose. This was the first season to produce two Bachelorettes, Andi Dorfman and Clare Crawley. Nikki Ferrell won the Season 18 Ring, although there was no proposal. She and Galavis broke up seven months after the Finale aired.

The Paradise Era (Seasons 19–23)

2015–2020

While much of today's game looks startlingly similar to the seasons from the Modern Era, something happened between Seasons 18 and 19 that drastically altered everything: the start of *BIP*. Season 1 of *BIP* aired immediately after Andi Dorfman's reign as Bachelorette, premiering on August 4, 2014. It was the second attempt at an "All-Stars" type of show after *Bachelor Pad* and it was much more successful, opening new doors for players postseason by creating goals beyond the Ring or the Crown. A loss in the main game didn't necessarily mean a player's career was over, and in many cases it might've only been the beginning.

Players found they were competing for appearance order in Paradise and story lines in this new, ancillary game. And just as the rise of the Beatles coincided with the mass adoption of television, Paradise was born in the upswing of the rise of Instagram. Followers became a prize worth as much as, if not more than, the Ring or the Crown by themselves and players began to realize the main game could be an audition for Paradise. Even without being a finalist in the main game, players could create a path to another two months' worth of screen time in Paradise, where they could become parasocial powerhouses, developing careers as influencers that last far beyond their time in-game.

Paradise also opened pathways for previous players to become the next Bachelor, such as Nick Viall and Colton Underwood, who used the extra screen time to prove to Producers they could handle the demands of being a lead. The promise of social media influence and the significant financial gain that came with it produced a level of competition the game had never seen.

SEASON 19

January 5–March 9, 2015

1 3-Hour Premiere, 10 2-Hour Episodes, 1 1-Hour ATFR

Players: 30

Bachelor: Chris Soules, a thirty-three-year-old farmer from Arlington, Iowa, who finished third in *The Bachelorette* Season 10 (Andi Dorfman)

The first season after *BIP* produced several household names, like Kaitlyn Bristowe, Becca Tilley, Jade Roper, and Ashley Iaconetti. These parasocial powerhouses all have over 1 million IG followers, the most 1M+ players of any season up to that point. As Instagram gave fans the ability to keep up with their favorite players even after their playing days were over, the game was at the height of its popularity and was rewarded with the first three-hour live premiere event, complete with a red carpet and All-Star players returning in formal wear to be interviewed by Chris Harrison.

Bo Stanley, a plus-size model, made history as the first diversity in body type, though she was eliminated Night One. Jimmy Kimmel became the first celebrity to guest host a date between Soules and Kaitlyn Bristowe. And the 2O1 saw a new element added—the first-ever hostile environment. Ashley Iaconetti and Kelsey Poe were pitted against each other in the rugged

Badlands of South Dakota. At the WTA, Ashley Salter received the first-ever on-camera invitation to be on *BIP* from Harrison himself. Bristowe made history by receiving the most GDRs in a single season with three. Becca Tilley also put her name in the history books by going the farthest of a PVC player, runner-up.

The Producers experimented with the presentation of the game this season, as well opted for multiple cliffhanger endings that denied viewers a Rose Ceremony at the end of some episodes. Whitney Bischoff won the Ring, but the couple broke up two months after the Finale aired.

SEASON 20

January 4–March 14, 2016

11 2-Hour Episodes, 1 1-Hour ATFR

Players: 28

Bachelor: Ben Higgins, a twenty-six-year-old software salesman from Warsaw, Indiana, who finished third on *The Bachelorette* Season 11 (Kaitlyn Bristowe)

For the first time social media was discussed openly and played an active part in the development of strategy. At the Night One Cocktail Party several women candidly discussed "stalking" Higgins on Twitter and Instagram, including the season's first Villain, Lace Morris. Twins made a comeback, having been absent from the game since Season 4 (except for Bachelor Brad Womack's twin making a brief appearance). Haley and Emily Ferguson were given the first joint intro package and they were also forced on the first sibling 2O1 when they were pitted against each other at their mother's house in Las Vegas.

This season was infamous, however, for what happened during the second round of play-offs—Fantasy Suites. While Season 10's Andy Baldwin told two women he loved them ten years prior, the game's most explosive growth in viewership happened in the Modern Era and so the majority of fans had never seen this historic event. Watching Ben Higgins tell two of his top three, Joelle "JoJo" Fletcher and Lauren Bushnell, that he loved them on two successive Fantasy Suite Dates sent shock waves through a growing Bachelor Nation thinking it was the first time this had happened. Fletcher herself seemed to think Higgins's admission of love meant she would be the Ring Winner, but she quickly learned that wasn't the case. The victimization she suffered after being dismissed by Higgins at the FRC led to an almost immediate announcement that she would be crowned the next Bachelorette. The Producers attempted to up the ante in the ATFR this season by flying out Higgins's pastor and the Ring Winner Bushnell's family in an effort to force the couple to get married live onstage, but they opted to hold off and ultimately split up a year and two months after the Finale aired.

SEASON 21

January 2–March 13, 2017

12 2-Hour Episodes, 1 1-Hour ATFR

Players: 30

Bachelor: Nick Viall, a thirty-six-year-old software sales executive from Waukesha, Wisconsin, and the previous runner-up in two back-to-back *Bachelorette* seasons: Season 10 (Andi Dorfman) and Season 11 (Kaitlyn Bristowe), and also a finalist of *BIP* Season 3 with Jen Saviano

---

Nick Viall was the most studied student of the game to ever wear the Crown after completing two full *Bachelorette* seasons and a full season of *BIP*. No Bachelor in history was as decorated or so versed in the specific nature of the game before wearing the Crown, and none has been since. Viall's legacy would encompass much more than his greatest-male-player-of-all-time status, however.

Season 21 marked a turning point for the game toward more diverse casting. About a third of Viall's players were not White, which was the highest percentage of diversity the game had seen in a single season. Jaime King pushed progress even further by appearing as the first openly LGBTQ player. The season's Villain, Corinne Olympios, pushed the envelope by breaking norms that seemed immutable when she skipped a Rose Ceremony in favor of a nap. And ultimately, this season was truly about the rise of Rachel Lindsay as the first Black player to ever win the FIMP Rose, make it through both rounds of play-offs (Hometowns and Fantasy Suites), and eventually go on to be the first Black player to wear the Crown as the thirteenth Bachelorette. Viall proposed to a Canadian player, Vanessa Grimaldi, but they broke off their engagement five months after the Finale aired.

SEASON 22

January 1–March 6, 2018

10 2-Hour Episodes, 1 3-Hour Finale, 1 2-Hour ATFR

Players: 29

Bachelor: Arie Luyendyk Jr., a thirty-six-year-old former race car driver from Scottsdale, Arizona, who was the runner-up on *The Bachelorette* Season 8 (Emily Maynard)

Although Luyendyk did finish second in a prior season of *The Bachelorette*, he was a surprising choice for Bachelor to many in Bachelor Nation because his last appearance in-game was six years prior, but Producers found themselves in a quandary when the runner-up from the most recent *Bachelorette* season, Peter Kraus, turned down their offer to wear the Crown.

Luyendyk was most known for "pulling a Mesnick." Becca Kufrin won the Ring and was a month into an engagement with Luyendyk when he broke it off with her live on-camera during the Finale in order to pursue the runner-up, Lauren Burnham, to whom he later proposed during ATFR. He and Burnham were married one year later and are still together, with three children.

The level of victimization experienced by Kufrin had never been seen up to that point and she was immediately awarded the Crown in a historic moment that involved beginning her Limo Exits at the ATFR, allowing her to meet the first five players before her official Night One. Also a notable first, the influence of the game reached into the political world as one of the members of the Minnesota House of Representatives signed a bill banning Luyendyk from Minnesota, Kufrin's home state, in retaliation for his actions.

SEASON 23

January 7–March 12, 2019

1 3-Hour Episode (Premiere), 11 2-Hour Episodes

Players: 30

Bachelor: Colton Underwood, a twenty-six-year-old virgin and former NFL player from Denver, Colorado, who finished fourth in Season 14 of *The Bachelorette* (Becca Kufrin) and played in Season 5 of *BIP*

An elaborate three-hour live premiere event opened this historic season that featured Chris Harrison hosting a traditional viewing party at a soundstage in Los Angeles as he checked in with pairs of *Bachelor* alumni hosting their own giant viewing parties all over the United States, two of which included on-camera proposals from fans. This premiere also featured the first open integration of Instagram into the game itself as Harrison directed Bachelor Nation to like a post on the official *Bachelor* ABC account in order to "unlock" a blooper reel.

Underwood made history as the first virgin Bachelor and the season focused on this element of his identity heavily, going so far as to produce an entire segment with a panel of *Bachelor* alumni and eliminated players sharing a Hot Seat during the Finale to speculate with Chris Harrison on whether Underwood lost his virginity. This was the first season to set up a rivalry in preproduction by casting two Pageant Queens (Caelynn Miller-Keyes and Hannah Brown) who were engaged in a prior adversarial relationship on the pageant circuit.

What Underwood's season can best be remembered for, however, is the fence jump. While one Bachelor had not chosen anyone in the Finale (Brad Womack), no Bachelor in history had ever attempted to end the game before its mandated conclusion in the Finale. Colton Underwood tried to do just that during his Fantasy Suite week when his front-runner, Cassie Randolph, quit the game after Producers flew her father to Portugal to convince her to quit. Underwood jumped a tall fence in protest of the entire production and then broke things off with his other two finalists in order to pursue Randolph and finish out the game's Fantasy Suite and Finale rounds with just her, making her the de facto Ring Winner. The couple broke up a year and two months after the Finale aired and then made headlines again in September 2020 when Randolph took out a restraining order against Underwood after several incidents of stalking including attaching a tracking device to her car (which he never, to our knowledge, denied). This season produced two historic Bachelorettes in Tayshia Adams, who was the first Black player to reach 1 million IG followers, and Hannah Brown, who currently has the highest IG count of any player in the game's history. Underwood has gone on to contribute even more to the historical record in his postgame career by coming out as the first and only gay Bachelor.

The Professional Era (Seasons 24–25)

2020–Present

After five seasons of steady social media growth for high-level players in the Paradise Era, the game began producing its first-ever members of the 2 million IG follower club in superstar players like JoJo Fletcher, Hannah Brown, and even male players like Colton Underwood and Tyler Cameron. Popular players were seeing massive increases in the rates they could charge for spon-con on their social media platforms, and using an appearance in-game to springboard into an influencer career had become the primary goal of almost all incoming players. So making a deep run to the Top 4 and beyond became an even more coveted goal in order to assure a big enough following to start a career in social media. And because the show had been on for so long at this point, many players had absorbed strategy and game mechanics simply through watching season after season starting in early childhood. This combination of incredible financial reward and instinctual understanding of the game at a new level produced the most competitive version of the game that has ever existed.

SEASON 24

January 6–March 10, 2020

11 2-Hour Episodes, 1 3-Hour Finale/ATFR

Players: 30

Bachelor: Peter Weber, a twenty-eight-year-old Delta Airlines pilot from Westlake Village, California, who placed third in Season 15 of *The Bachelorette* (Hannah Brown)

The first two recognized Professional players came from this season—the Ring Winner, Hannah Ann Sluss, and the runner-up, Madison Prewett. They both played rare errorless seasons that were built on impeccable Fourth-Audience play styles. But even beyond Sluss and Prewett, the game was firmly established as an influencer launchpad by this point and several of this season's players exhibited deep understanding of the game's intricacies. Kelsey Weier, for example, delivered the only 10.0 Huju in the history of the game to begin her international 1O1 Date. Multiple players gained over a million IG followers by the end of the season, including Sluss and Prewett, who are both now extremely successful influencers. Sluss operates a popular YouTube channel centered on cooking and Prewett has amassed over 2 million TikTok followers—the most of anyone from Bachelor Nation.

Weber's season is most known for the messiness of the Finale and post-season. Madison Prewett quit in the Finale and Weber proposed to Hannah Ann Sluss. However, Weber ended the engagement with Sluss during ATFR and was then forced to promote the idea that he would entertain a reconciliation with Prewett, which did not last beyond ATFR. Weber then reunited with the fifth-place finisher, Kelley Flanagan. The couple dated for almost a year before calling it quits.

SEASON 25

January 4–March 15, 2021

12 2-Hour Episodes

Players: 38

Bachelor: Matt James, a twenty-eight-year-old friend of Tyler Cameron who was initially cast as a player in *Bachelorette* Season 16 (Clare Crawley) but was fast-tracked to the Crown after pressure for more diversity in the game on social media following the 2020 Black Lives Matter demonstrations across America

---

The casting of Matt James as the first Black Bachelor was a long time coming but only actually happened as the result of several different circumstances of the year 2020. First the COVID-19 global pandemic pushed production of Clare Crawley's sixteenth *Bachelorette* season several months. During that time, the murder of George Floyd by a police officer energized the Black Lives Matter movement, which prompted the strongest call for diversity from within Bachelor Nation that had yet been seen. Although James never played in any prior seasons, he was cast as a player on Crawley's postponed season, and because he was friends with former player Tyler Cameron and former Bachelorette Hannah Brown (the two highest IG follower counts of all time) he was positioned as the perfect choice. Despite the hope that Bachelor Nation collectively felt for what James's season could represent, it turned out to be the biggest Producer-manufactured disaster in the history of the game.

Although there were two *Bachelorette* seasons shot during the national

COVID lockdown, completely on the grounds of different resorts with no travel whatsoever, there was only one season of *The Bachelor* and this was it.

Producers inserted five new players into the player pool midway through the season, which led to rivalries, infighting, and bullying on an unprecedented level. Producers also saw fit to include a potentially life-ruining and completely unfounded rumor that a player was a sex worker in the final edit. And as if this wasn't enough, a player named Rachael Kirkconnell became embroiled in a racism scandal that ultimately involved Chris Harrison himself inadvertently issuing racially insensitive comments of his own, which led to his forced departure from the show.

James broke things off with Kirkconnell in an official capacity at the ATFR, which was hosted by Emmanuel Acho instead of Harrison, who had been exiled at that point. But as of writing, James and Kirkconnell are back together and working on their relationship.

Thank You

Thank you so much to everybody who has come on this journey with us. We did our absolute best to accurately record the data from the first twenty-five seasons of The Bachelor, derive and calculate the most meaningful statistical metrics, and ultimately present it all here as coherently as we could. Given the Herculean and often insane effort of our Hyperbinge, we fully acknowledge the possibility of a margin of error. It's our hope that this book will serve as a starting point for a brand new era of our beloved game that will include an even more robust community of statisticians, writers, and commentators who will hone the data even further. We envision a day in the very near future when *The Bachelor* has an entire industry devoted to its coverage just like any other professional sport and we look forward to being a part of it.

Sincerely,
Lizzy & Chad

The Lexicon

Collected here in alphabetical order are the terms and phrases that make up the language we created to describe our beloved game.

After Party (AP)

Usually occurring at night, this is the final portion of a Group Date in which players join the lead for cocktails and conversation, allowing them a last opportunity to vie for the Group Date Rose (GDR). This term was generated by Producers.

All-Player Date (APD)

A date that involves the participation of all remaining players, which can sometimes include a Play For Time (PFT) or an APD Rose.

The Aloha

One of the eight Limo Exit types, in which the player greets the Bachelor in a language other than English.

The Bland Entrance (Blandy)

One of the eight Limo Exit types, in which the player greets the Bachelor with a hug, kiss on the cheek, or handshake accompanied by light, non-humorous conversation.

Blessing

Refers to a player getting a stated approval of their romantic partner, usually from a parent during the Hometowns round of play-offs.

Blocked Steal

When a player attempts to interrupt another player who is speaking with the Bachelor and the speaking player rejects the Steal attempt successfully.

Cocktail Party (CP)

An event held on the eve of each Rose Ceremony that allows players one final chance to engage with the Bachelor before he makes his final elimination determinations. This term was generated by Producers.

Colorful Narrator

A role any player can take on during the confessional portion of the game in which she continuously provides concise comedic recountings of the night's events and/or descriptions of the other players.

Complicit
English definition—involved with others in an illegal activity or wrongdoing. When applied to *The Bachelor* this refers to fandom of the franchise while operating with the full knowledge that it promotes certain regressive cultural tropes (homophobia, racism, misogyny, et cetera) that are in direct conflict with progressive ideals.

C.O.T.A.
Ceremony of the Ancients—an event usually reserved for play-off rounds of each season that involves the Bachelor and a player encountering an elderly couple in a public space who divulge the secret to romantic longevity.

Council of Crowns
An event that takes place at the beginning of each season in which two or more past Crown Winners converge to deliver advice to the incoming Bachelor over a round of alcoholic beverages.

The Crown
The award bestowed upon the player who ascends to take the title of the next Bachelor or Bachelorette.

Dynamic Duo
A close friendship between two players in the house that is played for screen time. Often helps a player in the postseason by joining social media forces.

First Flower
The rose that is given out first in the Rose Ceremony, often to signify a special interest by the Bachelor or Producers in the recipient. The Night One First Flower is actually statistically more advantageous than the FIMP.

First Impression (FIMP) Rose
Given to a single player on Night One, this is one of the most valuable Roses in the entire game.

First Responder
Designation given to the player who holds and eventually hands the Bachelor his first drink on Night One when he enters the Inauguration Chamber, where he delivers his first toast. Also refers to the first player who grabs the Bachelor first for time from a Cocktail Party.

First Sand
Designation given to the first player to enter the beach on The Bachelor's off-season show, Bachelor in Paradise. Designation can be made between First Female Sand and First Male Sand.

Floater

A player who makes it to the international travel round (usually Week 6) by drawing little attention to themselves, presenting no reason to be removed but also no reason to be kept into the play-offs.

Forced Nudity

A date element that demands a player remove some or all of her clothing in service of the stated date event.

For The Right Reasons (4TRR) (As Opposed to For The Wrong Reasons [4TWR])

This phrase describes the primary structural rule of the game, that a player is only participating to find love and any monetary gain or increase in IG followers, fame, or general clout is purely incidental.

Four Audiences

The four audiences that each player must appease at any given moment in-game:

1. The First Audience: The Bachelor
2. The Second Audience: The other players
3. The Third Audience: The Producers
4. The Fourth Audience: The viewers (Bachelor Nation)

The Full Royale

Designation given to the achievement of winning both the Ring and the Crown. To date, only three players have achieved a Full Royale—Jen Schefft, Emily Maynard, and Becca Kufrin.

The Gentleman

This is generally a move at the After Party portion of a date or at the Cocktail Party in which the player gets the Bachelor to give her his jacket.

Glow

When a player gets their family members to state that they physically look like they are in love, usually during a MOTF.

The Grand Entrance (or Grandy)

One of the eight Limo Exit types, the Grandy requires the player to forgo emerging from the actual limo in favor of arriving at the Mansion by grander means. Sports cars, ice-cream trucks, and even beasts of burden are all examples of modes of Grand Entrances.

Grim Reaper

The production staff member who enters the Mansion (or hotel if players are in a travel round) to remove an eliminated player's suitcase. This term was generated by Producers.

Group Date (GD)
A date involving three or more players, usually with one Rose available. This term was generated by Producers.

GTTC (Get To The Chopper)
A date element that finds the player in a helicopter for any reason.

Hail Mary
An all-or-nothing act of desperation employed by a player in an attempt to garner a Rose in the eleventh hour. Often performed by players who have found themselves Turtling during a Group Date or Cocktail Party.

Home Invasion
A date element that features the Bachelor sneaking into the Mansion or hotel while the players sleep in order to photograph them without their consent or force them into prematurely waking up in service of a date activity.

Hot Seat
The portion of Women Tell All or After The Final Rose where the player sits on the chair opposite the host for a one-on-one interview. This term was generated by Producers.

Huju
A shortened form of "Hug Jump"—a mandatory athletic display requiring a player to run toward the Bachelor upon first seeing him at the beginning of a date, then jump and cling to him in a tight hug as he stands supporting the player's full body weight. Standard form involves wrapping both legs around the Bachelor's torso, although there are variations.

IFI (Injury Fear Illness)
This strategy requires a player to suffer from the debilitating effects of an injury, fear, or illness (real or faked) in order to exempt herself from participating in a date activity (usually Group Date). If played properly the secondary effect is generation of One-On-One time with the Bachelor as he is forced to inquire about her well-being.

I Love Cleveland
The state of heightened excitement and enthusiasm Producers force the players to convey when a celebrity guest or travel destination is revealed, no matter how underwhelming these elements might actually be.

Inauguration Chamber
The large room into which the Bachelor always enters once all players have performed their Limo Exits. This is where he delivers his first toast and sets in motion the second half of the Night One Cocktail Party.

Italian Steal

Taking its name from a strategy first performed by local Italian players Cosetta Blanca and Agnese Polliza in Lorenzo Borghese's ninth season, which took place in Rome, this refers to a player immediately stealing the Bachelor back from the player who stole him from her.

ITM (In The Moment)

An ITM is a direct-to-camera confessional shot of a player speaking to the Fourth Audience, the viewers. These are often loosely scripted by producers and are frequently where plays are loaded. Sometimes they are filmed long after the show has shot to pick up some emotional reaction or narration of play. This term was generated by Producers.

The It Takes Two

One of the eight Limo Exit types, the It Takes Two requires the player to engage the Bachelor in some form of willing physical participation. Dancing, kissing, and feeling of heartbeats are all recognized It Takes Twos.

Knock Knock

An event designed by the Producers that allows a single player to visit the Bachelor outside the context of a normal date, usually at night. This term was generated by Producers.

Loading

"Loading" refers to a player projecting a play she will make before she executes it, either in an ITM or to the other players. Often, players load Personal Tragedy Cards, Personal Virginity Cards, Package Deals, and Love Levels.

Love Levels

The four tiers of emotional escalation that mark a player's progress through the game. Although there are variations and in some cases subdivisions, the four basic tiers are:

1. I Like You
2. I'm Starting to Fall for You
3. I'm Falling in Love with You
4. I'm in Love with You

Mi Casa

A date element that requires some portion of the date to take place in the Bachelor's or player's actual home or hotel room.

MMS (Make Me Stay)

Performable at virtually any time in the game, the MMS is a strategy that involves a player subtly hinting or overtly stating that she is on the verge of quitting the game unless she's given a strong sign from the Bachelor that he wants her to stay—usually a Rose.

MOTF (Meeting Of The Family)

A date element in which the player meets one or more members of the Bachelor's family or vice versa. Most MOTFs generally occur in the Hometown round of the play-offs, but early MOTFs can indicate front-runner status.

Not Here To Make Friends (NHTMF)

A Villain strategy in which a player outwardly states that they don't care about their Second Audience game.

Night One Curveball

A shocking event that occurs on Night One designed to shake up the Bachelor and the players. This can range from controversial figures crashing the game, such as the Bachelor's own mother or ex-girlfriend, to a change up in-game dynamics, like multiple First Impression Roses.

Night One Guy/Night One Girl (N.O.G.)

A player who is eliminated from the game on Night One without ever having won a single Rose.

One-On-One (1O1 Date)

A One-On-One Date between one player and the Bachelor. These dates often result in the binary choice of a Rose or elimination. This term was generated by Producers.

Package Deal

When a player reveals that she has one or more children. This can be loaded in ITMs or a player's intro video and is usually played pretty early in-game.

Peeping Tom

Refers to Producers constructing dates so that the players not on the date have to watch the date in some capacity. Sometimes they even provide binoculars as an aid.

Personal Tragedy Card (PTC)

A universal play that requires a player to divulge some past tragedy or hardship experienced before her time in-game to garner sympathy and, if used properly, a Rose from the Bachelor.

PFT (Play For Time)

A type of competition Group Date where the winner(s) get extra time with the Bachelor. This can be in the form of group time if the date requires team competition or One-On-One time if the date requires individual competition.

Praising the Process
An open declaration of support for and acceptance of any and all results, emotional or otherwise, that might come from participation in the game.

Precog
When a player tells the Bachelor that she would accept a proposal. Can be loaded via ITM or during a MOTF.

The Process
A term referring to the overall experience of attempting to find love in the unorthodox environment of the ten-round structure of the game. This term was generated by Producers.

The Ring
The award bestowed upon the Bachelor's final choice in a season, the winner. This selection is usually accompanied with an actual engagement ring designed by Neil Lane.

Rivalry
A hostile dynamic between two players that can be played up for screen time, often stoked by Producers. It frequently transitions into both players being put on the 2O1 Date at some point.

Rose
The standard signifier of a player's passage to the next round of the game, of which there are six types:

1. One-On-One (1O1) Rose
2. Two-On-One (2O1) Rose
3. Group Date (GD) Rose
4. First Impression (FIMP) Rose
5. Final Rose (FR)
6. Special Rose (SR)

Rose Ceremony
The final event in each week of play in which players are forced to stand before the Bachelor and either receive a Rose/berth into the next round or be eliminated. This term was generated by Producers.

Rose Quotient (RQ)
A statistical metric that illustrates a player's raw ability to win Roses outside Rose Ceremonies. After a player has received at least five Roses, the RQ is derived by adding the Rose Value of each Rose won and then dividing by the total number of Roses. Lower scores indicate higher levels of skill and 0 is a perfect score. It has never been achieved by any player in the history of the game.

Sabbatical
When a player (usually Professional archetype) tells the Bachelor that she quit her job in order to come on the show.

Sacred Word Defense
A preemptive conversation about the overwhelming, almost religious importance of uttering the phrase "I love you" initiated by a player or Bachelor in order to delay an impending Love Level raise.

The Santa Claus (or Kringle)
One of the eight Limo Exit types, in which the player bestows a gift on the Bachelor. Kringling also refers to any time in-game when a player gives the Bachelor an object.

Shoulder To Cry On (STCO)
Refers to a player providing emotional support to another player as a means of garnering screen time and appearing 4TRR.

The Sidecar
One of the eight Limo Exit types in which a player brings a third party with them to meet the Bachelor.

Slussian Protocol
The idea that players "know what they've signed up for"—based on Hannah Ann Sluss's line during Fantasy Suites.

Skeleton
Some person from a player's past who is brought out by Producers in an attempt to sabotage her play style. Exes, town gossips, and parents are all examples of Skeletons.

Special Rose (SR)
Any Rose granted to a player outside a standard-date Rose structure (One-On-One Date, Two-On-One Date, Group Date, First Impression, Final Rose) or a Rose Ceremony.

The Stand-Up (Standy)
One of the eight Limo Exit types, in which a player does a performance for the Bachelor, through song, dance, jokes, et cetera.

Steal
A strategic maneuver that allows one player to usurp One-On-One time from another, usually at a Cocktail Party or After Party.

Steal Fatigue

A phenomenon of diminishing returns that occurs after the first three to five players have performed successful Steals in a night that leaves the Bachelor less interested in all following players who attempt Steals of their own.

Tattling

"Tattling" refers to a player using her 1O1 time with the Bachelor to speak negatively of one or more of the other players. Tattling is almost always detrimental for the Tattling player and often ends in her elimination in the same week she Tattles.

Tears

An emotional device in every player's toolbox that can be utilized to accentuate Personal Tragedy Cards, display a tearing down of walls, and generally convey that a player is 4TRR.

The Trick-Or-Treat (or TOT)

A TOT is one of the eight types of Limo Exits, in which a player dons a costume to meet the Bachelor. This can range from the very first TOT, Shannon Bair wearing fake monster teeth on Jason Mesnick's thirteenth season, to Alexis Waters wearing a full shark outfit in Nick Viall's twenty-first season.

Turtling

Describes the situation in which a player fails to perform a Steal on a Group Date or at a Cocktail Party, resulting in her getting no time to speak with the Bachelor.

Two-On-One (2O1 Date)

A Two-On-One Date between two players and the Bachelor that forces head-to-head competition for what is most often a single available Rose. This term was generated by Producers.

Voluntary Nudity Play

A strategy in which a player elects to remove some or all of her clothing, usually on a date involving a hot tub, swimming pool, lake, ocean, or other body of water.

Walls

Explicitly stated emotional barriers that will provide a necessary obstacle for a player or the Bachelor to overcome through the course of the game.

The Bachelor Score Sheet

We proudly present to you the *Bachelor* Score Sheet. This document will allow you to conveniently follow along every season and track the important plays and players as they attempt to win the Ring and the Crown. It's modeled after a baseball score sheet but modified to suit our beloved game. We hope it elevates your interaction with the game and makes watching the show a little more fun.

The following elements of the Score Sheet have been filled out using Hannah Ann Sluss's groundbreaking run through Season 24 to give you an example of how to score various plays throughout the season.

Players	Night 1	Week 1	Week 2	Week 3
	1 2 3 4	1 2 3 4	1 2 3 4	1 2 3 4
	1 2 3 4	1 2 3 4	1 2 3 4	1 2 3 4
	1 2 3 4	1 2 3 4	1 2 3 4	1 2 3 4
	1 2 3 4	1 2 3 4	1 2 3 4	1 2 3 4
	1 2 3 4	1 2 3 4	1 2 3 4	1 2 3 4

KEY | **K:** # of kisses **T:** # of tears **RQ:** Rose Quotient **FT:** Family Tears **S:** # of Steals **KK:** Knock Knock

	Week 4	Week 5	Week 6	Home-towns	Fantasy Suites	Women Tell All	Finale
	1 2 3 4	1 2 3 4	1 2 3 4	1 2 3 4	1 2 3 1 2 3 4		1 2 3 4
	1 2 3 4	1 2 3 4	1 2 3 4	1 2 3 4	1 2 3 1 2 3 4		1 2 3 4
	1 2 3 4	1 2 3 4	1 2 3 4	1 2 3 4	1 2 3 1 2 3 4		1 2 3 4
	1 2 3 4	1 2 3 4	1 2 3 4	1 2 3 4	1 2 3 1 2 3 4		1 2 3 4
	1 2 3 4	1 2 3 4	1 2 3 4	1 2 3 4	1 2 3 1 2 3 4		1 2 3 4

A PDF of this Score Sheet is available for download at HowToWinTheBachelor.com

NIGHT 1

GRANDY	TOT	PTC	
ALOHA	STAND-UP		
KRINGLE	ITT	LOVE LEVELS	
		1	2
SIDECAR	BLANDY X	3	4

K	T	S	RQ
3		2	FIMP=0

Sluss began her Night One with an unassuming Blandy but went on to dominate the first round of Season 24 with 3 Kisses, 2 Steals, and a FIMP win, which garnered her 0 total points in her chase for a historic Rose Quotient.

KEY | **K:** # of kisses **T:** # of tears **RQ:** Rose Quotient **FT:** Family Tears **S:** # of Steals **KK:** Knock Knock

WEEK 1

<table>
<tr><td>GD
obstacle course ✓</td><td>R
does not win GDR</td><td colspan="2" rowspan="2">PTC/WALLS</td></tr>
<tr><td>1O1</td><td>R</td></tr>
<tr><td rowspan="2">2O1/3O1</td><td rowspan="2">R</td><td colspan="2">LOVE LEVELS</td></tr>
<tr><td>1</td><td>2</td></tr>
<tr><td>KK</td><td>R</td><td>3</td><td>4</td></tr>
</table>

K	T	S	RQ
			7

Sluss's first week saw her compete in an Obstacle Couse group date on which she did not win the GDR. Riding on the momentum of her Night One FIMP win, Sluss knew to hold back her PTC and Love Levels for later rounds, but she was demoted in the Rose Ceremony that week with a 7th Flower.

KEY | **K:** # of kisses **T:** # of tears **RQ:** Rose Quotient **FT:** Family Tears **S:** # of Steals **KK:** Knock Knock

WEEK 2

<table>
<tr><td>GD
artistic activity
modeling</td><td>R
does not win GDR</td><td colspan="2" rowspan="2">PTC/WALLS</td></tr>
<tr><td>101</td><td>R</td></tr>
<tr><td rowspan="2">201/301</td><td rowspan="2">R</td><td colspan="2">LOVE LEVELS</td></tr>
<tr><td>1 (circled)</td><td>2</td></tr>
<tr><td>KK</td><td>R</td><td>3</td><td>4</td></tr>
</table>

K	T	S	RQ
1	2		2

After avoiding a producer manufactured rivalry with Kelsey Weier in the infamous Champagne gate scandal, Sluss managed to get a kiss at the GD and up her RQ score to 2 for the week as she played a perfect Love Level raise at the After Party.

KEY | **K:** # of kisses **T:** # of tears **RQ:** Rose Quotient **FT:** Family Tears **S:** # of Steals **KK:** Knock Knock

WEEK 3

<table>
<tr><td>GD
forced violence football</td><td>R
does not win GDR</td><td colspan="2" rowspan="2">PTC/WALLS</td></tr>
<tr><td>101</td><td>R</td></tr>
<tr><td rowspan="2">201/301</td><td rowspan="2">R</td><td colspan="2">LOVE LEVELS</td></tr>
<tr><td>1</td><td>2</td></tr>
<tr><td>KK</td><td>R</td><td>3</td><td>4</td></tr>
<tr><td>K</td><td>T</td><td>S</td><td>RQ
5</td></tr>
</table>

Sluss manages to float through week 3 as much of the attention is focused on Victoria Paul and her rivalry with fellow pageant queen Alayah Benavidez.

KEY | **K:** # of kisses **T:** # of tears **RQ:** Rose Quotient **FT:** Family Tears **S:** # of Steals **KK:** Knock Knock

WEEK 4

<table>
<tr><td>GD
artistic activity
photo shoot</td><td>R
GDR!</td><td colspan="2" rowspan="2">PTC/WALLS</td></tr>
<tr><td>101</td><td>R</td></tr>
<tr><td rowspan="2">201/301</td><td rowspan="2">R</td><td colspan="2">LOVE LEVELS</td></tr>
<tr><td>1</td><td>2</td></tr>
<tr><td>KK</td><td>R</td><td>3</td><td>4</td></tr>
</table>

K	T	S	RQ
2			0

As Tammy Ly and Kelsey Weier become embroiled in a rivalry, Sluss sidesteps the drama on her GD to walk away with her first zero-pointer since the FIMP.

KEY | **K:** # of kisses **T:** # of tears **RQ:** Rose Quotient **FT:** Family Tears **S:** # of Steals **KK:** Knock Knock

WEEK 5

<table>
<tr><td>GD</td><td>R</td><td rowspan="2">PTC/WALLS

After divulging that she's never been in love, Sluss brings her wall down for a perfectly timed LL2.</td></tr>
<tr><td>101

when in Rome/COTA</td><td>R

101 R!</td></tr>
<tr><td>201/301</td><td>R</td><td>LOVE LEVELS

1 | (2)</td></tr>
<tr><td>KK</td><td>R</td><td>3 | 4</td></tr>
</table>

K	T	S	RQ
4	2		0

Sluss finally gets her first 101 in week 5, and when she senses Weber hesitating to give her the 101R, she deploys an incredible LL2 raise punctuated with tears to seal the deal.

KEY | **K:** # of kisses **T:** # of tears **RQ:** Rose Quotient **FT:** Family Tears **S:** # of Steals **KK:** Knock Knock

WEEK 6

<table>
<tr><td>GD</td><td>R</td><td rowspan="2">PTC/WALLS

Brings down walls with a handwritten letter outlining the reasons she's starting to fall for him</td></tr>
<tr><td>101</td><td>R</td></tr>
<tr><td rowspan="2">201/301

lavish estate</td><td rowspan="2">R

301R!</td><td>LOVE LEVELS</td></tr>
<tr><td>1 | 2</td></tr>
<tr><td>KK</td><td>R</td><td>3 | 4</td></tr>
</table>

K	T	S	RQ
	2		0

Sluss clinches a berth into the playoffs by sending frontrunner Kelley Flanagan packing on a 301 in the final round of the regular season.

KEY | **K:** # of kisses **T:** # of tears **RQ:** Rose Quotient **FT:** Family Tears **S:** # of Steals **KK:** Knock Knock

HOMETOWN

<table>
<tr><td colspan="4">HUJU</td></tr>
<tr><td>APPROACH
0</td><td>MOUNT
6.4</td><td>CLING
7.2</td><td>DISMOUNT
8.4</td></tr>
<tr><td colspan="4">NO HUJU</td></tr>
<tr><td rowspan="2">GLOW</td><td rowspan="2">BLESSING</td><td colspan="2">LOVE LEVELS</td></tr>
<tr><td>1</td><td>2</td></tr>
<tr><td>FAMILY TEARS
sister</td><td>PRECOG</td><td>3</td><td>(4)</td></tr>
</table>

K	T	1st AUDIENCE LL	RQ
9	1	3	1

Despite receiving neither a GLOW nor a BLESSING, Sluss carried her strong HUJU momentum through a 9-kiss Hometown punctuated with a LL4 raise that prompted Weber to respond with a LL3 of his own, and she walked away with a First Flower in this all-important Rose Ceremony.

KEY | **K:** # of kisses **T:** # of tears **RQ:** Rose Quotient **FT:** Family Tears **S:** # of Steals **KK:** Knock Knock

FANTASY SUITE

ORDER		
1 (circled) aquatic jet skis	2	3

FORGO?	LOVE LEVELS	
Y ✓ (circled)	1	2
N	3	4 (circled)

K	T	RQ
14		1

The Producers give Sluss the first Fantasy Suite, and she dominates with 14 kisses, a re-upping of her LL4 status, and an enthusiastic acceptance of the offer to forgo her individual room to stay in the FS.

KEY | **K:** # of kisses **T:** # of tears **RQ:** Rose Quotient **FT:** Family Tears **S:** # of Steals **KK:** Knock Knock

WOMEN TELL ALL

<table>
<tr><th>HOT SEAT ORDER</th><th colspan="2">DESCRIPTION OF HOTSEAT PLAY</th></tr>
<tr><td>1</td><td colspan="2" rowspan="6"></td></tr>
<tr><td>2</td></tr>
<tr><td>3</td></tr>
<tr><td>4</td></tr>
<tr><td>5</td></tr>
<tr><td>6</td></tr>
<tr><td>7</td><td rowspan="2">PROPS</td><td rowspan="2">TEARS</td></tr>
<tr><td>8</td></tr>
</table>

As a finalist, Sluss did not appear at the Women Tell All.

KEY | **K:** # of kisses **T:** # of tears **RQ:** Rose Quotient **FT:** Family Tears **S:** # of Steals **KK:** Knock Knock

FINALE

FINAL DATE TYPE		(tear drop) / (ring, circled)	
Animal Husbandry Kangaroos			
GLOW	**BLESSING**	**LOVE LEVELS**	
Mom Dad		1	2
FAMILY TEARS	**PRECOG**	3	4 (circled)

K	T	PT	RQ
5	3		0

Sluss finished off one of the greatest seasons of play in history with a double parental GLOW, a reiteration of her LL4, and the big win of the Final Rose.

KEY | **K:** # of kisses **T:** # of tears **RQ:** Rose Quotient **FT:** Family Tears **S:** # of Steals **KK:** Knock Knock

Players	Night 1	Week 1	Week 2	Week 3	
Hannah Sluss	X 1 2 3 4 3 2 FIMP=0	v 1 2 3 4 7	0 2 3 4 1 2 2	1 2 3 4 5	
	1 2 3 4	1 2 3 4	1 2 3 4	1 2 3 4	
	1 2 3 4	1 2 3 4	1 2 3 4	1 2 3 4	
	1 2 3 4	1 2 3 4	1 2 3 4	1 2 3 4	
	1 2 3 4	1 2 3 4	1 2 3 4	1 2 3 4	

KEY | **K:** # of kisses **T:** # of tears **RQ:** Rose Quotient **FT:** Family Tears **S:** # of Steals **KK:** Knock Knock

	Week 4	Week 5	Week 6	Home-towns	Fantasy Suites	Women Tell All	Finale
	1 2 3 4 2 0	1 0 3 4 4 2 0	1 2 3 4 2 0	0 6.4 7.2 8.4 1 2 3 0 9 1 3 1	0 2 3 ✓ 1 2 3 0 14 1		0 1 2 3 0 5 3 0
	1 2 3 4	1 2 3 4	1 2 3 4	1 2 3 4	1 2 3 1 2 3 4		1 2 3 4
	1 2 3 4	1 2 3 4	1 2 3 4	1 2 3 4	1 2 3 1 2 3 4		1 2 3 4
	1 2 3 4	1 2 3 4	1 2 3 4	1 2 3 4	1 2 3 1 2 3 4		1 2 3 4
	1 2 3 4	1 2 3 4	1 2 3 4	1 2 3 4	1 2 3 1 2 3 4		1 2 3 4

A PDF of this Score Sheet is available for download at HowToWinTheBachelor.com